£3

Tm

Sex, Money and Morality:
Prostitution and Tourism in Southeast Asia

Sex, Money and Morality:

Prostitution and Tourism
in Southeast Asia

Thanh-Dam Truong

Zed Books Ltd
London and New Jersey

Sex, Money and Morality: Prostitution and Tourism in Southeast Asia was first published by Zed Books Ltd,
57 Caledonian Road, London N1 9BU, UK, and
171 First Avenue, Atlantic Highlands, New Jersey 07716, USA,
in 1990.

Copyright © Thanh-Dam Truong, 1990.

Cover designed by Sophie Buchet.
Typeset by EMS Photosetters, Rochford, Essex.
Printed and bound in the United Kingdom
by Biddles Ltd, Guildford and Kings Lynn.

British Library Cataloguing in Publication Data

Truong, Thanh-Dam
    Sex, money and morality in South-east Asia.
    1. Asia. South-east Asia. Women. Prostitution.
    I. Title.
    306.740959

    ISBN 0-86232-936-1
    ISBN 0-86232-937-X pbk

Contents

Part I
The Analytical Framework for Prostitution

Acknowledgements

Writing this study has been a multi-level affair. Many people have provided much support, and have been part of this work in many different ways. I owe them all my most sincere appreciation. Cees J. Hamelink is thanked for having taken up the study as a thesis during its most critical stage, knowing that I was unwell, and for having guided me meticulously to the end of the exercise. Jeffrey Harrod is thanked for having stimulated my ideas since the very beginning of the project, even before his role was formalized. As a friend, a colleague and a supervisor, he never imposed boundaries on newly emerging ideas, or on his critical contributions which helped me to give these ideas shape and coherence. Although his gender is inappropriate to this compliment, to me he is truly an 'intellectual midwife'. Emmanuel de Kadt of the University of Sussex is appreciated for his extensive comments on my earlier attempts to come to terms with tourism as a research subject.

Many other colleagues and friends at the Institute of Social Studies have also read and commented on versions of the research proposal and/or drafts of various chapters, including George Irvin, Valpy Fitzgerald, Ken Post, Aart van de Laar, Jan Breman, Aurora Carreon, Loes Keysers and Mia Berden. I thank them for their suggestions and supportive comments. Wicky Meynen is warmly acknowledged for having initially given me the idea to identify the link between prostitution and reproduction. Colleagues in the Women and Development Programme at the Institute for Social Studies, The Hague, are thanked for allowing me to take a three-month leave during my convenorship to finalize my work, and for having shouldered my administrative burdens. In particular, Geertje Lycklama is thanked for her support, which enabled me to obtain funds and time for field research, and to participate in the Economic and Social Commission for Asia and the Pacific 'Workshop of Experts on Prevention and Rehabilitation Schemes For Young Women in Prostitution and Related Occupations', held in Bangkok in June 1985. Renée Pittin is sincerely appreciated for having read my first draft and for her critical, useful and humorous comments. Fellow-members of the informal 'Power-Study Club', Amrita Chhachhi, Carla Risseeuw, Ravni Rai Thakur and Brigitte Holzner, occupy a special place in this thesis because of their understanding, perception, patience and stimulation when I tried to concretize my thoughts, and for pointing out relevant material and ideas developed elsewhere. To Martin Doornbos, I wish to express my gratitude for his support and guidance during a critical period.

During fieldwork, many friends, including Edu Hassing, Robert Wihtol, Nora de Guzman, Siriporn Skrobanek, Nguyen Huu Dong, Gigi Duenas, have helped with practical as well as emotional problems. Some also have provided me with shelter during difficult times. To them, I wish to express my deep appreciation and friendship. John Kleinen must be acknowledged separately for having appeared coincidentally (but exactly when needed) on the scene to help me complete the last bit of fieldwork: that of getting in touch again with my initial point of departure before leaving the place of research. Leo Theuns has kindly allowed me to consult the material on tourism which he has collected and organized over the past ten years.

Throughout the project, I have learned a great deal from participants in the Women and Development Programme through my interaction with them as a lecturer and a supervisor of their research work. I have also enjoyed enormous privileges granted to me by the library staff, Leny Schrikker, Ettie Baas, Saskia Scheffer, Cynthia Recto-Carreon, Willem Bucking and many others. Not only have they bent their iron rules for me, they often did so with much affection. Without their help in searching for, and obtaining through inter-library loans, obscure journals on obscure topics, I would have been quite lost. Koos van Wieringen is thanked for the cover design and the illustration. Linda McPhee is thanked for her excellent editing. Aïda Jesurun, Ank van de Berg, and Barbara Kennedy in particular are thanked for their word processing expertise and assistance.

A number of friends have also provided attention, care and warmth to my uprooted mother and sisters, Ly Thi Minh, Truong Dieu De and Truong Anh Thu, while I neglected them and while they gave me unlimited love. Tine van den Burgh, Jan Zaadhof, Erik Fraterman, Truong Van Binh, and Trix van de Schalk are sincerely appreciated for their loyalty and understanding of human relationships. Kyaw Tint Swe is warmly thanked for having remembered what I am and who I am, in spite of the complex transformation I was experiencing. His gentle lessons are much appreciated. Nguyen Ngoc Luu is thanked for his wise advice on how to cope with mixed feelings. Carol Eggen and Mila Avramovic must be given a big hug as it means a thousand words. Last but not least, I must address myself to Pitou van Dijck, who gets too many hugs already and cannot be thanked sufficiently because of what he is to me. In the last instance, I am still alone in assuming responsibility for the views expressed here.

Preface

This book resulted from a developing awareness of a number of issues connected with prostitution, tourism and the traffic in women, issues which I once perceived as isolated and localized. Through my experience, and through discussions with many people, I began to see the interconnection between them, and I chose to analyse this interconnection for the following reasons.

Being Vietnamese, I witnessed the spread of prostitution in my adolescence in South Vietnam during the Indochina conflict. Forced urbanization campaigns, carried out for military reasons in the 1960s, uprooted millions of peasants in an effort to destroy the rural bases of communist guerrillas. Many rural women were drawn into the cities and to areas surrounding US military bases, where a service economy instantly sprung up and revolved around personal services provided to US military personnel. Brothels and sex establishments mushroomed in these areas and enriched many of their owners. The profitability of prostitution made the entrenched Confucian ethics of the society and its codes of sexual conduct almost irrelevant for many. While there was a certain awareness of the fragility of our social fabric during a period of major upheaval, the internal causes of prostitution were rarely discussed. It was far easier to blame American imperialism in order to defend one's own cultural integrity. From 1968 to 1973, as a student in the United States, I was exposed to the anti-war movement and the pertinent debates prevailing at the time, of which the controversy surrounding prostitution was one. At that time notions about prostitution were reversed. With some exceptions, the blame was placed on the loose sexual mores of Vietnamese women, or on the backwardness of Vietnamese men who found it legitimate to sell women, including their female kin.

In the early 1980s, the issue of sex tourism to Thailand caught my attention. The arguments casually propounded rang a familiar bell. Influenced by the feminist debate on the male–female relationship, I started this project basing my thoughts, with some hesitation, on the notion of 'male social power' which has guided feminist action groups against prostitution and pornography since the 1970s.

During fieldwork in Thailand and the Philippines I adopted a limited participant observation approach to see how this 'male social power' operated. The information gathered through unstructured discussions with clients, prostitutes and their managers, travel writers, and government officials, and the emotions evoked by this experience led me to raise more questions than when I initially started the project.

Some questions were latent while others were new. One of the latent questions was: 'why "Rest and Recreation" then, and why "tourism" now?' The question of 'why tourism?' had boggled my mind some thirteen years ago as a young co-ordinator of the United Nations Volunteers Programme in Upper Volta (now Burkina-Faso). Upon my arrival in the country, I was struck by the existence of the 'Ministere du Tourisme et de L'Environnement'. While I did not question the second function of this institution, I was puzzled by the 'why' of tourism in a country pressed by drought and food shortage. And of course, the classical and naive question often raised by young persons involved with volunteers programmes (sometimes also by mature researchers) did cross my mind: 'what's the meaning of development?' A new question which emerged during fieldwork was: 'how can I feel sympathy and disgust at the same time for what I see, hear and read about prostitution?'

The 'why' of tourism led me to probe deeper into the rationale of tourism as a development strategy. The 'how' of mixed feelings about prostitution made me recognize the significance of differentiation and the power of discourse. Of particular importance for me then was the differentiation between prostitution and prostitutes, the differentiation among prostitutes, and the differentiation between the moral position adopted by officials and the practices they follow.

Subsequent to my field experience, I became involved with organizations set up by prostitutes themselves in Western Europe, and to a lesser extent in the United States and Canada. Although my involvement was of short duration — mainly during the First and Second World Whores Congresses in Amsterdam and Brussels — I soon recognized that differentiation ran much deeper than I had previously believed. I felt compelled to understand its deeper roots.

Fieldwork and armchair research evoked in me a mixture of feelings, which educated me on differentiation, while the literature on power I consulted hung somewhere in my sub-consciousness. Emotions such as anger, guilt, embarrassment and despair were part of the process of looking, talking, reading, thinking, and writing. Experiencing these emotions helped me grasp the meaning of power at its centre and at its extremities.

Anger, evoked from looking, seeing, and reading, motivated me to deal ambitiously with this difficult subject, in as many dimensions as possible, as I began to recognize the central power of scientific discourse, of which I have become a part. In this process I ignored the valuable and wise advice of friends, family members and colleagues to 'not bite off more than I can chew'. I can only appreciate the liberty my supervisors granted me, and apologize that any undigested ideas in this study are the results of my own cognitive capabilities.

As my understanding increased, I have felt guilty for having earlier reproduced (learned) biases and assumptions during discussions with, and about women who confided in me, and for having caused them pain. But as someone who understands power has written:

It is quite possible that the major mechanism of power has been accompanied by ideological production . . . but basically, I do not believe that what has taken place can be said to be ideological. It is both much more and much less than ideology. It is the production of effective instruments for the formation and accumulation of knowledge, methods of observation, techniques of registration, procedures for investigation and research, apparatuses of control. All this means that power, when it is exercised through these subtle mechanisms, cannot but evolve, organize and put into circulation a knowledge, or rather apparatuses of knowledge, which are not ideological constructs. (Foucault, 1986: 237)

The fact that unintended words could cause pain is a manifestation of power at its extremities: the power of discourse at its point of application and its effects on inter-subjectivity and intra-subjectivity.

The intra-subjective effects of power on myself as a researcher and as a woman manifested themselves in the embarrassment I felt when being mistaken for a prostitute by some men during fieldwork. I felt the urge to prove the opposite. Yet simultaneously, I also felt embarrassed for having pretended that the dichotomy between 'madonna' and 'whore' could be erased through supportive action, and embarrassed at being awakened to the fact that there are prostitutes who can do without researchers or activists.

The glimpse I had of certain aspects of power in prostitution has also influenced my process of becoming an aware researcher, i.e. helped me to recognize complexity and to note the selectivity of advocacy. This creates feelings of despair in me. After having self-served a large plate with many courses (not to mention discourses), and having spent sleepless nights trying to digest this, only a modest plea is made to sympathetic organizations to support the rights of prostitutes to organization and welfare.

The usefulness of preventive and corrective measures seems distant. These measures are often advocated along the lines of improving women's social and economic conditions in general, or of changing the prevailing 'discourses' on sexuality and prostitution as they are expressed in the media, religion and parliamentary bills. However, they do not seem to bear a direct effect on the lives of prostitutes in the near future. Their realization depends on a wider political process of which prostitutes do not form a part, at least until they have access to better welfare, and are able to exercise their rights to organize and to articulate their views.

Introduction

A zeal to do right leads to the segregation of saints from sinners.

Edmunch Leach, 1967: 750

Object of Study

This study is a contribution to the on-going debate on prostitution. It focuses on the factors underlying the phenomenon, its transformation and convergence with one major industry, namely the international tourist industry. Breaking away from the common conception of prostitution as promiscuity and crime, the study formulates the problematic of prostitution from the angle of the political economy of women's labour and sexuality. The rupture with this common assumption stems from a recognition of its biases and critical consequences, and from the need for a more sensitive understanding of prostitution and its dynamics.

The study proposes the following as an alternative approach: firstly, the areas of sexuality and reproduction are disaggregated in order to name and locate their contents; and secondly, the interconnection of the two areas is reconstructed through an examination of the social relations which organize them. The processes which incorporate sexuality into labour relations for the purpose of meeting reproductive needs (maintenance) will be shown, highlighting the role of ideology, the state, and of economic agents. The diversification of labour relations in prostitution and the patterns of accumulation will also be discussed in their specific contexts.

The contemporary expression of prostitution through the venue of the tourist industry will be analysed from the following perspectives: (1) the international political economy of tourism as part of the larger sector of services, in particular leisure services; and (2) the place of female labour in the process of industrialization through tourism. In the study on Thailand, more specific aspects of prostitution and tourism will be shown, including the cognitive and material basis of prostitution, and the operation of the cognitive and institutional structures in combination with the class alliance and capital. This study will show how these combined social forces lead to the phenomenon of sex tourism.

Background

To some extent, the fury over prostitution in tourism expressed at various levels today is not new (Fernand-Laurent, 1983; Barry, 1984). It is a continuation of the last century's movement towards 'social purity' in the West. This movement has initiated discussions and action at an international level on the issue of 'white slave traffic' for the purpose of prostitution. This eventually led to the formulation and adoption by the United Nations of the Convention for the Suppression of the Traffic in Persons and of the Exploitation of the Prostitution of Others, in 1949. Subsequently, domestic legal measures were adopted by UN member states to criminalize prostitution and procuring syndicates.

However, evidence shows that such measures have brought about few changes in so far as suppressing the practice of prostitution and the traffic of women and children are concerned. In fact, two controversial trends have developed over the last few decades. Firstly, many studies have shown that the criminalization of prostitution has been selective. Law, and its enforcement, mainly affect women, while clients, pimps and brothel owners have remained relatively untouched (Smart, 1976; Jaget, 1980, McLeod, 1982; D'Cunha, 1987). Secondly, while prostitution is illegal in many countries, numerous forms of services related to sexual relations have emerged and are sanctioned by the law, e.g. escort services, eros centres, sex holidays, sex therapy centres, telephone sex-calls and dating services. The sex industry means big business in many countries.[1] Traffic in women for the purpose of prostitution is meanwhile being done through legally sanctioned overseas employment agencies and international mail-order bride agencies (Sereewat, 1983; Barry, 1984; Ohse, 1985; Mies, 1986).

Given this background, it is obvious that a revision of the notions of promiscuity and vice is needed. The old battle around the rights and wrongs of prostitution has been marked by the position, 'we hate sin, but we love sinners', i.e. criminalizing prostitution and rehabilitating prostitutes. Either the legal system is totally ineffective, or the barriers of morality have been seriously eroded, or this perspective is simply inadequate or incorrect. The expansion of the sex industry in many countries and of its international linkages through sex tourism clearly reflect the failure of many to live up to the ideal of moral conduct, if prostitution must be viewed as a sin.

Recent attempts to question the definition of prostitution as promiscuity were made by segments of the women's movement in the West in the 1960s and 1970s. The critique has been directed at the role of prostitution in patriarchal culture and its implications for women as a gender and as prostitutes. This led to the formulation of the issue of prostitution within the framework of the violation of human rights and of women's rights, in particular. In the process of the campaign against sex tourism, however, many more complex issues have been revealed, including racial discrimination, business ethics, economic policy, and international relations (cultural, economic, social and political).

Until today, at the international level, sex tourism is presented only as a violation of human rights and women's rights (de Vries, 1985). Its basis in economic policy and international relations has been somehow silenced.[2] Equally, the ethics of business and sexual conduct are rarely discussed. The present terms of the international discussion on sex tourism either 'womanize' the issue, or nationalize the issue. To put it differently, sex tourism is either seen as a form of violence against women, or as a problem which emerged from the specific social and economic conditions of a country.

Beyond the issues of the violation of women's rights and of poverty, which do reflect some aspects of reality, there remains the industrial basis of the production of sexual services. The moral and legal structures in many countries recognize only certain aspects of prostitution. It is therefore essential to show what is recognized and denied in prostitution, when, by whom, and why. It is very likely that, together with other factors, the contradiction between recognition and denial has contributed to today's thriving sex industry.

Before such aspects of prostitution can be shown, a number of questions must be dealt with. For example, what constitutes sex as a human need? What is the material basis of the relations which organize the satisfaction of this need? How are these relations related to the organization of production?

In dealing with these questions, it is reckoned that conceptual thinking on sexuality can have an effect in the sphere of politics and practices. Conceptual thinking does form a part of acquired and processed knowledge and a basis for practices. It is therefore important to show how particular forms of acquired and processed knowledge about prostitution emerge, how they are related to practices and their implications for prostitutes. So far, the conception of prostitution as promiscuity appears to be most powerful, as it permeates the cognitive and institutional structures of many societies. The source of this conception is deeply rooted in a scientific view of sexuality which is far from impartial.

Four main trends of thought on sexuality may be distinguished. The first trend of thought is built on the empiricist tradition and rests upon a definition of sexuality essentially as a biological urge. Here, two main positions may be distinguished, namely the bio-social view and the socio-cultural view. The bio-social view argues that patterns of sexual behaviour are natural outcomes of the sexual urge, with the male urge being stronger and more expressive. The recurrence of male dominance in sexual relations through time is explained as a consequence of the male biological construct and therefore as immutable (Tiger and Fox, 1974; Wilson, 1975; van den Berghe, 1978). Thus, promiscuity, polygamy, prostitution and rape are products of biology and not of history. By contrast, the socio-cultural view argues that sexual behaviour and institutions are products of the interaction between the sexual urge and specific socio-cultural systems. Influenced by Freud, this view maintains that although cultural regulations are necessary to hinder the sexual urge, they are not arbitrarily constructed, but follow the dictum of the sexual urge while performing their function in a given society. In loosely organized societies, sexual morality is equally loose, therefore the phenomenon of prostitution does not exist (Malinowski, 1932). By contrast, in highly organized societies there exists a repressive sexual morality which has its own costs, namely pathological sexual behaviour (Ellis, 1927). The idea that sexual pathology and promiscuity are products of the tension between cultural regulations and the sexual urge is pursued by many writers in the field of the sociology of deviance and sociological dysfunction (Davis, 1937; Lemert, 1951; Kelly, 1979). The existence of prostitution is explained in terms of its function of serving the male sexual urge, while women's entry into prostitution is explained in terms of economic dependence as well as their rebellion against repressive morality. This approach is male-centred and comes close to defining sexuality in terms of male sexual needs.

The second trend of thought defines sexuality as an expression of cultural meanings and symbols surrounding biological sex and sexual practices — commonly referred to as the social construction of gender. Based on the work of Lévi-Strauss (1969) who adopts an anti-empiricist position and argues that social phenomena are objectified systems of ideas, the social construction of gender approach identifies three realms of sexual expression (Ortner, 1974; Rubin, 1975). These realms are: the abstract, the intermediate, and the empirical. In its abstract form, the meaning of sexuality is found in symbols and language, sometimes also in what is loosely defined as ideology. In its intermediate form, such symbols and language express their meaning in religions, media, scientific debate, the law and popularized social norms. Empirically observed sexual practices and institutions are merely an expression of the abstract and the intermediate definition of sexuality and the power relations embodied in it. Here, biological sex and the social construct of gender become conflated. Sexual practices and institutions which are offensive to women's identity (prostitution, pornography, rape) are analysed as empirical expressions of a deeper phenomenon, i.e. male control over female sexuality and male violence against women. Rather than accepting existing explanations on promiscuity, this approach is female-centred and clearly defines sexuality as an expression of male social power (ideological, institutional, behavioural), and promiscuity and sexual violence as male creations.

The third trend of thought adopts a historical approach to sexual relations and is built on Engels' work (1981). This trend emphasizes the role of economic relations in shaping sexual norms and relations. Sexual morality and ideological assumptions about sexual roles are analysed in terms of the formation of subjects fit for historically specific socio-economic relations (Kuhn and Wolpe, 1978; Gimenez, 1978). Thus, rather than reducing the phenomenon of male dominance to patriarchal ideology, this trend of thought emphasizes the transformation of such ideology and its role in sustaining particular economic systems through history. Emphasis is on the control of female sexuality and labour in the social organization of child-bearing and -rearing, and of household services. Rather than discussing sexuality as a construct of cultural symbols and ideological assumptions, this approach relates these symbols and assumptions to socio-economic relations, to the formation of the sexual division of labour and to its effects on women's social and economic position in historically specified periods. Here, biological sex and the social construction of gender are separated. Biological sex is considered as static, while gender ideology responds to changes in economic relations inside and outside the household. This approach does not deal with consequences for their position in wage-work. Women in prostitution are often bypassed, except by those who examine the wider process of social reproduction beyond the confines of the family (Bujra, 1982; White, 1986). Those who maintain the rigid dichotomy between the household and market and who see prostitution as a form of violence against women rather than work, refer to prostitutes as scabs who represent a source of division among women and who make a sex-strike among housewives inconceivable (Ferguson, 1978: 300).

The fourth trend of thought is also historical but adopts an anti-essentialist notion of sexuality, and brings the debate beyond the male–female relationship. It rejects the notion that sexuality can be defined as something constant, whether on a biological or ideological basis (Foucault, 1980a). Emphasis is placed on the existence of a multiplicity of 'discourses on sex' (fields of knowledge), their diverse social and historical origins, and the equally diverse methods of regulation and control which are entailed. Sexuality is understood as an aggregation of social relations (male–female, state–civil, class) which are historically specific. 'Discourses on sex' extend themselves over the areas of fertility and eroticism and differ along historical as well as class lines. The dominant 'discourse' is related to a regime of power which regulates its practices, and to the forms of behaviour within which individuals recognize themselves as sexual subjects. Discourses on sex create diverse sexual categories which include those related to fertility (such as husband and wife) as well as those related to eroticism (such as 'the normal' and the 'perverse'). Through such categories, social power (e.g. that of communities and the state) is exercised over individuals and their subjective sexual experience. As pointed out by Weeks (1987: 23), this historical approach to sexuality re-examines the old question concerning the forces that shape sexual norms and behaviour from the angle of the history of ideas about sex and its relationship to social history. As such, it enables us to relate ideas about sex, regulations and practices to wider social change, in terms of their functional as well as political implications.

These approaches to the subject of sexuality show that there is no ready-made theoretical framework with which to analyse the interconnection between prostitution and tourism, let alone to formulate strategies and policies.

The first two trends of thought ascribe too much importance to the male–female relationship almost to the exclusion of class and ethnic relations. The third trend of thought touches upon the labour process and therefore can show labour-related transformations of sexual relations and ideologies. However, because of its focus on economic and social relations, sexuality is discussed on the basis of ideological assumptions about gender roles and their relationship with production, to the exclusion of the biological and subjective dimensions of sex. The fourth trend of thought is most comprehensive. However, as it minimizes the role of economic forces and stresses the area of subjectivity, it does not discuss how economic forces can utilize and benefit from particular sexual identities which have been created. While it stresses the domain of power relations inherent in sexual subjectivity, it leaves out the relationship between the constitution of sexual subjects and its application in economic relations. In other words, it does not give a place to notions about sex in the division of labour.

The analytical framework of this study will draw upon the third and fourth approaches to the subject of sexuality outlined above. Sexuality is seen both through the history of ideas and in terms of the relationship between such ideas and socio-economic relations. This framework can show the developmental nature of prostitution through the changing relations of production, highlighting the effects of class, race and generation.

Although the main focus is on Thailand, relevant secondary data on the phenomenon as it occurred or is occurring elsewhere will be used to support essential elements of the framework. The main aim is to show how the process of accumulation can take place from the labour embodied in prostitutes, emphasizing the effects of cognitive and institutional structures and the ambivalence between recognition and denial inherent in them. It is suggested that through prostitution and tourism a link is being fostered between the local sexual division of labour and the international division of labour in the production of welfare services. As unrecognized workers, the contribution of prostitutes in this division of labour remains invisible in spite of the blatant exposure of their flesh.

Organization of the Study

This study is composed of two parts. Part I deals with theoretical issues which are consequential to policies and practices. The aim is to provide a foundation for conventional wisdom and theories and for their critique, leading to the formulation of a more accurate analytical framework. In each approach of the social sciences, ranging from sociobiology and anthropological functionalism to Marxism, structuralism and the feminist paradigm, the causes and effects of prostitution and the place of the prostitute will be examined. This will be the basic task of chapter 1. In chapter 2, a less conventional framework will be considered for the analysis of sexual labour in prostitution, tracing the relation between the historical conception of the human body, its place in cognitive and institutional structure and the division of labour. The socio-economic and political processes which organize sexual labour in prostitution will be identified and discussed.

Part II deals with the international political economy of prostitution and tourism, using Thailand as an example. Chapter 3 demarcates leisure as a new terrain for capital investment and production, highlighting the main economic and political factors and policy decisions underlying the emergence of international tourism as a new leisure industry. The structure of power relations in the production of tourism and its operation will be described and discussed, showing how the interplay between discourse, culture and economy contributes to the incorporation of prostitution in the packages of tourism services. Chapters 4 and 5 present the experience of Thailand in the process of its integration into the political economic structure of international tourism. Chapter 4 explores the discursive and material origins of prostitution in Thailand prior to its incorporation in tourism. Chapter 5 illustrates the operation of the discourse on prostitution in combination with social alliance, economic policy and business practices, showing that the interconnection between prostitution and tourism is a product of this operation. The study concludes with a summary of its main arguments and some remarks on ethical questions regarding prostitution.

Notes

1. One source suggests that the yearly turnover of the pornographic industry in the United States alone stands at US$4 billion (Morgan, 1984: 110). Another source estimates the yearly turnover of the pornographic industry on the North American continent at US$8 billion and that there are more outlets for sexual and erotic goods and services than there are McDonald's fast-food restaurants (Bell, 1987: 161).

2. Since 1975, several attempts have been made by women's groups in the East and Southeast Asian region to bring governments' attention to the ongoing process of exploitation in the sex-related entertainment industry which sustains the tourist industry. Due to its effects on the balance of payments, only cosmetic gestures have been taken (such as requesting tour operators not to be so blatant in advertising sexual services; or discussing alternative employment creation strategies for women).

Part I
The Analytical Framework for Prostitution

The two chapters in this part deal with the main conceptual issues related to prostitution and their practical consequences. Social scientific writing on prostitution in this century has faced a major difficulty in coming to terms with the nature of sexual relations and sexuality. The conceptualization of prostitution is directly related to current views on the human body, its sexual faculties and functions. Such views are generally coloured by a prevailing cultural ethos which lies at the core of the social construction of sexual norms. It is therefore important to trace the process whereby the corpus of thought (theory and conventional wisdom) on prostitution emerged, the causes and effects assigned to it, and their implications on prostitutes as women. This is the main objective of chapter 1. In chapter 2, an alternative framework is developed for the analysis of prostitution from the angle of the political economy of women's labour and reproduction. Here, a relationship is established between sexuality and economy, placing the human body in social analysis and taking up the issue of sexual labour in reproduction. The chapter identifies the main dimensions of reproduction, separates its biological and social aspects, looks at the social relations which organize these dimensions, and how such relations are transformed. In so doing, it shows that there is a level of labour derived from the utilization of the body as an instrument of labour which has been concealed by cognitive and institutional structures (religion, morality, legal practices). The patterns of organization of sexual labour in prostitution will also be delineated and discussed, showing the diverse conditions under which prostitution takes place and the social structures which ensure such patterns.

1. Prostitution, Social Theory and Politics

> They say, 'you have a blue guitar
> You do not play things as they are'.
> The man replied: 'things as they are
> Are changed upon the blue guitar.'
> *Wallace Stevens, in Ruthven, 1979: 8*

Defining Prostitution

Social scientists dealing with prostitution are often affiliated with the following disciplines: history, sexology, sociology, psychology, and the interdisciplinary field of women's studies. The bulk of the work done by scientists in these disciplines concerns specific types of prostitution or some important aspects of the phenomenon taken as a whole. The contours which have been identified to define the phenomenon tend to be partial, and the arguments are fragmented.

According to the *Encyclopaedia Britannica* (1973–74), prostitution may be defined as 'the practice of habitual or intermittent sexual union, more or less promiscuous, for mercenary inducement. It is thus characterized by three major elements: payment, promiscuity, and emotional indifference'. The element of promiscuity underlines the assumption that sexual intercourse is morally accepted only within the confines of socially accepted unions. The elements of payment and emotional indifference reflect the assumption that sexual intercourse within socially accepted unions is unpaid and involves emotional attachment. Both assumptions merit reconsideration as they are not applicable in many situations.

Other definitions indicate an agreement among scientists that the element of payment is most basic, but clearly the economic criterion alone does not suffice. The areas of disagreement concern the social confines in which prostitution manifests itself. Thus, Davis (1937; 1976) argues that since some form of payment is found in social arrangements such as marriage and courtship, the element of promiscuity must be retained in the definition in order to differentiate prostitution from other types of relation between the sexes. This view is extended by Polsky (1967) who defines prostitution as the granting of 'non-marital sex as a vocation'. However, Polsky does not accept the inclusion of promiscuity since it denotes a certain bias, i.e. there are women who engage themselves in sexual intercourse on an indiscriminate basis, yet they are not considered as prostitutes by official agencies or the public. Although the element of vocation and its legal implications pointed out by Polsky can serve as important clues, his assumption of the public acceptance of 'promiscuous' women is debatable. In many societies, women who exercise their right to choose their own sexual partners are betokened as prostitutes, or may be severely and violently punished. More significantly, the term 'prostitute' and the stigma attached to it have been used in some societies to label women who are not necessarily 'promiscuous' but who directly challenge social norms governing their conduct.

A less moralistic definition of prostitution is that of Gagnon (1968) who sees prostitution as the 'granting of sexual access on a relatively indiscriminate basis for payment in money or goods, depending on the complexity of the local economic system. Payment is acknowledged for the specific sexual performance'. With this definition Gagnon hopes to be able to differentiate professional prostitutes from mistresses or from women who accept a range of gifts while having sexual contact with men. Thus, prostitutes are defined as professionals on the basis of monetary exchange and the scarcity of the services provided. These services are assumed to be unavailable within the confines of non-commercial sexual relations.

However, as many writers have pointed out, this differentiation is artificial since in patriarchal societies the social relationship between men and women is such that the control of women's sexuality and female prostitution form two sides of the same coin, i.e. male dominance. The separation between the wife (the respectable woman), the mistress (the kept woman) and the prostitute (the fallen woman) only serves to divide women and to strengthen patriarchal ideology, to conceal women's consciousness of their common conditions of dependence on men and of being a source of male pleasure and caterer for emotional demands. In this context, prostitution is seen as an expression of the 'cultural hegemony' of men over women (Rowbotham, 1973).

Based on Rowbotham's view, a more forceful approach is advanced by Barry (1981b), who showed empirically that women are forced into prostitution by men who use a variety of means ranging from deceptive promises of jobs, marriage or the 'invisible enslavement' of love and loyalty (for a pimp), to physical kidnapping and imprisonment. Barry argues that under male cultural hegemony women form a vulnerable social group, and that this vulnerability provides ample opportunities for men to abuse and exploit them sexually. Barry writes: 'Female sexual slavery is present in *all* situations where women and girls cannot change the immediate conditions of their existence; where regardless of how they got into those conditions they cannot get out; and where they are subject to sexual violence and exploitation' (1981b: 40).

Although Barry's definition brings out a very important dimension of prostitution other authors have ignored, namely coercion, it is both too wide and too narrow. While slave labour in prostitution has existed and still exists today, it is not the only source of labour in prostitution. Secondly, not all women who are subject to sexual exploitation can be regarded as sexual slaves, even when they cannot get out of the situation. Slavery carries the notion of the social outcast, of property, and compulsory labour (Watson, 1980). In many societies, there are women who are purchased as a piece of property through marriage, who must perform compulsory labour in the husband's household, and may be sexually abused, but they are not social outcasts. However minimal, the marriage contract still provides them with some legal protection.

Moreover, the labour extracted from their bodies at the household level is not always linked with the external system of trade and exchange. By contrast, there are women who are coerced into providing sexual services by pimps and brothel owners and kept under relations of confinement without any legal contract or protection. Their labour is directly connected with accumulation and they are discharged once their usefulness ends. Finally, there are women who practise prostitution as a profession to support a 'love object' (a man, a woman, parents, siblings, children) to whom they are 'invisibly enslaved' by love and loyalty. They may be considered as social outcasts, but they are the property of no one; they use their own labour as their own property to make money. Although their money may be used to support someone else, this should not be confused with any proprietary relationship. A distinction should also be made between sexual abuse within kinship relations, and sexual abuse under commercial relations. The former is often not connected with exchange and accumulation while the latter is. Although sexual abuse within kinship relations may lead to abuse and exploitation under commercial relations, these cannot be taken together under the category of slavery only on the basis of their similar relations of confinement.

On the whole, it may be observed that there are three main elements of prostitution which are widely recognized: economic, sexual, and psychological (emotional, individual psycho-structure). As all these elements are present in most sexual relations, the contested issue concerns how a prostitute can be distinguished from other women. One definition homogenizes prostitutes under the issue of vocation, scarcity of sexual services and skills, and promiscuous desires. The other definition homogenizes the female sex under patriarchal culture. As patriarchal culture defines female sexuality in male terms to serve male needs, no distinction can be made between prostitutes and other women. As such, prostitution cannot be accepted as a vocation but only as a form of violence against women's dignity.

Both definitions have problems stemming from overgeneralization about the economic aspect of prostitution (utility and scarcity of sexual skills) and the political aspect of prostitution (male dominance and male vice). While the emphasis on vocation and scarcity recognizes the utility and economic basis of prostitution, homogenizing prostitutes as professionals means that the element of political domination of men over women cannot be addressed nor coerced labour in prostitution be taken into account. By contrast, homogenizing women under male domination enhances the political aspect of prostitution and related forms of sexual abuse, but minimizes the social differences among women and among prostitutes. These differences are important and do form a source of conflict regarding sexual morality and practice as will be shown in the latter part of the chapter. An examination of old forms of prostitution may shed some light on the changes and continuity in prostitution.

The oldest form of prostitution is found in ancient countries such as India and ancient Babylon. As the concept of sexuality was connected with the sacredness of fertility or mysticism about birth and human life, practices of prostitution were closely connected with religious rituals. In ancient Babylon, women affiliated with a temple performed sexual intercourse with strangers who visited the temple to honour fertility and the sexual power of the goddess. Customary rewards took the form of a donation to the temple. These women had access to land, slaves and enjoyed social prestige (Lerner, 1986). Similarly, the *Devadasi* (temple prostitute) of India owed her social prestige and privileges to her 'dedicated status' to the deity of the temple and to her artistic and sexual skills which she exercised to maintain herself and her offspring (Srinivasan, 1985). *Devadasis* were recruited from lower castes and formed a distinct social group with access to religious goals in a context where the classical formulation of the salvation question was misogynic, i.e. women needed to be reborn as men before they could hope to undertake the quest of salvation (Marglin, 1985).

Non-religious prostitution was associated with the ruling class as well as with the lower social strata. In so far as the ruling class was concerned, prostitution was often not condemned but glorified in one way or another. In East Asian societies such as China, Japan and Vietnam, *Geisha* and *Ky Nu* were women who provided services which included cultural aspects such as music, poetry, dance as well as sexual services to men of the ruling aristocracy and the court. They were recruited from all classes, were socially respected as artists and could acquire significant privileges and some social influence, depending on the men with whom they were affiliated. In Western Europe, similar forms of prostitution were found among *courtesans* during the rule of kings and aristocrats. Courtesans were replaced by *demi-mondaines* with the advent of capitalism and the emergence of the bourgeoisie.

Existing in parallel with prostitutes serving the ruling class were those who served men of the lower stratum of society. They had to be identifiable, were isolated and bore social stigma. In the Middle Ages for example, prostitutes in Europe were allowed to form their own guild, but they had to wear clothes that distinguished them from 'respectable women'. This stemmed from the Christian conception of sex as sin and of prostitution as functional to male lust. The position adopted by Saint Augustine and Saint Thomas Aquinas clearly reflects this view. Saint Augustine condemned prostitution but argued: 'yet remove prostitution from human affairs and you will pollute all things with lust' and therefore 'harlots were a lawful immorality'. Saint Thomas Aquinas also defended the same position: 'Take away the sewage and you will fill the palace with pollution . . . take away the prostitutes from the world and you will fill it with sodomy' (Parrinder, 1980: 225–6). The tolerance of prostitution was mainly of a fiscal and moral nature, namely collecting taxes from brothels and prostitutes while protecting the integrity of the family upheld by law and religion (Chauvin, 1982).

As Perry (1985) has shown, legalized prostitution in pre-industrial Europe was not only a response to socio-economic problems but also an expression of a larger consciousness about women and sexuality. Increased urbanization, demographic instability, and the economic dislocation of women led to the acceptance of the social utility of the brothel in two senses. The brothel provided a place for men who were dislocated from their kin to satisfy their sexual needs, and a place for dislocated women to be sheltered in the absence of other possibilities such as marriage or cloister. Secondly, brothels provided a source of income for religious corporations and municipalities (Perry, 1985: 144–5). Thus, while witch hunts raged through Europe between the 12th and 17th centuries victimizing women who possessed skills and knowledge, prostitutes were not persecuted owing to the recognition of their sexual utility. Until the 14th century, prostitutes had their own guilds, their own place in Church processions and their own patron saint, Saint Magdalena (Mies, 1986: 81). However, from then onwards, owing to the spread of syphilis and other venereal diseases, tighter control was ensured through health inspection, registration and confinement which eventually led to the labelling of prostitutes as a source of moral and physical infection and the brothel as a place where 'bad' women were confined and distinguished from 'good' women.

Historical changes have transformed the position of privileged prostitutes as well as common prostitutes. Many of the categories of prostitutes affiliated with the monarchy and aristocracy have disappeared, as have prostitutes' guilds. With the emergence of the social purity movement in the 19th century and the affiliated abolitionist campaign, prostitutes lost their rights to organization and became legally singled out as a deviant sub-species of the female sex. The only known category which continues to exist under the guise of religion and culture is the *Devadasi* who has lost many of her traditional rights and is forced to work as a common prostitute within highly commercialized and exploitative relations (Ramesh and Philomena, 1984; Srinivasan, 1985; 1988). From these observations, it may be noted that the transformation of the confines of prostitution corresponds to the transformation of socio-economic relations as well as to the changing conception of human sexuality. Such transformation also affects the treatment of prostitutes and their ability to have control over their own lives.

Rather than assigning an historical property such as promiscuity or sexual violence to prostitution, it is more useful to start with the most basic element in prostitution, namely sexual services under exchange relations, and look how the nature of such services and the relations surrounding them are transformed. Prostitution must be understood as a set of social relations which involves the provider of sexual services, the receivers or buyers and the regulator. This set of relations assumes particular historical forms which are affected by wider social transformation (e.g. in kinship relations, relations of production and ideology). Skills, vice or violence are specific to the forms through which social relations in prostitution are expressed. The nature of the social relations of prostitution concerns the regulation and control of the exchange of sexual services, the distribution of material gains, and the constitution of prostitutes (as providers of sexual services) as subjects. These aspects vary with history and the particular sites through which prostitution is practised. Therefore a definition of prostitution must allow room for these variations.

What follows is an examination of the ways in which the major theoretical approaches in the social sciences — including sociobiology, functionalism, historical materialism, structuralism and the feminist critique — have dealt with the subject of prostitution. The attempt here is to delineate the main assumptions about the nature of human sexual and social conduct, to show how these assumptions manifest themselves in the analysis of prostitution, and to relate them to policies on and the politics of prostitution.

Sociobiology and Prostitution: Phallocracy and One-dimensional Sex

The main objective of this section is to identify the basic assumptions about the naturalness of the human anatomy in sociobiology and to discuss their implications for the analysis of prostitution. It is argued that the danger of the sociobiological approach lies in its reduction of complex social institutions to a limited number of biological traits, and thereby ignores social power relations. Sociobiological arguments can provide a basis for the justification of oppressive social structures and practices.

Sociobiology is a research strategy which attempts to explain the nature of human behaviour by applying the evolutionary principles advanced by Darwin. For this reason it is also known as social Darwinism. Emerging in the 19th century, social Darwinism was used to explain human individual and collective social evolution. As regards to the male–female relation, the main position adopted by social Darwinists was the location of the unequal progress of men and women in differences in biological faculties. Spencer, for example, saw nature as having fitted the male and female sexes in their social roles — women as homebound child-bearers and men as actors in the public domain. Women were seen as less socially evolved than men through 'the a priori inference that fitness for their respective parental functions implies mental differences between the sexes' (quoted in Sayers, 1982: 35). Seeking to relate biological faculties to social differentials was the fundamental feature of sociobiology.

Although orthodox social Darwinism has been discredited for some time, in the last decade it re-emerged with the new sociobiology, maintaining more or less the same principles, while abandoning crude biological approaches and concepts such as craniometry and *atavism*. Three influential authors who represent the new school of sociobiology are Trivers (1972), Wilson (1975), and Dawkins (1976). The new school attempts to convince us that the genetic component of the human body cannot be ignored by those who try to explain human behaviour, and that the knowledge provided by sociobiology is important for ethical and political decisions made by those who govern a 'planned society' (Wilson, 1975: 575). Wilson thus advises that 'it is time we start viewing ourselves as having biological, genetic and natural components to our behaviour, and that we start setting up a physical and social world to match those tendencies' (Wilson quoted by Lowe, 1978: 124). While the pretension that human society can be modelled and executed by a handful of scientists and policy makers is not new and not particularly limited to sociobiology, the basic assumptions of this approach to human nature are essentially static and ahistorical, and therefore do not capture complex social relations.

Sociobiology has no theory of human nature to use as the ontological basis of its methods and theory. Central to the sociobiological approach to human nature are the concepts of genes and adaptation. Human nature is defined in terms of genetic composition. Behaviour and genes form a positive backloop, i.e. if any behavioural trait has genetic components, then that trait is adaptive to the given environment (Lowe, 1978; Harris, 1980; Sayers, 1982). That is, it has developed so far as to maximize the number of genes favouring that behaviour to pass on to other generations. The goals of sociobiology are: (1) to explain the consistent recurrence of certain traits of human behaviour as a consequence of human nature; (2) to elevate these to the level of universality on the grounds of their historical and cultural validity; (3) to explain the cultural variations of these traits in terms of environmental differences. The consistency of these traits is further backed up with observations of primate and other animal behaviour since it is assumed that *Homo sapiens* evolved from lower order primates and therefore share certain genetically controlled traits with such species.

Studies on prostitution which adopt the theories and methods of sociobiology can be categorized into two types, namely those within the confines of criminology and those that consider prostitution as an aspect of human sexual behaviour. The former sees prostitution as a moral crime and the act of prostituting oneself as a result of moral idiocy. The latter places prostitution in the context of human sexual behaviour, and analyses it in the context of the relationship between biology and society, and argues that the institution itself is a social imperative to accommodate the overpowering male sex drive.

The field of criminology emerged in 18th-century Europe, and was heavily influenced by orthodox sociobiological principles. Central to the classical approach to criminology applied in early studies on prostitution is the concept of *atavism*, which embodies the assumption that anti-social elements found in individuals are in fact a recurrence of traits found in ancestors who are more remote than the parents. The first studies of this kind emerged during the 19th century in Europe where the increasing numbers of prostitutes found in large cities somehow seemed to have represented a violation of the Victorian image of a 'civilized' society.

As shown by Ellis (1927), those who have adopted this approach simply used arrested prostitutes as study samples, examining their physiques including shape of hands, jaws, brain size etc., and deriving their conclusions from these observations. They proposed that the organic constitution of these women represented a biological degeneration, causing moral idiocy which in turn caused them to avail themselves as sexual objects in exchange for money (Lombroso and Ferrero, 1895, in Ellis, 1927 and Smart, 1976). A milder version of the deterministic influence of *atavism* is reflected in the work of Kemp (1936) whose observation of the lineage of arrested prostitutes led him to conclude that prostitution had a hereditary dimension, as a number of them had mothers and grandmothers who were themselves harlots.

The major problem with the concept of *atavism* is the fact that it regards human 'civilization' as a linear process characterized by high standards of morality based on reason and rationality. Immoral people are those who fail to adhere to such standards as the result of their lack of capacity to reason, itself biologically determined. This concept ignores the role of socio-economic forces that give rise to a particular morality and other forces that contribute to the failure of those who do not adhere to its standards. It only takes into account biologically determined forces. Moreover, the concept of *atavism* denies the dimension of social stigmatization and/or male coercion which may constitute the major barrier preventing the departure of prostitutes and their children from harlotry. The danger of defining morality on the basis of biological traits is that it negates the exploitation of those who are defined as biologically inferior, legitimizing the perpetuation of such exploitation. It is important to point out here that although the concept of *atavism* was abandoned some time ago, the evolutionary principle embodied in this concept has been largely retained. Thus, the idea that moral idiocy is a feature of the lower class and that the act of prostituting oneself is the result of a lack of morality still permeates contemporary thinking with varying degrees of explicitness.

The contemporary body of literature on prostitution which treats the subject as one aspect of human sexual behaviour determined by human anatomy, claims that humans have a striking resemblance to primates. Firstly, there is a biologically determined difference between male and female sexual behaviour. Secondly, this difference has consequences for other types of behaviour with non-sexual motives. The biological construct of males dictates that their behaviour be assertive, while female biology is constructed in such a way that their sexual behaviour is passive (Sayers, 1982). The dominant role of the male is further enhanced by the fact that he can impregnate an unlimited number of females whereas the female capacity to have intercourse is limited because of pregnancy, childcare and lactation even though biologically she can always be responsive. Thus, the male tends to be interested in all females and tries to collect as many as possible while the female is more pressured to draw the male who has impregnated her towards herself by granting sexual favours in order to ensure that he will provide for her and her offspring (Wilson, 1975). This creates the pressure of sexual selection, i.e. the battle among males for females, and the desire of females to choose among the males to ensure the recurrence of the best genes in her offspring (Trivers, 1972).

Furthermore, sociobiologists argue that sexual dimorphism in humans and animals also entails a difference in parental investment. Mammals (humans in particular) have longer gestation, lactation and maturation periods with the heavy burden of parental investment falling mainly on females. Heavy parental investment leads to the restriction of physical mobility and ultimately to dependence on males for survival. This sets the conditions of the struggle for survival of females (and their offspring) who tend to use sex for non-sexual ends (Trivers, 1972).

The contention here is that the biological construct of the male determines the institution of polygyny, at least in part, while the biological construct of the female determines her tendency to grant sexual favours for survival and to use her assets to her own advantage (Lewontin, et al., 1984: 260). More explicitly, this view is phrased as follows:

> Some primates use sexual behaviour for non-sexual purposes: female chimpanzees and baboons will sometimes present themselves sexually to a male in order to avoid attack or distract the male while the female purloins his food. It is a small step from such primate behaviour to accepting coitus for food. Consequently, it seems likely that the exchange of food for coitus began in the transitional period between man and ape, and that with the subsequent development of more elaborated rules of social behaviour, the restrictions of marriage, the concept of parenthood, prostitution was eventually defined in some form and set apart as an entity to be accepted or condemned. (*Encyclopaedia Britannica: Macropaedia*, 1973–74: 76)

As has often been pointed out, among the many conceptual and methodological problems inherent in the sociobiological approach, the most important is that it simply selects certain characteristics from human history in particular cultures and times, elevates them to the level of universality and makes its theoretical departure from this point (Lewontin, et al., 1984). Thus, metaphysical categories such as altruism, selfishness, aggression, oppression, and historically specific social categories such as slavery, entrepreneurship, investment and competition are used by sociobiologists as conceptual tools to study animal behaviour. When these traits are confirmed in animal behaviour, sociobiologists then rely on the evolutionary principle to conclude that these are characteristics of human anatomical development (genetic adaptation) and are therefore the unchangeable products of nature. Furthermore, because they use ahistorical categories, sociobiologist arguments become caught in anthropomorphism rather than providing new explanations (Lewontin, et al., 1984).

In the context of prostitution, three main issues may be identified: (1) the reduction of the complex social and biological relationship between male and female to the male sex drive, (2) a static conception of the human body, and (3) the assumption that the female is both the seducer and exploiter of the male.

The reduction of complex sociosexual relationships to biological instincts leads to the justification of polygamy and prostitution on the basis of the male sex drive, and of the total dependence of women on men, on the basis of biology regardless of forms of exploitation this dependence may entail. As van den Berghe writes (1978: 44): 'Even prostitutes who are promiscuous for gain, experience the need of pimps in defiance of any economic interest'. It has been widely recognized that complex sociosexual institutions cannot simply be reduced to biological origins. The assumption that polygamy is a product of male sex drive and biological strength has been refuted by several studies which show that although polygamy is a common form of human mating, it is not the only one, that polyandry has existed and still exists in contemporary societies (Rodman, 1971; Harris, 1980). Equally, it has been shown that the system of multiple mates is conditioned by socio-economic factors rather than by biological needs alone (Reddock, 1984). Sexual rules and monogamy for women are part of the political process of male domination over females, and need to be understood within the context of the development of male sociopolitical power (Millett, 1971; Mitchell, 1975; Rubin, 1975). This complex process cannot be reduced to a few biological principles and the attempt to do so is in itself a reflection of sexism in scientific thought (Reed, 1978; Easlea, 1981).

Even if one accepts the argument that the sex drive is the sole determinant of sociosexual institutions, still, the static conception of an unchangeable biological drive in both male and female is known to be erroneous. Studies have shown that the so-called nature of human sexuality has been subject to biological evolution, i.e. the loss of oestrus in the female in the course of human evolution and its recurrence influenced by non-biological factors (Caufield, 1985). Thus, the human anatomy itself is a dynamic entity and theories about its behaviour cannot be deduced from its specific and visible organs.

Sociobiological arguments on the male–female relationship based on the assumption that the female is both the seducer and exploiter of the male, a behavioural trait determined by the fact that she must bear offspring, is loaded with flaws. At the level of evidence, studies have shown that all animals forage their own food and that males do not provide food for the female as a rule. In human societies, the thesis of male-the-hunter and provider has been increasingly exposed as a myth both by anthropological studies as well as by studies on the socioeconomies of contemporary societies (Martin and Voorhies, 1975; Tanner and Zihlman, 1976). Therefore, being endowed with a womb to bear offspring does not necessarily cause economic dependency leading to a tendency to accept coitus in exchange for food. While such a tendency may be accepted to be a pan-human trait, its cause cannot be located at the level of biology alone but must be searched for in the specific context of social organization.

At the level of subjective interpretation of sexual behaviour, many studies on the major patriarchal religions such as Islam, Christianity, Buddhism and Hinduism have shown that these so-called female behavioural characteristics have been derived from men's own subjective perception of human sexuality (Paul, 1979; Parrinder, 1980; Mernissi, 1982; Harris, 1984). In fact, studies exploring archaic cosmology have shown that such dichotomized notions of human sexuality did not exist in archaic thought. Human sexuality was seen as an interaction with nature which represented the wholeness of being and existence, and the mystic unity between human life and nature (Carmody, 1979; Parrinder, 1980). Subjective perceptions of human sexuality and their implications for sexual rules will be discussed in chapter 3, and in the case study on Buddhism in Thailand. Here, it is important to point out that the shift from a holistic approach to human sexuality to one which is marked by the dichotomy of two separate sexualities indicates that the social processes from which these notions emerged can neither be ignored nor accepted as biologically determined.

The conceptualization of prostitution on the basis of biological differences between the sexes is far too narrow and potentially dangerous. Such a framework essentially regards prostitution as an issue directly related to female anatomy and makes no provision for other types of prostitution such as homosexual prostitution and child prostitution. Accordingly, prostitution constitutes an issue pertaining mainly to the female sex and not to society at large. Furthermore, by seeing commoditized sexual intercourse as a natural evolution from the simple barter of sex and food, the sociobiologist conceptualization of the male–female relationship and of prostitution conceals social inequality between the sexes. It also fails to provide an explanation for complex relations in the system of commoditized sexual intercourse, which are not static and not always heterosexual. Moreover, due to the use of biological characteristics as basic tenets to justify social practices in a rather simplistic way, sociobiologist arguments can be easily popularized by those who want easy answers to complex social problems. In this sense sociobiologist arguments can be misused in different ways. It can serve to legitimize non-action against procurers or sex syndicates engaged in the traffic of women and children. It can serve to endorse the practice of purchasing the virginity of young girls by older men who can afford to spend, to fulfil their illusion of rejuvenation by deflowering a child under ten years of age. This issue will be taken up in chapter 5. Finally, the acceptance of male sexual aggression as biologically determined serves to justify the argument that prostitution helps reduce the incidence of rape.

Thus, rather than providing any guidelines for ethical and political decisions as it has presumptuously claimed, sociobiology can provide the necessary arguments for the legitimation of oppression and exploitation.

Functionalism and Prostitution: The Dilemma of Rationality

Functionalism in anthropology emerged as a challenge to biological reductionism, pledging to reject crude racist and sexist theories of behaviour derived from the sociobiological approach. Instead, the focus is placed on the relationship between social and biological facts, in which the sphere of the social is defined as 'culture', something beyond the biological. In the functionalist tradition, 'culture' is conceptualized as a result of social processes which shape human behaviour, and which subjugate biological facts to social ones. In Benedict's words (1934: 235–6):

> cultural interpretations of behaviour need never deny that a physiological element is also involved . . . To point out, therefore, that the biological bases of cultural behaviour in mankind are for the most part irrelevant is not to deny that they are present. It is merely to stress the fact that the historical factors are dynamic.

Functionalist anthropology attempts to defend the importance of pluralism and relativity of cultures on the basis of the different historical experiences of human societies.

The roots of functionalism can be traced to the work of Durkheim who left a mark on the thinking of contemporary sociology and anthropology. Two main Durkheimian principles may be identified: (1) social forces exercise an external constraint over individuals, and (2) individuals are themselves hierarchically organized by the action of these forces (Gane, 1983). Central to Durkheim's approach is the concept of 'collective conscience' defined as a set of ideas external to any given individual but endowed with coercive force over individual thought and behaviour (Harris, 1980: 166). With this concept, Durkheimian sociology moves from the material realm of biology to the realm of ideas as a reflection of social life. Society is seen as a holistic entity with its complex institutions and their interdependencies, and individual action is analysed mainly as determined by social structure rather than by volition.

Adopting the framework of liberal philosophy, functionalists define human nature in terms of reason, i.e. the ability to think, to create and control. 'Collective conscience' and social institutions are seen as products of reason which are functional to society since they represent a collective reaffirmation of society itself. It is further assumed that although humans have the same potential for rationality, the way in which they can develop this potential depends on the immediate physical milieu, hereditary antecedents, and social influences. Consequently, consciousness and action are diversified. The definition and treatment of an individual act depends on the criteria established by the collective and on the extent to which a given society has the power to judge (Durkheim, 1979), and thus on the cohesive force of the 'collective conscience'. The power of a given collective to judge is derived from the fact that in the process of individual subjugation to society, 'the qualities of civilization are developed by the dominant strata who become social beings of a more elevated type, and whose mode of domination is by virtue of their possessing moral superiority' (Gane, 1983: 244).

From a material perspective, Durkheim uses the concept of division of labour to differentiate qualitatively the character of 'collective conscience' of social groups. In primitive society, 'collective conscience' was archaic — mechanical solidarity — and based mainly on individual subjugation to the likeness of their conscience and similar needs (religion, magic). Social evolution, specialization and division of labour brought about a new type of 'collective conscience' — organic solidarity — which, in spite of social differentiation, provides a higher form of social cohesion. Out of a strong and repressive organic solidarity emerges a regression from collective sentiments, e.g. suicide or crime (Durkheim, 1951; 1979).

Durkheim saw social evolution and division of labour as having affected the male–female relationship in the following way. Initially based on sexual functions (procreation), the division of labour between the sexes became extended to other social functions. As a result, two great functions of psychic life (affective and intellectual) became dissociated. The former became primarily female and the latter male. Based on findings and inferences of craniometry and physical anthropology which suggested evolutionary dimorphism, Durkheim concluded that the female physique has regressed and the male has progressed as a result of social evolution (Gane, 1983: 239).

If social evolution has generated the costs of differentiated biological constructs and psycho-structure of the sexes, it also contributed to the creation of a new form of bonding essential to modern society, i.e. conjugality. Among the categories of organic solidarity, conjugal solidarity is the most important, representing to Durkheim the highest form of sexual union which rests upon the difference and division between the two sexes. He writes:

> If the sexes are not separated, an entire category of social life would be absent: the order of conjugal solidarity. Mutual dependence caused by functional differentiation produces a complex conjugal solidarity which carries ramifications throughout societies. Conjugal solidarity as it exists among the most cultivated people makes its action felt at each moment and in all the details of life. (Durkheim, 1960: 61)

The main assumptions which bear on later work within the functionalist framework can be discerned here:

- the assumption that 'collective conscience' is both a unitary and supreme subject both in a functional sense of affirming society as well as in the coercive sense over individual action;

- the assumption that human reason is evolutionary, the highest stage being a total adherence to collective ideas and values (religion, morality, social norms) and the lowest being anomie or a state of being without any moral or ideological affinity with the group;

- the assumption that human action is guided on the one hand by the different potential for reason determined by social milieu, and on the other hand by the cohesive power of collective values;

- the assumed link between heredity and social conduct;

- the assumption of a division of labour according to sex, whereby the female sex assumes affective roles and the male sex intellectual roles, is functional to society.

These assumptions show that while biological reductionism has been more or less abandoned, the biological model remains the main intellectual source providing the functionalist approach with a basic orientation to conceptualize the structure and functioning of social systems and to examine the evolutionary process of individual and collective behaviour through adaptation.

In functionalist anthropology, society is described as an organism with institutions as its constituents, presumed to be rational since they are the products of human reason. Culture is tripartite, divided by time, by space, and by space and time, i.e. geographically distinct contemporary cultures; cultures which developed in the same area as the society in question but in an earlier period; cultures which existed earlier in time and occupied a different area. In spite of the fact that functionalist anthropology acknowledges the relativity and diversity of cultures, a hierarchical order is built into this relativity by virtue of the fact that it uses categories derived from the history of Western culture as units of reference (Gaboriau, 1970). Coupled with its assumption that an understanding of the common logic governing this triple diversity will shed light on the gradual development of humanity and on the ways in which one kind of society evolves into another, this hierarchical relativity brings functionalism to a cultural evolutionist view of human societies scaled from 'primitive' to 'civilized'.

From this model, two main theoretical propositions on human sexual behaviour can be discerned. One adheres to the conceptualization of human sexuality formulated by sociobiologists, i.e. the overpowering male and the passive female, an animal instinct dictated by our biological construct. The other stresses the significance of social confines.

The first approach locates the function of sex at the level of the individual and thus as external to society, and considers society as an autonomous and neutral intervenor that introduces mechanisms to regulate this drive and channel it into distinct institutions. Without such institutions there would be serious social disruption as a result of competition for sexual partners, something which will prevent the development of 'culture'.

One of the most prominent anthropologists who sought to universalize the thesis of the emergence of culture through the control of sex on the basis of his studies of 'primitive societies' is Malinowski. Malinowski defines culture in terms of social responses to a hierarchy of biological needs. The concept of culture in Malinowski's thoughts is from the outset tied to biological functions. Cultural variation is seen as the variety of ways in which specific human needs are satisfied. Since all societies experience some forms of control over sexual conduct, sex, to Malinowski, constitutes the most important biological need. He writes: '"sex is really dangerous", a powerful and disruptive force which demands powerful means of regulating, suppressing and directing' (Malinowski, in Weeks, 1985: 102). The function of sex is not just the direct satisfaction of needs, but 'rather the satisfaction of what might be called *instrumental needs*, that is, needs for instruments, for means to an end, the end being the biological well-being of the individual, the procreation of the species, and also the spiritual development of the personality and the establishment of a give-and-take in social co-operation' (Malinowski, 1932: xxxvi).

While Malinowski cautions us to disassociate ourselves from the tendency to interpret culture purely on the basis of instincts, the way in which he conceptualizes human sexuality ties it narrowly to an animalistic drive, an antithesis of a human nature based on rationality. To him, if all cultures exhibit some rules of sexual conduct, these must be functional both in a biological and social sense. Thus, sex is an irrational individual desire, and society shows its rationality by subjugating this drive and by creating and promoting forms through which it can be distributed to satisfy human needs. The conclusion that can be drawn from this argument is that the more society places control on sex, the better the chance for human civilization. Thus, loosely structured sexual rules among 'savages' are seen as residues of history, while Victorian monogamy is seen as the mirror of civilization.

The main problem with this approach is that it uncritically accepts the theoretical proposition provided by sociobiology which reduces human nature to the level of instinct, a reduction which already contains some biases. Then, it combines this notion of instinctual determination with the notion of rationality of the human mind, thus providing a 'rational' basis to instinct. This combination can only view institutions through which sex expresses itself as being functional in so far as the sex drive is concerned, and as having little to do with the economy and organization of labour. It is precisely the narrow conceptualization of sexuality which led Malinowski to treat sexuality and culture in dualistic terms and to his failure to show the dynamic linkages between the two.

By contrast, the second approach argues that sex in itself is not such a crucial drive. What is important to understand is the social confines through which it expresses itself. Through these confines one may arrive at an understanding of the nature of human sexuality, as flexibly determined by culture and social conditioning rather than as raw instinct (Mead, 1949). As pointed out by Weeks (1985: 105), here the notion that contemporary mores form an evolutionary necessity which transcends primitive ones is rejected. The attempt is to show the flexibility of such mores and to advance the view that humans are capable of an enormous range of sexual behaviour which is subject to sanctions by 'culture', defined in terms of human responses to the demands of environmental conditions. Just as sexuality is flexible, so too is culture.

Although the apparent plasticity of this approach urges one to understand sex as a social construct, to be understood in relation to the diversity of social forces rather than in a biological vacuum, the central thesis remains the same: without rules governing the sexual conduct of both sexes, there can be no culture. As Mead writes: 'If any human society is to survive, it must have a pattern of social life that comes to terms with the difference between the sexes' (1949: 7). While the validity of this statement might be recognized, Mead leaves the question of 'coming to terms' unexplored, as if reason alone could bring about these terms. Furthermore, by placing the functionality of sex at the level of society, and by adopting a relativist approach to culture, Mead deletes the question of the origins of the control of sexuality, of social institutions, norms and sanctions altogether. By leaving out the question of the origins of the control of sexuality, Mead falls into the circular argument that socialization and behaviour reflect cultural patterns, which in turn condition individuals to reproduce their culture.

Both approaches bring out the right issue, but raise the wrong questions. While it cannot be disputed that all societies exhibit some form of control over human sexuality, and that the sexual need is biologically as essential as the desire for food, the forms of control of human sexuality are dynamically linked with the organization of the productive base of societies. Any change in this base entails a change of norms of sexual conduct which affects the social construction of desire (Ross and Rapp, 1981).

What appears to be the source of bias and circularity in both arguments is the acceptance of contemporary mores in sexual behaviour as products of nature (a theoretical inheritance from sociobiology) rather than as products of social and historical processes. As has been shown in the previous section, the theory of sexual dimorphism and its implications contain many inconsistencies. The acceptance of the elements embodied in this theory leads functionalists to perpetuate the same biases. Sexuality is seen mainly as functional to individuals or to society in general. What is left unquestioned are issues pertaining to the social and economic origins of the control of sexuality and the ways in which this control benefits the social, economic and political interests of particular types of social organization. Sex drive is discussed mainly as the male sex drive and control of human sexuality is left in general terms without making it explicit that it is *female* sexuality which is subject to more diverse forms of control than is male sexuality. With the exception of a few tribal communities, no society places strict rules of sexual conduct on males. Most societies tend to prescribe stricter norms of sexual conduct for females and to execute more severe forms of punishment for deviating from the norms prescribed. These norms are bound to the reproduction functions of both males and females and to the subjective value attached to their biological organs.

Many studies on prostitution have combined the assumptions advanced by functionalist anthropologists about human sexuality with elements of the sex-role theory developed by Parsons and Bales (1956). Writers on the sex-role theory have themselves combined on the one hand Durkheim's concept of conjugal solidarity with Mead's theory on role formation through socialization and acculturation. They argue that the different social positions men and women occupy result from the different roles ascribed to them by society on the basis of their biological and social functions. These roles are functional to the management of society since they complement each other. In this context, the division of labour between the sexes is not to be seen as socially oppressive but as natural and biologically given.

The point of departure of functionalist studies on prostitution is that all institutions through which sexual contact between men and women occurs are functional in one way or another. Courtship is functional to the preparation of wedlock, prostitution is functional to deviant desire not to be accommodated in marriage, or to purely biological urge without social responsibility. Within this broad assumption, these studies focus either on the functional relationship between society and the various sexual institutions (e.g. marriage, courtship, prostitution) or on sexual behaviour external to heterosexual monogamy. Such behaviour is assessed on the basis of pathology and deviance. The first approach seeks to show the rationality of existing sexual institutions, while the second attempts to enhance further this rationality by arguing that 'deviant' institutions help subsume deviant behaviour.

The work of Davis (1937) exhibits a clear institutional approach with an apologetic undertone as far as the male sex drive is concerned. To him, every institution has several motives and performs several functions. Thus, strictly speaking, each institution embodies a multiplicity of motives and functions, which show the validity of its existence at the individual and social level. Sex is valid for both levels. He writes:

> Sex, like other elements in human nature, is drawn to integration, and thus controlled . . . Sexual appetite like every other, is tied to socially necessary functions. The function it most logically and naturally relates to is procreation. The nature of procreation and socialization is such that their performance requires institutionalized primary-group living. Hence the family receives the highest estimation of all sexual institutions in society, the others receive lower esteem as they are remoter from its *Gemeinschaft* character and reproductive purpose. Commercial prostitution stands at the lowest extreme; it shares with other sexual institutions a basic feature, namely the employment of sex for an ulterior end in a system of differential advantages, but it differs from them in being mercenary, promiscuous and emotionally indifferent. From *both* of these facts, however, it derives its remarkable vitality. (1937: 747–9)

The implication here seems to be that men prefer not to be tied down in wedlock, something which is functional to society and therefore highly regarded, but want to have their cake and eat it too, so that prostitution remains a vital institution.

The main assumption of the institutional approach is that prostitution emerges from the rigidity of a moral system which glorifies the family and represses sexual intercourse outside marriage. Since sexual energy cannot always be channelled through marriage, harlotry performs an accommodating function. To avoid contesting the rationality of religion as 'an expression of the universal necessity of certain functions in society' (Davis 1948: 371), Davis attempts to bridge the gap in his argument by turning to economic rationality. He writes: 'Since the economic means are distributed unequally between the classes but female attractiveness is not, some women of the lower economic means can exploit their attractiveness for economic gains' (Davis, 1976: 345). Those with few positive physical attributes will try to have their security through marriage, while those with positive physical attributes will maximize their profit by using them.

The focus on economic rationality on the basis of sexual attractiveness and individual motives of prostitutes leaves out the role of clients, pimps and sex entrepreneurs. It simply assumes that there is a constant demand by men for female sexual services and that there is a constant supply to be channelled through either marriage or harlotry. 'The demand rests upon a constant imperative need, not always conveniently satisfiable by substitutes' (Davis, 1937: 751). Implicitly, this argument accepts the male biological drive as the major determinant of the institution of prostitution as well as that of marriage. It only differentiates the two institutions in terms of legal arrangements and social esteem. It provides no further insights into the complex sociohistorical basis from where these two institutions emerged, nor does it explain the internal dynamics of either institution. From the perspective of prostitutes, the argument rests very much upon the assumption of the rational individual act in terms of the available comparative advantages, without touching issues of structural inequality and relations of power and domination between prostitutes and agents operating within the confines of the institution itself. To view the act of selling one's sexual services as well as the act of buying such services strictly as a rational individual choice is to ignore the economic interests grounded in the institution at the state, community and enterprise level.

Furthermore, while it touches upon issues of inequality between men and women, i.e. women tend to prostitute themselves more than men because men are in a more favourable position to offer payment (Davis, 1937: 754), inequality here is far too narrowly conceived along the lines of economics, leaving out other aspects of inequality such as legal, social and political inequality. Leaving these aspects of inequality unaddressed bypasses many questions, e.g. who gains from prostitution and how prostitution is related to women's social conditions in particular and to wider social transformation. Equally neglected are the forms of prostitution which are constituted through physical and emotional coercion, as well as the issue of social stigma and the ideological aspects of oppression in prostitution.

The other approach which treats prostitution within the framework of social pathology (Lemert, 1951), takes its point of departure from the assumption of contemporary sexual mores (monogamous nuclear family) as a product of nature legitimized by morality. Acccordingly, prostitution is seen as a 'formal extension of more generalized sexual pathology in our culture, of which sexual promiscuity and thinly disguised commercialization of sex in informal contexts play a large and important part' (Lemert, 1951: 238). Thus, prostitution subsumes other forms of sexual conduct which are not tolerated by morality. Desires for these forms are regarded as 'unintegrated impulses' which require outlets. Thus, as an institution, prostitution is functional to society in the sense that it accommodates such impulses. However, far from seeing this pathology in terms of male demand, Lemert locates it in the psychological construct of the prostitutes themselves. He writes: 'A girl with a strong sense of inferiority may have a compulsive need to be sexually promiscuous, and some such girls may even find an adjustment as prostitutes. Urgent need to rebel against authority may be expressed by a woman through flagrant violations of the community sexual taboos . . . A far greater proportion of sexual aberrancy is situational, i.e. the product of the numerous stresses, strain, and conflicts in our culture which surround the sex act and which lead to segmental integration of normal and sociopathic sex behaviour' (Lemert, 1951: 246).

Here, Lemert criticized culture for being oppressive in sexual relations resulting in a kind of anomie, i.e. the refusal to subjugate oneself to social norms. Prostitution forms an act of this anomie. Elsewhere he asserted that 'in fact a strong case may be made that our culture normally disposes women to utilize sex for many purposes outside of the marriage relationship. There are elements of prostitution in the behaviour of most women in our culture' (Lemert, 1951: 246). The underlying implication of Lemert's statement about prostitution is that 'culture' has created a woman's nature which is inclined to use sex for non-sexual ends, and the institutions through which this 'nature' expresses itself are subject to a degree of anomie. Lemert's view comes very close to Durkheim's position on organic solidarity and its relation with regression and anomie. The higher the form of civilization, the more repressive collective conscience becomes and the more pathological are the emergent trends.

The limits of the functionalist explanation of prostitution are grounded on four fundamental issues. Firstly, because it accepts uncritically some elements of evolutionary theory concerning the relationship between sex roles and biological constructs, it can only confirm this theory and perpetuate its biases by providing a more elaborate description of the institution of prostitution in contemporary societies. The social function of prostitution is kept mainly within the context of biological needs and of the repressive function of morality. As such, functionalist anthropological and sociological approaches to prostitution do not address the politico-economic basis of the institution of prostitution. They mainly focus on the individual prostitute and her economic motivation.

Secondly, because the functionalist approach uses a theory of sex roles which was developed on the basis of ahistorical as well as class and culture-specific data, i.e. the middle-class in Western industrialized countries during the post World War Two period, its validity is limited and cannot be generalized.

Thirdly, because the functionalist approach accepts the affective role of women, it can only conceptualize prostitution as an extension of this role and does not question the role itself. The social difference between women is seen mainly as one of a normative character (i.e. the legal status of a wife versus the status of a prostitute), but essentially it is accepted that there is an aspect of prostitution in all types of female sexual behaviour. It is tautological to argue that women tend to prostitute themselves because of the character of their sociosexual roles, while at the same time they have such roles because they are women. As will be shown in the next section, the failure to question the notion of sex roles at the root level has led many feminists to come to the same functionalist conclusion.

Fourthly, the functionalist approach betrays its own goals on the issue of morality. The point of departure of functionalism is to show the logical cohesive force of morality by virtue of it being the highest form of psychic life. To argue that prostitution is a rational institution because it serves to accommodate the male sex drive and to protect the purity of the nuclear family, and that morality itself is irrational because it does not accept this functionality and punishes prostitutes who themselves are rational to have chosen this profession, in terms of the comparative advantages available to them, is to stand in contradiction with the very goals of functionalism. Here, one sees the danger of accepting 'culture' as something which stands above and beyond history. Because functionalism accepts 'culture' as such, it allows itself to use ahistorical categories which then bring it either into a tautological argument, or into one which contradicts its own goals.

Historical Materialism, Socialism and Prostitution: Alienation and Lumpen-Proletariat

Before discussing prostitution and socialism, a distinction must be made between socialism as a set of political principles derived from the writing of Marx and Engels who applied a scientific method known as historical materialism, and socialism as an historical experience of countries whose governments have chosen to apply such principles. As historical experiences, socialist countries share two main features as regards to prostitution: (1) a similar moralistic position which stigmatizes and criminalizes prostitutes in spite of the acceptance of the argument that they are victims of pauperization, poverty and residual capitalist relations; and   (2) the failure to eradicate prostitution. Both features call for a re-examination of socialist views on human liberation in general and women's liberation in particular. This section will show how Marx conflates prostitution with all relations of exchange of labour for monetary gain, how Engels reduces it to property relations, and how Lenin categorizes prostitutes as part of the lumpen-proletariat, not to be enlisted as members of the socialist movement.

One of the most important contributions of Marxist theory is the location of abstract categories such as human nature, human need, human consciousness and liberty in historical processes. Two main concepts used to explain the transformation of such categories are *praxis* and *alienation*. Marx sees the human being and the natural world as being dialectically related. Human beings transform the natural world to satisfy their needs, but in the process of transforming the natural world, they themselves are created anew. This process is called *praxis* and human nature is seen as being continuously constructed by *praxis*, thus not reducible exclusively to biological needs or to the intellect. In *Grundrisse*, Marx suggests that human nature is a historic result and that each historical epoch produces specific characteristics of human nature. 'The human being is in the most literal sense a political animal, not merely a gregarious animal, but an animal which can individuate itself only in the midst of society' (1973: 83–4). At a more general level human nature is defined by Marx essentially as human labour, i.e. the transformation of nature to produce human subsistence. Historically specific human nature is determined by the social relations which organize human labour. Thus, rather than something external and beyond material existence, human nature is to be understood both as human labour itself as well as the ways it expresses itself within the material confines of specific periods of history.

Under the capitalist system of production the value of labour power is concealed. Human nature is characterized by alienation, or the powerlessness of workers derived from the particularities of capitalist relations of production which cause the human being to become alien to: (1) the products of his/her own activity and/or to the activity itself;   (2) the material conditions in which he/she lives;   (3) his/her own historically created human possibilities, i.e. the potential to change his/her own material conditions. Through alienation, workers live in false consciousness and do not realize that the social productiveness of their labour is brought about at their own cost and is benefiting capital. Means of production are turned into means of domination and exploitation of the producer who become degraded to the level of an 'appendage of a machine' and whose intellectual potential is destroyed in the process. Here, alienation refers to all relations of exchange in which the one who is forced by the economic system to exchange that which is most his/her own, i.e. labour power, is devoid of any power and control over the act of exchange as well as over its product.

Relations based on the exchange of labour for money are seen as humanly degrading and oppressive, a view which is best expressed in the following analogy: 'Prostitution is only a *specific* expression of the *universal* prostitution of the worker, and since prostitution is a relationship which includes both the one who is prostituted and the one who prostitutes (and the latter is much more base), so the capitalist etc. comes within this category' (Marx in Jaggar, 1983: 221). As noted by Jaggar, Marx either sees the prostitute as forced to work by economic necessity, or perhaps he is to be interpreted as saying that economically forced labour is the basis of alienation. In view of the few comments made by Marx on prostitution and given the lack of attention afforded to the male–female relationship in Marxist theory, Jaggar appears correct when she asserts that it is not the institution of prostitution which constitutes Marx's concern; rather, he uses the metaphor to make explicit a moral judgement of capitalist relations of production and to undermine the bourgeois ideology of love.

By conflating prostitution with all relations of exchange of labour for monetary gain, Marx implicitly accepts the liberal definition of prostitution as being devoid of 'true love' and therefore sees the act of exchanging one's own labour power under capitalist relations of production as one which is devoid of pleasure and creativity. Through the analogy between wage work and prostitution, Marx seems to indicate his subjective judgement that work without pleasure and satisfaction derived from creativity is prostitution. To him, under capitalism 'labour always appears as repulsive, always as external forced labour; and not labour by contrast as "freedom and happiness"' (Marx, 1973: 611). It appears that since he views creativity, freedom and happiness as the ultimate goal of human liberation, for him these subjective categories share the same sacredness as 'love' in a religious sense of liberation. Marx's moral judgement about the character of work under capitalism comes very close to the conventional view about prostitution, i.e. sex without the blessing and sacredness of love. Just as the implicit assumption here seems to fall into the moralist charge that sex without love is vice, so too, exploitative working relations without pleasure and creativity are charged as evil.

Marx's analogy between wage-labour and prostitution seems influenced by earlier attacks on the hypocrisy of Christian morality made by those whom he calls Utopian Socialists, namely Fourier (1771–1837), Owen (1771–1858), Saint-Simon (1760–1825) and Tristan (1803–1844). While the writings of Marx and Engels showed that they accept some of the ideas advanced by Utopian Socialists, the way in which they address the concept of sexuality, monogamy and property indicates fundamental differences as far as their theoretical arguments and strategies for political practice are concerned.

The critiques made by Utopian Socialists were directed at the institutions of monogamy, private property and religion. They pointed to the contradiction in Christian morality, which on the one hand worships sentimental love and on the other debases sexual love, whereas in reality sexual love in their view constitutes one of the most fundamental human desires and an essential aspect of human existence (Boxer and Quataert, 1978; Mies and Jayawardena, 1981). Monogamy as enforced by this morality does not guarantee 'true sexual love' as it is tied to property interests and becomes marriage of convenience, which is viewed as a form of prostitution from both the male and female sides. In Fourier's words: 'As in grammar two negatives make an affirmative, so in matrimonial morality, two prostitutions pass for a virtue' (in Engels, 1981: 135). Thus monogamy is seen as an instrument of private property which prevents men and women from finding 'free love' and passion and thereby the integrity of their hearts and minds.

In Utopian Socialist thought, private property is oppressive because of the acquisitive mentality it fosters, and because this mentality in turn cultivates the tendency to possess one's sexual partner and thereby oppress her/him. In the sphere of production, Utopian Socialists argue that this possessive mentality also conditions property owners to produce for profit and not for human needs; and in the process workers are driven to produce for others and not for themselves while the pleasure and creativity of artisans' work disappear. Utopian Socialists use the concept of private property essentially to refer to the ability of the owner to exercise property rights, or to refer to an object of such rights. Their notion of oppression is not tied to the process of accumulation and therefore is largely existential. Work is seen as a source of pleasure. The central question is how to organize working relations so that people can derive the most pleasure from it and thereby be most productive. Because of this narrow conception of property and oppression, Utopian Socialists see the solution to oppression mainly in the existential realm of 'free love' and free emotional expression as a condition to egalitarian relationships. Therefore, they advocate that only through passion and free sexual love could men and women find the condition for non-hierarchical and egalitarian relationships.

By contrast, the Marxist approach ties the concepts of property, labour and oppression to the historical process of accumulation and class formation. Women's subordination and prostitution (as its extension) are analysed by Engels in the *Origins of the Family, Private Property, and the State* (1981) within the framework of the social division of labour, accumulation and the changing forms of property. Essentially, Engels locates women's subordination in two dimensions, both related to the development of private property. These dimensions concern the character of social rules governing women's sexual conduct and the character of their work. As regards the first dimension, Engels argues that double-standard sexual rules which prescribe monogamy only for women and not for men emerged from the contradiction between the propagation of children and private property. Under savagery, there was no private property, no strict rules of sexual conduct, and the care of offspring was a communal responsibility. The transition from savagery to barbarism and eventually 'civilization' was marked by the emergence of property and pairing marriage and the disappearance of group marriage. This disappearance, however, occurs for women only, while for men group marriage still exists through conjugal infidelity.

Monogamy arose from the concentration of considerable wealth in the hands of a single individual and from the need to bequeath this wealth to the children of that man and to no others. 'For this purpose, the monogamy of the woman was required, not that of the man, so this monogamy of the woman did not in any way interfere with open or concealed polygamy on the part of the man' (Engels, 1981: 138). Monogamy further enhances the asymmetrical relation between men and women by reducing women to reproducers, thereby restricting their work to serving their husbands and children in the home. In the social division of labour which emerges from this trend women are relegated to the sphere of reproduction and cease to produce for society. This is seen as the origin of women's dependence and eventual subordination to men. In combination, these dimensions give rise to a system of exchange of sex for property interest. The bourgeois marriage 'is determined by the class position of the participants, and to that extent always remains a marriage of convenience' which 'often enough turns into the crassest prostitution — sometimes on both sides, but more generally on the part of the wife, who differs from the ordinary courtesan only in that she does not hire out her body, like a wage worker, on piece work, but sells it into slavery once and for all' (Engels, 1981: 134). Furthermore, because bourgeois men enjoy less restricted social rules of sexual conduct, and because they control the means of production, they also benefit from the system of exchange of sex for money, which is prostitution.

From this analysis, it appears that Engels shares with Fourier the idea that double-standard rules of sexual conduct are related to private property. But, whereas Fourier sees these rules as oppressive to both sexes in the subjective sense of the prevention of 'true sexual love', Engels ties sexual love down to historical materialist development, whereby the first historical form of sexual love or passion is seen 'as the highest form of sexual impulse', something which 'was by no means conjugal'; passion is transformed into 'individual sex love' in the historical development of monogamy and becomes something 'which had hitherto been unknown to the entire world' (Engels, 1981: 132–3). Individual sexual love under the system of private property is to be seen as false and unreal, since women's feelings are tied to property interests. 'Sexual love in the relationship with a woman becomes and can only become the real rule among the oppressed classes, which means today among the proletariat —

whether this relation is officially sanctioned or not' (1981: 135).

By tying sexual love to property relations, Engels distorts the issue in two ways: (1) the diversity of sexual feeling which may find its expression in short-lived passion or more profound relationship between married couples (or in other types of bonding) is universal and trans-historical, and is not necessarily always related to property interests; (2) by analysing the different historical stages of sexual love in terms of property relations, sexual love can only be seen as an area of oppression and not as fulfilment, therefore the value (economic or other) created by this experience is excluded from the analysis. These distortions lead to other equally distorting interpretations such as that true sexual love is a class issue (i.e. a reality only for the working class, which owns no property), and the denial of the material meaning of sexual feelings, i.e. that of maintaining and renewing human physical and psychological energy for production. Although Engels recognizes that sexuality has a material existence, he conceptualizes it only in terms of property relations and thereby betrays the historical materialist definition of human nature as labour. To transform nature to produce for human subsistence includes the transformation of both the material world and the human body. In this sense, subjective feelings of sexuality are directly related to labour, a fact ignored by orthodox Marxists, and later discovered by Marxist psychoanalysts such as Wilhelm Reich.

These distortions lead to a dismissal of the meaning of sexual passion in the life and productivity of human beings as a bourgeois and decadent intoxicant of the working class. Engels notes that:

> next to intemperance in the enjoyment of intoxicating liquor, one of the particular faults of the English working-men is sexual licence. But this too, follows with relentless logic, with inevitable necessity, out of the position of a class left to itself, with no means of making fitting use of its freedom . . . the working-men, in order to get something from life, concentrate their whole energy upon these two enjoyments, carrying them to excess . . . the failings of workers in general may be traced to an unbridled thirst for pleasure, to want of providence, and of flexibility in fitting into the social order, to the general inability to sacrifice the pleasure of the moment to a remoter advantage. (1971: 118–19)

The problem here is the distortion of sex as a universal basic human need into a class-based expression of this need. Whereas free sexual rules among bourgeois men are seen as a result of the tension between the property system and the male sexual urge, sexual licence among the working class is seen as a result of alienation. The points missed are: what constitutes sex as a human need, what is the material basis of the organization of sexual rules to satisfy this need, and how this organization is related to the economy. Without exploring the material basis of human sexuality and its relationship to society, Marx and Engels simply speculated that with socialism a new morality would emerge: there would be no more marital infidelity, prostitution nor double-standard sexual rules of conduct. It does not seem too far-fetched to conclude that the issue of prostitution as presented by Marx and Engles has only a metaphoric value in mobilizing workers in their struggle against capitalism.

The lack of scrutiny at this level results in the theoretical inconsistencies which Marx shows when categorizing prostitutes as 'lumpen-proletariat', the unproductive and 'dangerous' class (1974: 602). If all relations of exchange under capitalist relations of production are to be seen as an expression of prostitution, why then should prostitutes be singled out as 'dangerous'? Marx and Engels never address themselves to this point, leaving us to assume that prostitutes are to be categorized on the basis of their unproductivity, something which affects their class consciousness. Therefore, the direction which they may take in political action is unpredictable, unlike the working class which, by virtue of its working conditions, constitutes a revolutionary class. Moreover, as Marx places prostitutes among 'vagabonds and criminals' who together form the 'dangerous' class, he seems to regard them not only as a threat to the revolution, but as dangerous remnants of bourgeois society which can potentially infest the new socialist order. As such, the character of their work, the social relationships surrounding it as well as the value this work creates, remain a non-issue in Marxist thought.

This moralistic approach, which systematically discards the importance of sexual expression to human existence, is translated into Lenin's refusal to accept prostitutes as an oppressed class of wage labourers which must be organized. In his debate with Clara Zetkin in the 1920s, he expressed his disapproval as follows:

So what makes your comrades, the proletarian women of Germany, enthusiastic? What about their proletarian class consciousness; are their interests, their activities concentrated on immediate political demands? What is the mainspring of their ideas? I have heard peculiar things about this matter from the Russian and German comrades. I must tell you. I was told that a talented woman communist in Hamburg is publishing a paper for prostitutes and that she wants to organize them for the revolutionary fight. Rosa (Luxemburg) acted and felt as a communist when in an article she championed the cause of the prostitutes who were imprisoned for any transgression of police regulations in carrying on their dreary trade. They are unfortunate double victims of the bourgeois society. Firstly, by its accursed property system, and secondly, by its accursed moral hypocrisy. That is obvious. Only he who is brutal or short-sighted can forget it. But still, that is not at all the same thing as considering prostitutes — how shall I put it? — to be a special revolutionary militant section, as organizing them and publishing a factory paper for them. Aren't there really any other working women in Germany to organize, for whom a paper can be issued, who must be drawn into your struggles? The other is only a diseased excrescence. (Zetkin, 1973: 91)

From the refusal to listen to the cause of prostitutes on the basis of morality, Lenin moved to dismiss the issue of sexuality from socialist discourse altogether. The firm stand he took finds its expression in the following statement:

> I mistrust the sexual theories of the articles, dissertations, pamphlets, etc. which flourish luxuriantly in the dirty soil of bourgeois societies. I mistrust those who are always contemplating the several questions, like the Indian saint his navel. It seems to me that these flourishing sexual theories which are mainly hypothetical, and often quite arbitrary hypotheses, arise from the personal need to justify abnormality and hypertrophy in sexual life before bourgeois morality, and to entreat its patience . . . There is no place for it in the Communist Party, in the class conscious, fighting proletariat . . . Dissoluteness in sexual life is bourgeois, is a phenomenon of decay. The proletariat is the rising class. It does not need intoxication as a narcotic or a stimulus. Intoxication as little by sexual exaggeration as by alcohol . . . Self-control, self-discipline is not slavery, not even in love'. (Zetkin, 1951: 80)

Discarding the issue of sexuality as a bourgeois phenomenon had two important implications. At the level of practice, prostitutes were identified as those who intoxicated revolutionaries. In August 1918, an order was sent by Lenin to Fedorov, head of the local Soviet province of Nizhni Novgorod with the following instruction: 'No efforts to be spared; mass terror to be introduced, hundreds of prostitutes who have intoxicated our soldiers, and former officers, etc., to be shot and deported' (Medvedev, 1974: 32). At the level of theory, there is a conflation of sex as a biological need with sexual rules as a social construct and sexuality as the subjective meaning of how this need is individually satisfied. This conflation leads to the neglect of the entire domain of power relations between the sexes and the ways in which women's lives and work are shaped by these relations.

This neglect triggered a debate among early feminists such as Zetkin (1857–1933) and Kollontai (1872–1952), who attempted to convince leaders of the socialist movement that they had ignored the social relations which govern women's lives and their work, and that by focusing mainly on the area of production, Marxist theory did injustice to women. Kollontai, in particular, pointed to three major dimensions of women's oppression neglected by Marxist theory, namely, the role of domestic labour under capitalism, the implications of the so-called second-shift for women, and the way in which family life and subjectivity are shaped by economic constraints (Field, 1982).

Furthermore, Kollontai recognized the double standard adopted by Marxist leaders who dubiously equated the wage worker and the prostitute as products of the same social conditions, i.e. pauperization under capitalism, and yet at the same time singled out prostitutes as 'dangerous' remnants of a bourgeois society not to be enlisted in the socialist struggle. While maintaining the Marxist position that 'to fight prostitution is to fight the foundations of capitalist society', Kollontai urged the state to take responsibility for prostitutes; if it were to tolerate them and thereby support their profession, 'it must also accept housing for them and even — in the interest of social health and order — institute houses where they could pursue their profession' (in Ericsson, 1980: 352). With this demand, Kollontai showed an awareness that the Marxist assumption that the demand for prostitutes' services is essentially a phenomenon of the bourgeoisie which intoxicated the working class was unfounded, and that either the state was incapable of suppressing prostitution or had some interest in maintaining it. It is also possible, judging from her ideas on the socialist communes and other writings on sexuality, that Kollontai perceived a relationship between sexuality and productivity (Farnsworth, 1978). However, the lack of specificity provided by her analysis, as well as the fear among socialist leaders that by expending energy on sexual excess, people might cease to work purposefully for a socialist society, led to the suppression of discussion on the issue altogether. This suppression was exemplified by the expulsion of Marxist psychoanalysts such as Reich, who tried to organize sexual education in Soviet Youth Communes.

The strength of the Marxist approach to prostitution lies in its attempt to locate it at the level of political economy. Its main weaknesses can be clustered around the following issues. Firstly, it misconceptualizes sexuality and confuses biological sex with social rules of sexual conduct by reducing them to property relations. This leads to the dismissal of the subjective dimension of human sexual life as a bourgeois issue without acknowledging that sexual satisfaction and psychological nurturance also constitute a dimension of human existence, bourgeois and working-class included. Secondly, because it uses property as a fundamental concept, it also demarcates the confines of production only in so far as it derives from property. This leads to the narrow understanding of productivity and productive labour only as labour that produces value which adds to the circulation of capital. However, it has been argued that the notion of economic value conceived in Marxist thought (as well as in orthodox economic thought) is far too narrow, being limited to the monetary economy and ignoring the entire area of invisible work performed by women, work which contains values concealed by the assumption that it is a natural, biological imperative rather than part of the economy.

As has been pointed out by feminist writers, the combination of the misconception of sexuality and the narrow conception of production has led Marxist theorists to ignore the specificities of the social dimension of reproduction, i.e. biological reproduction; reproduction of the labour force through domestic services and psychological nurturance; and reproduction of the social relations which sustains women's subordination inside and outside the household. Reproduction has a material link with society but is barely dealt with by Marxist theory.

As will be shown in chapter 3, despite the feminist criticism of Marxist theory for omitting the dimension of sexuality and reproduction, the critique continues to use Engels' notion that sexuality constitutes an area of social oppression and struggle. Therefore, feminist theory also fails to capture fully the link between sexual fulfilment and the renewal of labour power. While it is acknowledged here that the sexual fulfilment of some may take place at the expense of others, it is argued that to arrive at a more profound understanding of prostitution, the area of sexuality has to be redefined and social labour reconceptualized in order to capture the specificities of the social process and the conditions under which sexual services are mutually provided in the context of love and personal fulfilment, or become commoditized or appropriated with sheer physical force.

Structuralism and the Exchange of Women: From Phallus to Brain

Structuralism essentially rejects positivism, taking an idealist and Kantian approach to knowledge which emphasizes the construct of the human mind. Initiated by Lévi-Strauss, structuralism emerged in an attempt to fill in the missing link in Marxism, i.e. to build an adequate theory of superstructure or ideology (Lévi-Strauss, 1985). The focus of Lévi-Strauss's work is the psychological structure of social systems, through which empirically observed phenomena are manifested. In order to understand social systems, models of their deeper structure must be decoded. The methodology used to decode such models is derived from theories in linguistics. Structuralism has had a profound influence on feminist writings, including those that focus mainly on ideology and the realm of symbolism, as well as those that try to relate symbols and signs to the material expression of sexual inequality. The purpose of this section is to show the ways in which the writings of Lévi-Strauss have influenced feminist writers, focusing mainly on those who stress the importance of ideology and psychology in gender formation.

In his most important work, *The Elementary Structures of Kinship* (1969), Lévi-Strauss suggests that all patterns of marriage, kinship relations and sexual relations are to be understood not as they are observed, but as manifestations of deeper structure to be found in the innate capacity of the human mind to think, to differentiate and to create rules governing this differentiation. He assumes that, in humans, there is an innate, genetically transmitted and determined mechanism that acts as a structuring force. This innate force generates a specialized structure for a particular type of activity — in this case, kinship organization — which in turn produces an observable pattern of social phenomena — in this case marriage patterns. Ontologically, human nature is defined as something which is neurologically reducible, since the physiological processes of the human brain are equated with the operation of the human mind (Lévi-Strauss, 1985: 119). The human brain is endowed with the capacity for binary thinking, which enables humans to create rules governing their interactions.

The two central concepts used to explain the operation of this deeper structure are: (1) binary opposition; and (2) reciprocity and exchange. Binary opposition is defined as the capacity of the human mind to structure and order thoughts into pairs of opposed ideas, e.g. self *vs* other; life *vs* death; culture *vs* nature. Reciprocity is defined as the most basic form of social intercourse that results from the capacity for binary thinking. Simple reciprocity may be casual and occasional, but when integrated into economic life it becomes exchange because of the utility attached to the object of exchange. Therefore, elaborate rules are created to regularize social intercourse. In the light of these two concepts, social life can be explained in terms of a systematically instituted mode of exchange between individuals and groups. Exchange constitutes a means of mediating between binary oppositions.

Using these concepts and theoretical principles, Lévi-Strauss posits that kinship rules constitute the origin of human culture. Universally, these rules are marked by the exchange of women as the most precious gift, since such an exchange creates permanent bonding between groups and widens the network of kinship, thus strengthening social solidarity. He writes: 'It is always the system of exchange that we find at the origin of rules of marriage . . . , it is always exchange that emerges as the fundamental and common basis of all modalities of the institution of marriage' (1969: 478–9). According to Lévi-Strauss, to ensure that the woman is available as an item of exchange, a mechanism of exclusion is instituted, namely incest taboo. Incest taboo makes the woman unavailable to her own kin group and therefore available to another. This mechanism is an instrument which has transported humans from 'nature' to 'culture', since any disorderly choice of sexual partners would lead to the weakening of and eventual disappearance of groups.

Accordingly, 'exogamy provides the only means to maintain a group as a group, avoiding the endless break-up and separation that consanguine marriage would mean' (Lévi-Strauss, 1969: 593). Women are to be seen as the first property traded to consolidate bonds between tribal groups controlled by men. To ensure continuity of the exchange of women, the sexual division of labour was created as a device to institute a reciprocal state of dependence between the sexes. The sexual division of labour is a taboo which prevents the sameness of men and women. It exacerbates biological difference between the sexes and thereby creates different social identities for men and women. The implication of Lévi-Strauss's thesis is that sexual hierarchy develops from the needs for exchange between groups to consolidate their social ties and predates the class hierarchy formed with the emergence of property. Male and female as genders are created by this process, and are universal. The meanings attached to gender vary in different contexts (Lévi-Strauss, 1970).

As pointed out by several writers (Lane, 1970), Leacock, 1980, MacCormack, 1980), Lévi-Strauss's thesis contains some major flaws. Broadly speaking, these flaws can be clustered around the following issues: (1) by resting his thesis on a single universal fact (mental structure), Lévi-Strauss oversimplifies social life and denies the complexity of the social world;   (2) the deeper structure which he uses to explain social forms is in itself static, biologically determined and male-biased; and   (3) by refusing to search for causes and effects at the empirical level, Lévi-Strauss treats social phenomena as timeless, illustrating a variation of forms but leaving out entirely the question of social origins emerging from specific historical contexts.

In spite of the flaws in Lévi-Strauss's thesis, many feminist writers have seen in his work a new avenue beyond the materialist constraints of Marxist theory which hypothesizes that women's oppression begins with property and class. They have accepted his postulate on the exchange of women as the origin of culture for several reasons. In the wake of the second wave of the women's movement during which the sexual and the personal were identified as political, there was a need to substantiate the issue of social power derived from sexual difference and the operation of such power. In this context, Lévi-Strauss's argument is particularly attractive because it implies that the exercise of male control over females is structurally tied to kinship rules and thus to norms of sexual conduct. Furthermore, because the argument negates women from social action by considering them as passive objects of exchange to consolidate male ties, it harmonizes with feminist concern over the exclusion of women from social theory, from the public sphere, and the treatment of women as 'the Other' (de Beauvoir, 1974) and as objects.

Derived from the feminist political arena of the 1960s and 1970s and from Lévi-Strauss's theoretical contribution is the notion that to understand the phenomenon of male dominance and its ramifications, it is necessary to delineate its ideological structure, i.e. the supporting signs and symbols. Such a structure is embodied in personal and sexual institutions such as wedlock and love, and all kinds of sexual practices such as rape, prostitution and pornography. These institutions and practices are connected to the more profound phenomenon of male dominance. The use of Lévi-Strauss's arguments in the construction of a feminist theory on the ideology of male dominance is very complex because of the mixture of methods which have been applied. Given the constraints of this study, the discussion here will focus particularly on the structuralist Marxist tradition so as to provide continuity to the argument.

Among the feminist writers who have made explicit use of Lévi-Strauss's theoretical principles are Ortner (1974), Mitchell (1975) and Rubin (1975). Whereas Ortner remains within the boundaries of structuralism, Mitchell and Rubin combine structuralist principles with those advanced by other authors such as Marx, Freud and Althusser. They find the basis of the theory of exchange of women elucidating when combined with Freud's thesis on the Oedipus complex and the establishment of the law of the father, with Marx's historical materialist method, and with Althusser's conception of ideology and ideological interpellation. The usefulness of these three major contributions lies in the fact that they each and independently show three things: (1) women's oppression is a product of historical processes; (2) women's oppression is an outcome of social and economic imperatives rather than biology; and (3) women's oppression has an important psychological and subjective dimension which re-creates itself through socialization.

In Mitchell's version (1975), the source of women's sex-specific oppression today can be located in the human psyche, or the unconscious, the contents of which were established at an earlier period of history through the Oedipus crisis and the establishment of the law of the father. These contents enabled patriarchal culture to establish itself and to impose four structures of ideological oppression on the female sex. These are procreation, sexuality, production and socialization. These structures are needed for patriarchal culture to maintain itself and to subordinate women for its own interests.

Gender identities are formed and enhanced by these structures, which coalesce in the particular form of sexual division of labour found in today's nuclear family, creating two specific sex roles and two autonomous spheres of women's oppression, i.e. the ideological sphere of patriarchy and the material sphere of capitalist production. Added to these four structures proposed by Mitchell is the concept of the 'sex/gender system' developed by Rubin to describe a 'set of arrangements by which society transforms biological sexuality into products of human activities . . . sex as we know it — gender identity, sexual desire and fantasy, concepts of childhood — [which] is itself a social product' (1975: 159). Thus, gender formation — masculinity and femininity — is not to be regarded as the logical extension of biological characteristics. Gender formation is a historical and social process, hinged on biological characteristics to create social characteristics. The key is to understand the product of gender formation, i.e. gender as a cultural category, its reproduction and effects on women's material conditions.

The focus on patriarchy, male culture and gender identity was an attempt to provide more specificities on the issue of how men have managed to acquire political, social and economic power in society. It was also an attempt to overcome biological reductionism. The concepts of patriarchy and gender identity have been used to illustrate the ideological dimension of sexuality. Patriarchy is not to be seen merely in its expressions through a discriminatory legal system, or unequal economic opportunities, but in the broader context of male dominance over nature, and male dominance over women who are symbolized as nature. This domination is facilitated by women themselves by virtue of their internalization of their own gender identity, or the cultural self which women are not born with but have become (de Beauvoir, 1974; Chodorow, 1978). Thus from the concept of sex as a distinct social class advanced by earlier theoretical propositions on male social power (Firestone, 1971; Millett, 1971), the debate moved on to the concept of gender created by cultural meanings rather than by purely biological or economic relations. This brings the issue of women's oppression to the realm of the symbolic, which, to a large extent, confuses the specificities of biological sex with gender construction.

Two main lines of critique of the structuralist approach may be discerned. One focuses on the sexual division of labour, the other on the exchange of women. As pointed out by MacCormack (1980) and Hartsock (1983), feminist writers who have developed their argument on the basis of the nature–culture–gender model maintain a dualistic position that treats male and female as separate and opposite categories. Nature is seen as female, culture as male and gender as the symbolic separation of the two. By maintaining a dual difference between male and female on the basis of symbols and ideas, and by failing to attach forms of women's oppression to their productive base, they make of gender a static and unchanging category. As a result, the definition of men as actors and women as acted upon is perpetuated. Therefore, there is no provision for a view of women as part of the social formation (MacCormack, 1980). To accept the sexual division of labour merely as an ideological device which maintains the binary opposition between two biological units is to ignore the complexity of material forces which are capable of introducing gender hierarchy as well as of changing it. The sexual division of labour is not merely an allocation of tasks on the basis of ideological imperatives, but also entails access to and exclusion from resources (Edholm, et al., 1977). Therefore the sexual division of labour must be seen in terms of a dynamic process of social change and not as a symbolic synchrony of sexual inequality.

The other line of critique takes the position that matriarchy predates patriarchy. This position is advanced by Reed (1975) and is difficult to test due to the lack of data. Nevertheless, the questions raised open a new dimension which merits consideration. Reed argues that exchange and reciprocity predated patriarchal culture, and were already known in the archaic maternal clan period. At that time, the system contained no element of purchase, sale or barter. Exchange emerged from the need to overcome the fear and hostility that separated kin from non-kin, strangers and enemies, and to bring them together as allies and friends (Reed, 1975: 151). Thus, society can exist with a kind of bonding other than kinship. Therefore, the phenomenon of exchange of women and its facilitating mechanism — incest taboo — cannot be explained by the innate conceptualizing capacity of the human psyche. Furthermore, Reed argues that the exchange of women in marriage is an historically specific phenomenon and cannot be generalized as constituting the origin of culture and society. The fact that the social history of women has been suppressed and unrecorded does not mean that women do not constitute an important agency of social change. More specifically, if the exchange of sexual partners is a prerequisite for the formation of society, then why is it that women, as a social category, constitute the objects of exchange? The exchange of women as well as the sexual division of labour require an explanation and cannot be considered as a cause of the creation of different gender identities (McDonough and Harrison, 1978).

In this connection, a substantial suggestion is made by Leacock (1983: 270), who argues that 'changes in women's position are neither secondary phenomena, as some imply, nor prior to economic hierarchy as argued by others. They are at the core of, and inseparable from, profound transformation that takes place in conjunction with the development of exchange and division of labour.' The creation of gender hierarchy is connected with that of class, and an explanation of the interconnection between the two categories — gender and class — cannot be simply reduced to the principles outlined by the structuralist method, which, by leaving the productive base untouched, implies that male dominance is not only universal, but also a product of the human brain.

The main argument advanced in this section is that, despite the acknowledged importance of ideology and symbolic meanings, women's oppression cannot and should not be reduced to this level. Feminist writers who have developed Lévi-Strauss's theory of the social construction of gender have carried the argument too far, disconnecting this construction from historical processes. Neglecting historical and social variations of gender construction and maintaining a dual difference between men and women on the basis of gender means that transformations in the productive base are bound to be dismissed whereas the mind and ideology are granted the supremacy and autonomy of a unitary subject. As will be shown in the next section, the influence of Lévi-Strauss's writings on feminists who have adopted the nature–culture–gender model have affected the politics of prostitution in various ways. The tendency to homogenize women as a gender, and prostitutes as victims of male violence means that prostitutes continue to be regarded as a sub-species of the female sex, not on the basis of promiscuity but on the basis of victimization.

Prostitution and Feminist Politics of Social Change: From Victimization to Glorification

Social theories and politics generally emerge with some mutual re-enforcement. Gaps in theory are often reflected in the politics of social change. Prostitution is not an exceptional case. The politics of prostitution may be discerned as having two main trends: abolition and regulation.

Prior to the emergence of the social purity movement and the demand for the abolition of prostitution as a violation of human dignity, the family, public morality and the community, prostitution was regulated under various forms of licensing in many countries (Chauvin, 1982). Regulation was based on the definition of prostitution as promiscuity but functional to male needs and to the sociosexual order. Abolition was based on the rejection of promiscuity and the exploitation of prostitutes, particularly as related to the traffic in women (Barry, 1984). Unable to abolish prostitution through legal measures, many governments have found a middle way through rehabilitation of prostitutes as promiscuous women into chaste women, while at the same time maintaining the criminalization of prostitutes and prostitution.

Although it is not possible to say where theories influence politics and where it is the other way around, it is important to bear in mind that theories and politics of prostitution have not been neutral. Partiality can be traced according to the characteristics of social groups, the ways in which they raise the issue of prostitution, and how far they are willing to pursue this issue to its logical extension, namely prostitutes' rights.

Social movements, such as the labour and women's movements that emerged in defence of the oppressed strata, did take up the issue of prostitution as a form of social and sexual oppression. However, the challenge against the established order lost its momentum when the interests of prostitutes became apparent. Within the labour movement, the issue of prostitution has been raised in connection with the emergence of capitalism, wage labour and exploitation, but was discarded as a phenomenon of bourgeois decadence. Yet, empirically the phenomenon is closely connected with the renewal of the working capacity of labourers themselves.

Within the women's movement, seeking to overcome male-biased thinking and practice, prostitution is considered as a product of male vice and a violation of women's dignity. Support provided to prostitutes' organizations by segments of the women's movement initially stemmed from the desire to erase the dichotomy between the chaste and the deviant. But the reality of prostitution shows that there may be more differences than originally assumed. Women's rights and prostitutes' rights share some similarities, but also many differences. Thus, while the oppression of prostitutes is recognized by the women's movement, prostitutes' demands for their own rights have created some division between prostitutes and their supporters (Barry, 1984; *Observer*, 21 September 1986; Bell, 1987). For the women's movement, the politics of prostitution are caught between abolition and regulation. It is necessary to look at how the feminist movement has dealt with the issue of prostitution in order to delineate the area of controversy.

The contemporary debate on prostitution raises three main questions: (1) is prostitution an issue of sexual oppression?   (2) is prostitution an issue of economic exploitation? and   (3) can the issue of oppression and exploitation be separated?

Most feminist writings on prostitution share a common feature inherited from mainstream social theories, namely a dualistic approach to sexuality. This dualistic approach is manifested in several ways: the dual opposition between male and female, the dual morality in marriage and prostitution and the dual opposition between the private and public. It must be noted here that feminist writings on prostitution, with few exceptions, share the tendency of not making their methodology explicit. Therefore, the task of clustering them is both difficult and perhaps unfair to authors who do not necessarily associate themselves with the approaches demarcated here. Nevertheless, it might be useful to cluster them on the basis of the arguments advanced and the concepts used. It is hoped that such an attempt will enable the clarification of the issues at stake and the distinction between the different levels of analysis. There are three main themes pertinent to the women's movement upon which various arguments about prostitution have been built. These are: (1) sexual politics;   (2) female autonomy; and   (3) domestic work. What follows is an attempt to bring out the essential characteristics of these arguments and their political implications.

Sexual politics and prostitution

Arguments casting prostitution against the domain of sexual politics are based on the assumption of the existence of a dual opposition between the male and female sexes that is independent from class. Within this opposition, the relationship between the sexes is conceptualized as a relationship of domination. This relationship is called 'patriarchy' and operates according to two sets of principles: that male shall dominate female, that older male shall dominate younger male (Millett, 1971). Male domination of female derives from control over female sexuality and the social institutions through which this control is exercised (the family, heterosexuality, prostitution).

The family as the major patriarchal unit forms the locus of female oppression since it socializes children into differentiated sexual roles and therefore contributes to the maintenance of male power. The female role itself is dichotomized into one of chastity and one of lust, which are mutually exclusive. The family accommodates female chastity while prostitution acccommodates male lust. With chastity, female sexuality is being denied and yet glorified. With prostitution, female sexual desirability (instead of female sexuality) is being promoted and yet stigmatized as sexual deviance. This dichotomy serves to divide women by concealing their consciousness of their common position as sexual objects serving male interests, and therefore contributes to the perpetuation of male domination (Lindsey, 1979). However, the argument advanced so far only deals with the normative and dualistic relationship between male and female within marriage and prostitution but does not explain the foundation of male power. Its main contribution is the identification of the control of female sexuality as a basis of this power, and of learned sexual behaviour as its manifestation.

Several attempts have been made to contextualize the issue of the control of female sexuality to bring out more strongly the issue of disciplining women as a gender which is seen as the basis of male power (Brownmiller, 1975; Barry, 1981a; 1981b; 1984; Rhodes and McNeill, 1985). According to these authors, the control of female sexuality is supported by patriarchal ideology, which defines women as sexual objects, deprives them of their own sexuality and enables various forms of violence against them to take place. Here, patriarchy is defined as an unchanging and cross-cultural ideological force. This ideological force shapes a male culture which sees sex as a male right and which sustains the practice of male sexual aggression and violence against women. Rather than being placed in binary opposition with marriage and the family, prostitution is equated with all kinds of other systematic forms of sexual violence against women such as wife-burning (*suttee*), rape, pornography, foot-binding, clitoridectomy, child marriage and sexual abuse etc. These systematic forms of violence serve the sole purpose of controlling female sexuality, through which oppression is exercised.

In the words of MacKinnon (1982; 1–2): 'Sexuality is to feminism what work is to Marxism, that which is most one's own, yet most taken away . . . sexuality is that social process which creates, organizes, expresses and directs desire, creating social beings we know as men and women, as their relations create societies'. This social process is facilitated by patriarchal ideology which constitutes:

the male pursuit of and control over female sexuality . . . men not as individuals or as biological beings, but as a gender group characterized by maleness as socially constructed, of which this pursuit is definitive . . . rape in marriage expresses the male sense of entitlement to access to the women they annex, incest extends it . . . pornography becomes difficult to distinguish from art and ads since it is clear that what is degrading to women is compelling to the consumer. Prostitutes sell the uniterality that pornography advertises . . . rape, incest, sexual harassment, pornography and prostitution are not primarily abuse of physical force, violence, authority or economics. They are abuse of sex. They need not and do not rely for their coerciveness upon forms of enforcement other than sexual. (MacKinnon, 1982: 18–19)

Within this approach, women's entry into prostitution is not regarded as a free choice but as a result of specific strategies of pimps who traffic women into prostitution by playing on women's economic and emotional vulnerability (Barry, 1981a; 1981b). Because female sexuality becomes a tool of male domination, feminists should reject any sexual practice that supports that domination (Ferguson, et al., 1984). As pointed out by Barry (1984: 26): 'Acceptance of prostitution as an inevitable social institution is lodged with the assumption that sex is male right, whether it is bought, sold, seized in rape, or more subtly coerced as in sexual harassment'.

It follows that within this perspective prostitution cannot be accepted as work, and prostitutes must be categorized as victims of patriarchy regardless of how they got into the trade (physical or emotional coercion, abduction, purchase, or economic incentives). In a similar vein, beneficiaries from prostitution, i.e. clients who benefit from prostitutes' services and pimps who benefit from their earnings, must be treated undifferentiatedly as a privileged social group born with the right to have access to women's bodies as a source of pleasure and profit.

The main problem with viewing prostitution as part of patriarchal sexual politics is the overloading of the concept of patriarchy with all types of social relations which involve the male and female sex. Patriarchy is viewed as a synchrony of male dominance, therefore static and unchanging. Its historical forms are not taken into account. 'Maleness' and femaleness' as socially constructed genders are accepted as an extension of biological sex. The material process of their formation is omitted or regarded as unchanging. This leads to the conflation of the biological and the social, with male social power reduced to the unsubstantiated domain of male culture. Just as earlier explanations of male social power reduce it to an anatomically given male sex drive, so too, the sexual politics approach takes for granted that the process of gender formation is somehow anatomically given, albeit by a different part of the anatomy, namely the brain which creates oppressive systems of thoughts and ideas.

Whereas sociobiologists see prostitution as functional to male biology, the sexual politics approach sees it as being functional to male social power. The only difference between the two approaches is the identification of norms and symbolic meanings surrounding maleness and femaleness as a domain of the social and political rather than of the biological. Furthermore,this perspective does not address sufficiently the economic basis of prostitution, the proliferation of its forms and vested interests. Subsequently, prostitutes and their vested interests are not taken into consideration. Equally, their relationships with procurers, pimps, employers in the sex industry, the law and the state are overgeneralized.

The dualistic approach to male and female in sexual politics also implies a dilemma in political practices. The root of this dilemma is the acceptance of male aggression and violence as given, and the oversimplification of social power. Essentially, this oversimplification stems from the failure to distinguish oppression from exploitation. Although the process of oppression (political) is linked with exploitation (economic), this does not mean that they should be treated as the same category and used interchangeably. The failure to recognize this distinction leads to the formulation of strategies for social change which face a paralysing dilemma in the following dimensions:

1 Ideologically, if all women are considered as sexual objects then what is the significance of the social stigma attached to prostitution? Is it only a male device used to divide and control women, as often argued, or does it contain more serious implications for the lives of individual prostitutes? Does the fight against stigmatization imply the acceptance of prostitution?

2 Politically, what does the elimination of prostitution imply? Can the institution of prostitution be differentiated from prostitutes as individuals? Does the abolition of prostitution mean the decriminalization of the act of prostitution, or the closing down of institutions through which prostitution takes place? If the sole purpose of prostitution is to support male dominance, would decriminalization condone it?

3 Economically, if prostitution cannot be considered as work (whether under the conditions of slavery, bondage, self-employment or other types of social relations) how can one speak of exploitation and economic benefits derived from it? By the refusal to recognize that prostitution is work and therefore governed by many types of social relations, the issue of consciousness among prostitutes is discarded. And to treat them as victims whose consciousness embodies patriarchal ideology itself the significance of consciousness derived from social relations of production is virtually to ignore.

4 Strategically, how can women fight against the argument that prostitution and pornography help reduce the incidence of rape if all these institutions are seen as being functional to male aggression? On what terms can the feminist movement foster an alliance with prostitutes' organizations?

As pointed out by Barry (1984: 29) 'In examining the relationship between the feminist movement with prostitute organizations, we face the serious question of how to support and work with individual women in prostitution without supporting the institution, something that will place us in opposition to the prostitute organizations which do support the institutions.' The questions raised require specific answers which the concept of patriarchal culture or male cultural hegemony cannot provide, mainly because it overgeneralizes social power and conflates the issues of oppression and exploitation.

Given the complex system of commoditized sexual intercourse found in today's societies, and its multiple relations of production, feminist writings on prostitution built on the issue of sexual politics and patriarchal culture have limited value as regards to strategies and policies. The main difficulty in trying to understand the interrelationship between prostitution and the economy is defined by the fact that prostitution remains largely an underground activity concealed behind other types of legal jobs such as bartenders, masseuses, porno models, escorts, etc. Moreover, there is a great deal of mobility between these different occupations. This is further complicated by the fact that each category of worker in the sex industry tries to maintain a separate identity to avoid the social stigma entailed in prostitution without taking into account that they are all part and parcel of the same industrial structure. It is therefore essential that the different relations and patterns of employment in prostitution are disaggregated from broader notions such as patriarchy so as to enable a more precise understanding of the issues at stake as well as to demarcate the areas of social responsibility.

Female autonomy and prostitution

From a liberal feminist perspective, prostitution is analysed in the context of occupational sociology which sees women's disadvantageous position in the labour market as being derived from male-biased norms and values. This structure gives women a limited range of occupational choices that are segregated into a series of stereotyped and low-paid servicing functions. In this context, women's entry into prostitution is understood as an 'entrepreneurial move' or a rational choice women make under the conditions of inequality and discrimination in the wage-labour market, and given the comparative advantages they have (Rosenblum, 1975; Heyl, 1979; Phongpaichit, 1982; McLeod, 1982). The problem is located in the irrationality of the legal framework governing prostitution, shaped by male-biased norms and values. The main aim of this approach is to challenge the view that prostitution is a form of social deviance, sexual pathology or delinquency, and to make a case against the stigmatization of prostitutes.

Restricted within the sex-role theory, this approach draws parallels between the attributes of the female sex role and the characteristics of prostitution arguing that the moral and social distinction between the wife and the prostitute is largely artificial. According to Rosenblum (1975): 'Prostitution utilizes the same attributes of the female sex role, and uses those attributes towards the same ends.' So long as prostitution occurs as a 'rational choice' under the conditions of unequal access to employment opportunities, the struggle should be directed at demanding legal reforms which protect women and minors from discriminatory and exploitative practices. The focus is thus placed on the need for the state to prosecute pimps and procurers more vigorously instead of criminalizing prostitutes. In so far as 'free choice' prostitution (with full consent of both partners) is concerned, it is propounded that the state should not intervene in the privacy of sexual conduct as this would violate individual human rights. The call is for decriminalization which neither prohibits prostitution nor regulates it through zoning and registration.

A major flaw in the liberal perspective is the emphasis on the condition under which the act of prostitution takes place (coercion versus 'free choice'), rather than the institutions which support it. The danger of disconnecting the act of prostitution from sexual institutions such as brothels, clubs, eros centres and other segments of the entertainment industry is the negation of complex socio-economic processes which lead to their formation and the process of accumulation from sexual labour. Consequently, the relationship between employer and employee and the legal framework governing the sex industry is inadequately dealt with. Ultimately, this results in an oversimplified view of prostitution which fails to address the social relations surrounding this work, and therefore 'free choice' and 'full consent' are accepted in a vacuum external to the social context of the individual prostitute herself as well as to the context in which she acts. Thus, in spite of the fact that this approach accepts prostitution as work, it fails to address coherently the issue of exploitation. Instead, it only refers to formal discrimination in terms of unfair legal practices and informal discrimination in terms of moral stigmatization of prostitutes.

The failure to address coherently the issue of exploitation in prostitution is inherent in the limits of liberal feminism which took as its point of departure the issue of sexual discrimination and the subsequent social disadvantages of women. To liberal feminists, discrimination is exercised through formal and informal patriarchal practices. Formal discrimination is executed through the legal system and informal discrimination is based on cultural norms, traditions and customs. The issue of prostitution is located at two levels, the double-standard morality in sexual conduct and discrimination in the wage-labour market.

On double-standard morality, liberal feminists have taken a position similar to earlier arguments on sexual politics, considering this morality as part of the patriarchal norm which represses and controls female sexual conduct. However, whereas the sexual politics trend emphasizes the control of female sexuality as structural male violence (and therefore no form of prostitution should be allowed), the liberal approach considers the issue of stigmatization of prostitution as a matter of discrimination against sexual minorities (Jaggar, 1983).

The discrimination against prostitutes is considered as one form of a more generalized trend of discrimination through sex-stereotyped occupations in the wage-labour sector where women are crowded into a limited range of low-paid servicing functions on the basis of assumptions about the female role. Here, a parallel is drawn between prostitution and other sex-stereotyped occupations (e.g. waitress, secretary, fashion models, etc.). All these occupations reflect the characteristics of the female role. Therefore, 'prostitutes should not be castigated as the only women opting for work which in some ways panders to male dominance. In a society riddled with sexual disadvantages, the choice presented to women generally by way of wage labour or domestic work is likely to lead them into the same trap' (Lawton, in McLeod, 1982: 135). Given the prevailing social structure, the female role defined by patriarchal norms is built upon marriage, prostitution and various forms of sex-stereotyped wage work.

This brings the issue of prostitution into the context of scales of sexual discrimination. The argument is that formal and informal stigmatization of prostitutes deny them, as a sexual minority, their basic human right to self-determination, liberty and autonomy. As Scott writes: 'a woman has the right to choose prostitution for a livelihood and the fact that she is choosing the worst form of economic slavery could not deprive her of basic human and legal rights' (in McLeod, 1982: 134). This reflects the main logic of liberal feminism over the last century: sexual discrimination constitutes the denial of liberal political values to women. Therefore, the struggle should be directed at demanding the extension of such values to all women, including prostitutes. One controversial issue connected with the demand for the acceptance of 'free choice' prostitution is the conflation of sexual behaviour and sexual practices under commercial relations, and the legal implications of this conflation.

The acceptance of prostitution as an occupational category would necessitate some kind of regulation, as in any other occupation. Prostitution cannot be accepted at the same time as a form of freedom of sexual expression (private) and an occupational category which requires no regulation (public intervention) because it takes the form of a private sexual expression. The problem is how to define norms of regulation which do not entail stigmatization and which take into account other forms of prostitution which are not based on 'free choice'. In many cases, 'free choice' and coercion cannot be separated. Entry to prostitution may initially stem from coercion. However, internal mobility may occur and prostitutes who have gained some independence from pimps can choose to operate on their own. There is a gradual process in the life of a prostitute and a transformation of the social relations surrounding her work which cannot be discounted. Not all prostitutes succeed in emerging from coerced prostitution to 'free choice' prostitution. Without addressing this process, the issue of accumulation from prostitutes' labour under different relations such as confinement, indentureship, patronage, etc., and the role of organized sex syndicates, cannot be addressed. The implication of the demand for the recognition of 'free choice' prostitution is that law pertaining to the traffic in women must be disconnected from law pertaining to prostitution. But this is not possible, since the traffic in women is one of the main means through which sexual labour in prostitution is supplied. The question is not only to recognize that prostitution is work, but also to question how labour is being supplied for this type of work.

Domestic work and prostitution

Writings on prostitution based on the theme of domestic work attempt to relate the character of work which is called women's work to different types of social organization of production (Jaget, 1980; James, 1983). The domestic labour debate took its point of departure in the ideas advanced by Marxists such as Engels and Kollontai who argued that the loss of social signifi-cance of domestic work derives from the process of privatization and the dichotomy between work and home. Thus, work which is essential to the reproduction of labour power — child-bearing and rearing, sexual and nurturing services, and other types of servicing work in the home — is categorized by society as unproductive since it falls into the sphere of personal and private relationships. However, this work is socially necessary since it renews the labour power of workers and produces generations of new workers. That this work is necessary yet unrecognized and unpaid is both an indication of the patron–client relationship between husbands and wives (patriarchy) and of the subsumption of household relations by capitalist relations of production. This subsumption has been enabled by the fact that the family mode of child-rearing, sexual and affective services and domestic chores has been built on family and kinship relations in which women occupy a subordinated position. Male dominance derives from male control of both the capitalist mode of production (wage-work) and the domestic mode of reproduction (consumption) through the family wage (Malos, 1980). The other side of the coin is female poverty which results from sexual discrimination and low wages in the labour market or wagelessness in domestic labour. Against this background, prostitution is to be understood as a female strategy for survival under the conditions of poverty.

The issue of prostitution emerges most sharply along the lines of the militant demands for wages for housework. Protagonists of these demands argue that domestic work produces a particular commodity, i.e. labour power, which is sold by the workers to capitalists. Because domestic work is unpaid and yet necessary, it produces surplus value for capital. In this context, the work of prostitutes as well as housewives should be recognized and paid for according to its merits. The focus is placed on the demand for wages for housework from the state and industry to enable women to be autonomous from men on whom they are now dependent. Consequent upon this demand is the demand for the recognition of female poverty as the major cause of prostitution and consequently for the abolition of laws against prostitution. As succinctly formulated by a collective of prostitutes supported by the International Wages For Housework Campaign: 'Outlaw poverty and not prostitution' (*English Collective of Prostitutes Newsletter*, 1983). It is argued that prostitution is one form of women's struggle to get paid for housework — by getting paid for the sexual services all women are expected to give for free. 'After all, who are prostitutes but housewives who go out for an evening job?' (Jaget, 1980).

In the merging of the campaigns of prostitutes with the International Wages for Housework Campaign, a parallel is drawn between the housewife and the prostitute, both of whom are portrayed as poor and dependent, and who are striving for their own survival and independence from men by changing their praxis.

There are several shortcomings in this parallel. Firstly, there is a confusion between housewives and housework, and between prostitutes and prostitution. Housework is not necessarily performed by housewives, and not all facets of prostitution can be associated with prostitutes. Wages for housework would also benefit housewives who already have domestic servants, and the abolition of prostitution laws would also benefit those who control prostitution as a business. Secondly, relations surrounding prostitutes' work and the work of housewives are not the same, and therefore the control over such work, the legal framework and rewards are different. The social conditions of a housewife and a prostitute cannot be homogenized, even though they both are engaged in reproductive tasks.

While the Marxist–feminist perspective touches upon the significance of domestic labour and reproduction, it tends to oversimplify social relations within the household and prostitution. Since the concept of domestic work is substantiated by experiences drawn during a specific historical period, i.e. reproduction under capitalism, it shows only two extreme forms of reproduction, namely reproduction through unpaid housework, and reproduction through commercial relations in prostitution.

It is necessary to recognize that the sexual act and sexual relations cannot be disconnected from their complex social and historical context. Thus, while sexual intercourse between a man and a woman may occur purely in an existential context of sensuality, intimacy and social significance, the same act can also occur as a form of sexual abuse and violence against women, direct or indirect. Direct violence occurs in the form of rape, while indirect abuse often takes place within different forms of patronage (e.g. husband and wife, landlord and peasantry, domestic servant and employer). When incorporated into market relations, the act of sexual intercourse — whether in the form of erotic art or physical abuse — becomes part of the institution of the brothel through which accumulation from prostitutes' labour takes place.

Given the fact that market relations are extremely dynamic, the social context under which commoditized sexual intercourse takes place also responds to market forces. Such forces can either bring 'free' women into 'detention', as in the case of forced prostitution in brothels using bonded or abducted labour (Truong, 1986: 18), or change the conditions of patronage into the relation between employee and employer as in the case of 'free choice' prostitution in some segments of the entertainment and sex industry. Therefore, social relations in prostitution should be seen as being inter-linked with the process of social change and the process of change in a woman's life.

Finally, the sites through which reproductive work and prostitutes' work take place are very diverse and therefore the social conditions of women as reproductive workers cannot be homogenized. There are two aspects of reproductive work which are purely based on biological sex, namely biological reproduction as in the case of female reproducers under slavery, and the provision of sexual satisfaction and significance as in the case of prostitution. Sometimes social aspects of reproductive work (cooking, cleaning, washing, entertaining) may be part of the work, but a distinction should be made between the sexual aspect and the social aspect of reproductive work. Social change induced by many factors can change the relationship between the social and sexual aspects of reproduction.

Biological reproduction may be separated from the social role of mother as was formerly the case under specific systems of slavery which used female slaves as biological reproducers. Equally, the recent introduction of birth technologies (surrogate reproducers) can potentially alter the situation of middle-class women in the West as reproducers. The only difference is that unlike under slavery, surrogate reproduction involves some kind of wage and meets other needs than the creation of needed additional labour force. Technological change can also have wider ramifications in changing the area of reproduction. As will be shown in chapter 3, technological change in the area of air transport and information have contributed to the process of integrating social and sexual aspects of reproduction (accommodation, entertainment, sexual services) into the congealed form of the sex package tours, bringing men and women from separate corners of the world together in the commercial transaction of sexual services in which the women may be expected to play the role of prostitute or wife for a specific period of time.

It is important to keep in mind that the relationship between the sexual and social aspect of reproductive work is not static and uniform. It is changing and can be diversified, as can its social, economic and political effects on women. It is not possible to equate a housewife with a prostitute on the basis of female poverty and wagelessness. Not all prostitutes are poor, and not all poor housewives enter prostitution.

The perspective of prostitutes: from victimization to glorification
Prostitutes who try to make their voice heard depart from all the issues raised by feminists regardless of their political position and its implications. It appears that the affiliation of prostitutes with particular trends of feminist political thought stems from the influence of supporters and the choice of spokesperson. Therefore, it must be kept in mind that the voice of prostitutes emerging from their own organizations must be carefully assessed. There are contradictory tendencies within the prostitutes' movement itself (e.g. wages for housework, individual choice and self-determination). At this stage of the prostitutes' movement it is very difficult to differentiate the underlying trends because their political stances and the link with feminist issues are confused. Nevertheless, a clear difference emerges between feminists and prostitutes in so far as the targets of attack are concerned.

While feminists condemn male clients and pimps as oppressors and exploiters, prostitutes direct their target at the level of the state, the law and the community. To prostitutes, the hypocrisy of morality does not manifest itself so much in their clients' demands, but more fundamentally in the fact that, while the state and municipality claim to be the guardians of legal and moral order, they profit at the same time from prostitutes' work through taxes levied on brothels and entertainment establishments, and through fines imposed on street soliciting. Stigmatization denies their rights as workers and as citizens, brings them into social isolation and exposes them to all kinds of economic and physical abuse.

For example, in many countries prostitutes must pay income tax but are not entitled to welfare benefits such as health and pension schemes as other workers are. Furthermore, a known prostitute (or common prostitute) may not file charges alleging theft, rape or attempt to murder since she is already labelled as sexually immoral and criminal. Those who wish to keep their identity unknown must pay fees to pimps, police and club owners for protection. Pointing to these unfair practices, prostitutes argue that it is the denial that prostitution is work which leads to the abuse of sex. In other words, by criminalizing prostitution, society allows the abuse of prostitutes as women (Jaget, 1980).

Inherent in the arguments put forward by prostitutes is the differentiation between the structure of male dominance, i.e. law and morality, and individual men. Clients are portrayed as sexually handicapped men who are also victims of repressive sexual morality and who need prostitutes' services. Pimps are presented in the context of personal and emotional relationships while the state and owners of sex establishments are denounced as sex capitalists and 'white-collar pimps' who profit from prostitutes' invisible labour (Jaget, 1980; James, 1983; First World Whores Congress, Amsterdam, 1985 and Second World Whores Congress, Brussels, 1986).[1] Thus, the target of the campaign shifts from sexual abuse by men to economic exploitation by capitalists and the state, whose interests are converging.

Some sections of the prostitutes' movement claim that sex is an erotic art and that prostitutes are mistresses of the art. They stress their role as sex educators and social workers, and prostitution as a profession which is functional to but denied by society. The prostitute herself is portrayed as a prototype of the revolutionary whose praxis not only defies male-defined morality but also empowers her economically. The housewife is portrayed as a prototype of the oppressed, namely a woman whose sexuality has been denied by patriarchal ideology and practice, who has no chance to select partners except her husband and who is economically dependent (First World Whores Congress, Amsterdam, 1985). Within these sections of the prostitutes' movement, there is a tendency to attack only the state and to leave out the capitalist enterprises engaged in the sex business such as those in pornography and entertainment establishments. The state is accused for interfering far too much in private sexual choices, for regularizing the sex business and for censoring pornography, all of which restrict the freedom of sexual expression.

As pointed out earlier, how far the voices expressed through prostitutes' organizations reflect the consciousness of the majority of prostitutes is not known. Given the fact that many prostitutes still fear the effects of stigmatization on their private life in the community, it may be assumed that until prostitutes' organizations are allowed to become more broadly based, no firm conclusion may be drawn about the views expressed above. Nevertheless, two issues which prostitutes have confronted the women's movement with are the issue of sexual morality and its praxis (politically correct sexual conduct) and the issue of pimping.

Traditionally, pimping is defined as the act of deriving benefits from immoral sexual conduct, while moral sexual conduct is defined as that which does not involve commercial dealings and is confined to matrimony. Feminists who oppose pimping draw a parallel between this act and forced marriage of young females, in order to expose the hypocrisy of sexual relations in matrimony, and to denounce organized syndicates who use various means including emotional and physical coercion to traffic women and children and bring them into prostitution (Barry, 1981a; 1981b). However, feminists fail to offer an alternative sexual morality, except to say that it should reflect self-determination and control over one's own body, and emotional intimacy rather than commercial interests. The assumption that these liberal values are neutral and can be adopted as reflecting the prototype of morally and politically correct sexual conduct is directly contested by the reversal of the comparison between the housewife and prostitute by some segments of the prostitutes' movement, with the underlying assumption that the former is sexually deprived and the latter is sexually liberated.

This shows the limitation of understanding prostitution within a dualistic approach: the dual opposition between male and female, the dual morality in marriage and prostitution, and the dual opposition between reproduction and production. The dual opposition between male and female homogenizes all women under the issue of male vice and male violence, and all victims of sexual violence under male-controlled relations of confinement. The dual morality in marriage and prostitution homogenizes all women under sex-stereotyped roles and prostitutes under stigmatization. The dual opposition between reproduction and production homogenizes both women under female poverty and prostitutes as women who struggle for their survival. While all the issues raised so far are relevant, by placing them into pairs of opposed categories the dualistic approach to prostitution bypasses complex social processes. It is the dualistic approach to prostitution shared by many feminists which enables the shift of the argument from victimization to glorification.

This shift is particularly significant in terms of the issues raised which show the meagreness of feminist solidarity and international sisterhood. It is also significant because of its omission of particular issues which concern prostitutes from Third World countries who either work within the informal sector, the tourist industry or as migrant prostitutes in industrialized countries. For many of these women, the issue is not just sexual freedom or oppression but concerns deeply-rooted dimensions of social inequality exacerbated by social change such as agrarian change, urbanization, foreign currency crisis, international labour mobility, and militarization.

In fact, prostitution in the context of sex-tourism has been labelled as a form of 'sexual imperialism' by segments of the Asian women's movement who point to the profits made by tour operators from industrialized countries by incorporating prostitutes' services in their packages of services sold to male tourists.[2] This could only occur, because of the inferior economic position of some Asian countries, which sought gain from international trade through tourism by allowing the trade in women. Clearly, if this perspective is taken into account, then the analysis of prostitution cannot be limited to questions pertaining to the male–female relationship alone, but must take into account the process of internationalization of production in the area of leisure and entertainment facilitated by state and capital intervention.

Conclusion

This chapter assesses the ways in which prostitution has been conceptualized in mainstream social theory. It is shown that the analysis of prostitution tends to be reduced to a single level, e.g. to the level of biological instinct, morality/ideology or class structure and economic imperatives. The prevailing trend is to adopt an ahistorical approach to the conception of sexuality, to dichotomize sexual categories under the broad notions of male and female and to conflate three categories which are interrelated but not always interchangeable. These are: sex as a biological category, gender as a socially constructed category (masculine and feminine) and sexuality as an ideological apparatus which emerges from a particular social formation, can carry different conceptions of biological sex at different times and does not always have the same effects on humans. This conflation has obscured the nature of social relations in prostitution. Advocacy for change is thus bound to be partial and inconsistent with broader principles of equality and emancipation.

Notes

1. Field notes T. Truong and T. Cordero as participants and observers in the First and Second World Whores Congresses held in Amsterdam in 1985 and Brussels in 1986 respectively.

2. The term 'sexual imperialism' was coined by the Japanese Women's Christian Temperance Union in 1973 when protests were carried out simultaneously in Japan and South Korea against Japanese sex tourism (*Far Eastern Economic Review*, 14 March 1975). The term was adopted by women activists in the Philippines and Thailand in 1980 when similar protests were carried out against Japanese and Western European sex tourism.

2. Sexual Labour in Prostitution

Poor Louise, she went from a frying pan into the fire. But then, with us women it's always a question of frying pan or fire, and it's hard to say which is worse. At best our situation is critical.

Eleanor Marx to her sister Laura on the marriage of Louise Kautsky, in
Janssen-Jurreit, 1982: 103

The long history of prostitution inevitably implies diverse and inconsistent social relations in which it is embedded. Nevertheless, various forms of prostitution do exhibit a clear relationship with the state through its regulation and intervention. In particular, organized prostitution in many countries is connected with the service sector lodged in capitalist relations of production, adding yet another dimension to sexual transactions. There is sufficient evidence which indicates that a proper discussion on prostitution cannot be initiated exclusively from the perspective of the male–female relationship. A link must be established between sexuality, reproduction and political economy to provide analytical space for sexual labour as an essential constituent of prostitution.

Reproduction and the Structure of Gender Relations

One of the major contributions made by feminist theorists in recent years has been to bring into focus the area of women's labour in reproduction. While the significance of this labour is recognized, interpretations pertaining to how it is organized and who benefits from it remain contested. Reproduction itself is a confusing concept, introduced in Marxist theory and enlarged by feminist theory to include women's labour. Hearn (1987: 47) has identified six different interpretations of reproduction:

1 biological reproduction (propagation);

2 maintenance of labour through consumption of necessities;

3 reproduction of labour-power by converting part of capital, and so augmenting the value of capital;

4 reproduction of capital by converting every form of capital into accumulated capital, or capitalized surplus value;

5 reproduction of production, as a mere repetition of the proceeds of production; and

6 reproduction of capitalist relations on an extended scale.

Most feminist writings on reproduction use the term to mean biological reproduction, maintenance of the labour force and reproduction of social relations. Whereas Marxist writers consider biological reproduction as one of the natural human instincts of preservation, feminists argue that there is nothing instinctual about the biological reproduction and maintenance of the labour force. As Jaggar (1983) argues, human needs extend beyond food, shelter and clothing to include biological reproduction, sexual satisfaction, psychological nurturance and physical maintenance. Just as the satisfaction of human needs assumes specific historical forms, so too do needs for biological reproduction and regeneration, sexual satisfaction and nurturance.

In general, the feminist debate on reproduction seeks to provide answers to the following questions: what factors influence the formation of social structures that mediate sexual satisfaction, social significance, childbirth and the maintenance of living human beings; and how are these structures articulated in the economic, social and political spheres? What is the relationship between the spheres of reproduction (propagation, maintenance) and production?

Several concepts have been introduced to describe and analyse the organization of women's labour in reproduction, including the family mode of production (Delphy, 1977), mode of reproduction (Gimenez, 1978), sex-affective production (Ferguson, 1978), social relations of gender (Edholm, et al., 1977), and household forms of social relations of production (Harrod, 1987). The main concern is twofold. The first is to establish a list of activities undertaken by women in the reproduction of the labour force — which constitute a significant proportion of productive activities in society. The second is to identify the social relationships under which these activities take place in order to draw conclusions about the economic position of women.

Defining what is biological and what is social in pleasure and procreation presents major problems. As regards the social relationships under which women's labour in reproduction takes place, the difficulty has been to identify their sites of expression, something feminist theory has not yet resolved. Feminist authors diverge on the question of sexuality, and converge on the question of site. To put it differently, while feminist authors see the family, household, and kinship relations as a major site of expression of the relations of reproduction, there are two different interpretations of what is social and what is biological about sex.

One trend of feminist thought conflates the biological with the social, and the other trend separates them. Those who conflate the biological and the social see gender as a static expression of biological sex (male and female) and also tend to conflate the productive and the unproductive. Social conflict is regarded mainly as a conflict of interests between men and women. Capitalism simply takes advantage of this conflict for its own perpetuation (reproduction). Men benefit from capitalist organization of reproduction and therefore will fight to maintain it. Those who separate the biological from the social also separate the productive from the unproductive and demand more specific observations of social relations before conclusions can be drawn about gender conflict and class conflict.

Initially, the debate on reproduction abstracted the experience of women in domestic work in industrialized societies to highlight the significance of this work to capitalism in order to show the economic class position of women. Building on the existing internal structure of the male-dominated nuclear family, which is referred to as the sexual division of labour, feminist authors have tried to link this structure with the ways in which women's labour becomes incorporated in the production process (industry, commerce, services). Consequently, the contextualization of women's work remains by and large very ethnocentric and class specific. The discussion is restricted to sex roles in the family and sex-stereotyped functions in the labour market.

The main structure mediating reproduction has been identified as patriarchy. This is regarded as a structure predating capitalism that has become incorporated by and is functional to the operation of capitalist relations. Under capitalism, patriarchy functions as an ideological force which transforms the traditional sex-roles in the family into the sexual division of labour and sex-stereotyped skills in the labour market. Women's labour in the family and in the labour market benefit capitalism (Ferguson, 1978; Beechey, 1979b; Eisenstein, 1979; Hartmann, 1981). Patriarchy is loosely defined as male culture/ideology, male choice, male bonding and male political interests in dominating women as producers and reproducers.

Defined as such, patriarchal relations in reproduction are seen on the one hand as serving to structure women's position in the family as mothers, wives, and unrecognized domestic labourers, and on the other hand as reinforcing women's low position in the wage-labour market through sex-stereotyped functions. Thus, the organization of women's labour in the family is considered essential to the sustenance of the organization of their labour in the market. Accordingly, capitalism derives benefits from both types of organization, which provide women's labour at low prices. Eisenstein writes (1979: 27–8):

> Male supremacy, as a system of sexual hierarchy, supplies capitalism . . . with the necessary system of order and control . . . [which] is necessary to the smooth functioning of the society and the economic system and hence should not be undermined . . . Capitalism uses patriarchy, and patriarchy is defined by the needs of capital . . . At the same time one system uses the other, it organizes itself around the needs of the other in order to protect the specific quality of the other.

Here, the relationship between capitalism and patriarchy is seen as reinforcing sexual differentiation.

There are several problems with the use of the concept of patriarchy in the conceptualization of reproduction. Firstly, by defining sexual hierarchy in terms of sex roles, the argument is tautological. While stressing that the organization of women's labour in the household determines women's work situation outside the household, these authors leave the question of what determines the character of women's labour open to cultural determinism, or see male bonding and male choice to dominate women as a universal characteristic. Such explanations are not only untenable but are also far from materialist since they do not explain the basis of the 'male choice' to dominate women.

Secondly, by treating the family as an autonomous unit of consumption, this approach bears a class and ethnic bias. Such a discrete model of the family is not always applicable, particularly among low-income groups in non-Western societies, but also in the West. The majority of households in the world are units of both production and consumption and are not always governed by the same relations. In some households several relations of production may coexist and operate in combination with each other (Wallerstein, et al., 1982; Smith, et al., 1984; Harrod, 1987).

Thirdly, adding a new type of women's work, i.e. domestic work, to procreation as part of sex roles does not make the concept of reproduction clearer, as it still adheres to a dualistic vision of the domestic/private and the public spheres. The emergence of wage relations in essentially domestic reproductive work (housework, physical maintenance) is not taken into account. Only the content of the work of married women and the social relations governing this work are described.

While women's work in the production and maintenance of people is important, it is not carried out under the same conditions by all women. Therefore, this organization of reproductive work cannot be considered as the main structure which exacerbates the socio-economic position of men and women. The lack of clarity finds its expression in statements such as 'while motherhood is an important mechanism for patriarchy, patriarchy is also an important mechanism for motherhood' (Ferguson and Folbre, 1981: 319). Such a statement provides no room for other types of social bonding and households in which relations are less dichotomized and are governed by very different dynamics of production than the separation of work and home.

Overgeneralization leads to the failure to capture the social experience of many women who are living and working outside the modern nuclear family structure. Therefore the character of their work, the social relations governing such work and the implications on their class position have been marginalized by the analysis. This marginalization leads this approach to contradict itself on its own ground when trying to deal with prostitutes as a category of women working outside the domestic sphere but providing similar services to men. Within this functional framework, prostitution is seen as a product of capitalism serving to reinforce male supremacy. As such, it obstructs women's struggles by making any conceivable 'sex-strike' to be organized by housewives totally ineffective, because 'there are always scabs (i.e. prostitutes) available to men to get those needs met' (Ferguson, 1978: 300). This shows that while initially, social conflict has been conceptualized as a conflict of interest between men and women, at the level of analysis conflict of interests between women are noted but not explained. Conclusions drawn on the economic position of women are limiting because the social relations which organize their work are conceptualized within the limits of the dual interaction between capitalism and patriarchy.

A number of important questions relating to the domain of reproduction are left unanswered, particularly those pertaining to social differentiation among women and to the distribution of resources in reproduction. Social relations which govern the area of reproduction are historically specific and cannot be reduced to patriarchy.

Attempts to give some explanation of the complexity of reproduction were taken up by the social relations of gender approach. Based on the empirical material drawn from non-Western and developing countries, this approach offers the following propositions:

- the rejection of the term patriarchy and of women as a social category defined by patriarchal relations since such a category obscures biological and social factors;

- the rejection of the family as a unit of analysis since it confuses kinship relations with household relations of production and consumption;

- the rejection of the distinction between exploitation and oppression and its replacement by the concept of subordination, which should be specified according to the historical and locational context;

- the distinction beween 'social' and 'socialized' to avoid the misspecification of women's work as private, which implies that it is neither social labour nor socialized work;

- the distinction between social division of labour (production of different commodities within different sectors) and technical division of labour due to their correlation with the sexual division of labour.

The focus is placed on the male–female social relationship, referred to as social relations of gender, a term which depicts different forms of subordination at different phases of capitalist development. Women's social and economic positions are then specified accordingly.

At the conceptual level, the rejection of patriarchy as a cultural force leads to the rejection of gender as a cultural category which is ahistorical (feminine and masculine, male and female). Rather, a distinction is made between 'gender ascriptive' and 'gender characteristics' (Whitehead, 1979: 11). This distinction aims at tying the concept of gender to concrete social and economic relations. 'Gender ascriptive' refers to gender identity, i.e. to describe a position is to describe gender. In other words, 'gender ascriptive' is a category which reflects the social ascription of particular qualities to a gender. Thus, mother and housewife are 'gender ascriptive' categories since they describe the reproductive role and the economic position of women. 'Gender characteristics' refer to the relations in which 'gender ascriptive' notions are transposed. Such relations are called bearers of gender.

Conjugal relations are 'gender ascriptive' relations; they involve opposite sexes with specified social roles defined by law and with resources attached. By contrast, social relations which are bearers of gender are those which selectively use certain aspects of women's reproductive roles as their ideological constructs and apply them in wage relations. Examples of such bearers of gender are found in export-processing zones in newly industrialized countries where female docility, endurance and 'nimble fingers' are used as ideological constructs to attract foreign capital investment as well as to discipline the female labour force (Elson and Pearson, 1981).

With these distinctions, the social relations of gender approach seeks to specify the context under which gender relations operate. The hypothesis is that, although the male–female relation universally depicts the asymmetry of social power between the sexes, the sites of its expression are different in a cross-cultural sense, and entail different forms of asymmetry or subordination. Indicators of subordination include factors such as access to resources (e.g. political position, food, land, physical and social mobility), responsibilities in the maintenance of and caring for the young and old, command of labour and confinement of sexuality (Young, et al., 1981). Any understanding of the forms of subordination and how they are maintained and recreated must be based on the analysis of the division of labour along gender lines, its mechanisms of inclusion and exclusion from access to resources, and their impact on the organization and control of women's labour.

To analyse the forms of subordination, their maintenance and recreation, the concept of sexual division of labour is introduced and defined as 'a system of allocating the labour of the sexes to activities, and highly importantly as a system of distributing the products of these activities' (Whitehead, 1981: 90). The sexual division of labour is an empirical and structural phenomenon found both in the household and the labour market. Its complexity and the multiple levels at which it functions must be recognized.

The multiple levels at which the sexual division of labour operates are described broadly as social reproduction, i.e. the process by which the main social relations that structure a particular empirical situation are constantly re-created and perpetuated. Social reproduction must be seen as a totality which takes place at three levels of theoretical abstraction: (1) human or biological reproduction (e.g. kinship and marriage systems); (2) reproduction of the labour force through the daily maintenance and services within the household that renew its working capacity; and (3) reproduction of social relations (Edholm, et al., 1977).

The specificities regarding male–female relations and relations of production, as afforded by the social relations of gender approach, provide the necessary tools to periodize and localize the historically specific forms these relations may take. These specificities also help to overcome reductionist arguments derived from overgeneralization about patriarchy. However, there are several conceptual and methodological shortcomings.

Conceptually, although this approach treats social reproduction as a totality, the conceptualization of women's labour within this totality is based on the separation of biological and social issues and on the conventional distinction between productive and unproductive labour. As Whitehead writes, 'sex is the province of biology, gender is the province of social science'

(1979: 10). This separation makes it impossible to analyse forms of work in which biological sex is used as a source of labour. The conceptualization of women's labour subsumes issues concerning biological sex under social phenomena such as the control of female sexuality for the purpose of the transmission of resources and property, and population control. This conceptualization treats female sexuality only in terms of social manipulation rather than granting sexuality its significance in its own right.

The reproduction of class relations is conceptualized within the limits of the transmission of property. The concept of property is restricted to tangible forms of property such as land. As has been pointed out (Hirschon, 1984), there is a tendency to equate property as object and property relations as the relation between subject and object. Anthropological findings indicate that in many societies there exists a category of property which is non-material, sometimes referred to as 'incorporeal' property which may include certain privileges that constitute sources of wealth such as information, knowledge (songs, legends, rituals) or special skills (Hirschon, 1984).

Thus, property may also be a socially valued resource relating subject with another subject. A house slave is valued by the master for the labour embodied in him/her. A herbal medicine man or woman is valued by the community for the knowledge he or she possesses. A *courtesan* is valued for her entertainment and sexual skills by the monarchy and aristocracy. Equally, attributes which are perceived as a threat to society e.g. particular political affiliation, sexual identities, criminal and deviant identities may lead to people's exclusion from production. The difference may be located in the ways in which such 'intangible property' is constructed, valued and utilized, and the kinds of rewards received. While form and content may vary, their source remains with the conception of the human body and the relations which institute it as a subject.

Rather than reducing women's social position to their access to property, the concept of property must be disaggregated to take into account other forms of 'intangible property'. This disaggregation will enable a more precise understanding of what constitutes socially valued resources and women's access to or exclusion from them.[1] Instead of using access to property as the basis to explain sexual differentiation, sexual hierarchy must be understood in the context of the formation of socially valued resources, including those associated with the human body as a biological entity and as a social subject. The concept of class can encompass more structures than the one derived from the utilization and transmission of tangible property and may include other types of social stratification derived from the use of attributes to gain access to production, or from exclusion from production because of certain attributes. Such attributes are historically specific and do change in conformity with ideological and social changes. Class and sex relations do respond to such changes and therefore cannot be reduced to property ownership.

Methodologically, the marriage-based household whose division of labour is based on property relations (among other factors) continues to be emphasized as a unit of analysis (Young, et al., 1981). This results in a confusion of the different levels of analysis. For example, social reproduction is defined as the 'structures [which] are reproduced in order that social reproduction as a whole can take place' (Edholm, et al., 1977). These structures are identified as the transmission of property or access to resources (Beneria, 1979) or sexual division of labour (MacIntosh, 1981; Whitehead, 1981). The concept of sexual division of labour is used to describe the structure which conditions the maintenance of the same patterns of social reproduction and to describe the content and character of women's work inside and outside the household. In this context, it does not differ from the concept of social reproduction of the labour force which is defined as the allocation of agents in the labour process and/or the mechanisms of inclusion and exclusion of workers in such a process (Edholm, et al., 1977; Beneria, 1979). The three concepts of social reproduction, reproduction of the labour force and sexual division of labour are used interchangeably.

At the level of interpretation, there is a teleological bias in the social relations of gender approach inherent in the conceptual and methodological issues mentioned above. This approach first identifies a synchronic structure, then argues for its cardinal significance on the basis that it not only repeats itself but also transforms itself in different spheres of social activity. This offers an explanation only in the context of the transformation of forms of subordination, and of the formation of female subjects fit for specific socio-economic relations. The approach still omits the material basis of ideological formation.

The concepts of sexual division of labour and gender relations so defined only provide an explanation in so far as the ideological assumptions about women's work are concerned and their manifestations in different contexts. In other words, since the sexual division of labour is treated as a technical issue, only the transposition of notions about sex roles on labour relations are discussed (allocation of women's position in the social division of labour) in relation to forms of accumulation. But accumulation from sex as labour is omitted. While the significance of ideological assumptions as mechanisms of labour control is recognized, whether such mechanisms could be located at the level of structural causality remains an open question. As the domain of production is extremely dynamic, any predetermined identification of structural causality will lead to a predetermined understanding of change in a given context.

Sexual hierarchy embodies a much more complex system of control and regulation which is not static and unchanging across history or classes, and which is not always tied to property relations. By tying it to property relations, the social relations of gender approach separates the analysis of biological reproduction from the social maintenance of the labour force, the former belonging to biology and the latter to sociology. While this separation is necessary for conceptual clarity, either a way must be found to establish the link between the two areas or biological sex must be deleted from social analysis. This deletion has consequences for the understanding of women's labour as there exists a level of labour which is purely sexual.

Historically, the manifestation of women's sexual labour — the use of the body as an instrument to produce a service — has taken different forms under various types of social relations such as slavery, patron–client relations or wage relations (e.g. wet-nursing, biological reproducers under slavery, surrogate reproducers under wage relations, and prostitution). The social relations governing sexual labour correspond to the dominant social relations of production. Thus, sexual labour can be organized purely on a communal and household basis, or can be taken outside the household and linked with a (limited or wide) network of commercial relations. The link between relations which organize sexual labour and the social relations of production prevailing at any given time must therefore be understood. Dominant social relations of production not only transpose on to wage relations notions that are ascribed to a gender. They can also encroach at a level beyond the social ascription of gender, directly related to the utility of female biological functions (in Firestone's words (1971), to 'a woman's body as a means of reproduction').

Therefore it is necessary to go beyond issues pertaining to the ideological assumptions about women's labour. It is equally necessary to move beyond debating whether women's labour in the household is productive or unproductive. It can be both, depending on the context. The household is only a site through which various kinds of work are performed. It can be a site for domestic labour alone, and it can be a site for production for the local market or for export (food processing, crafts, garments) as shown in case studies on home-based production in the Third World (Piñeda, 1981; Mies, 1982). Thus, the link between women's labour in the household and the wider process of production and accumulation may not be overgeneralized. It would be difficult to show that domestic labour performed by Western housewives today produces surplus value. At the same time, labour performed by women in many households in the Third World is directly linked with accumulation at an international level. Therefore, the household cannot be confused with the kinds of labour that take place within it (Harrod, 1987). By limiting itself within ideological assumptions about women's labour in the household, the social relations of gender approach can show only how such assumptions are transposed into relations of production, but cannot show the process which transforms the social relations surrounding reproductive work (procreation, maintenance), nor its effects on women's social and economic positions.

Another confusion that needs to be avoided is the confusion between household relations and relations which organize reproductive work. Within reproductive work, there are categories of sexual services and social services of maintenance. These services may be organized on the basis of household relations, or they may be incorporated in the sphere of production. The question is when and how the social and the sexual aspects of reproduction are integrated into household relations, and when and how they become disintegrated and incorporated into the sphere of production and accumulation.

For example, the existence of organized domestic labour under the form of 'cleaning services' in some industrialized societies is a clear indication of its utility and profitability, in a situation in which more and more women are refusing to do housework and can afford to do so because of higher wages. In this case domestic labour has nothing to do with household relations but is performed under relations which are external to the household, although the site of its performance is still the household. Similarly, sexual services in the sex industry and social services for the physical maintenance of single workers through institutions such as boarding houses are organized entirely under commercial relations and bear little resemblance to household relations, although both services fall within reproduction as physical maintenance. Here not only the sites of reproduction but also the social relations governing reproductive labour are different.

In the sphere of production, sexual services and social services of maintenance can exist independently in a given locality in the forms of brothels and boarding houses respectively, or they can be integrated within specific forms. As will be shown in chapter 5, sexual services and social services of maintenance can also converge in an organized commercial form found in some Asian societies today, i.e. the 'hired wife' who comes with a furnished flat for a fixed period, or the sex package tour with sexual services included for specific time periods chosen by the travellers prior to departure. They can also converge in the form of ad-hoc prostitution by women whose main work is to provide maintenance services to single male workers under 'casual' labour relations (Nelson, 1979; White, 1983b).

The social conditions which contribute to the integration or disintegration of sexual and social services of maintenance are historically, socially and culturally specific. So too are the patterns of accumulation. Thus, rather than conceptualizing the sexual division of labour and reproduction in the given context of a marriage-based household and treating other forms of reproduction as derivative, it would seem more useful to start with the basic elements of reproductive work, to look at how the relations surrounding them are transformed and how certain categories of women and men are included or excluded from the various dimensions of reproduction.

In summary, while the insights provided by feminist analysis of reproduction are important, insufficient attention has been given to processes which organize reproduction outside the family. As a result, in spite of their recognition of the provision of domestic services, psychological and sexual satisfaction as important aspects of women's work in the maintenance of the labour force, there remains a tendency to gloss over the character of such work beyond the household. As the theoretical propositions of the socialist feminists conceptually separate biology and gender, the level of labour which is purely sexual has been deleted from the analysis. Using the household as a basis of analysis contextualizes women's labour in reproduction in the home, but does not expose those forms of reproduction which are not mediated through the family or household.

It is essential to understand the main constituents of reproductive work, under which conditions they coalesce into one unit, under which conditions they are kept separated and how this separation affects the social position of women. Changes in the production system may fundamentally alter the traditional forms through which human needs for sexual pleasure and physical maintenance are fulfilled. These changes may lead to the separation of biological sex, procreation, and physical maintenance, all conventionally defined as part and parcel of women's work in the family. Gender relations also encompass the dimension of sexual identity which is derived from the ways biological functions are utilized for the production of a service which has some utility outside of conjugal relations (surrogate reproduction, prostitution). The next section seeks to show the relationship between sexuality and production and the constituents of sexual labour under various forms of social relations of production.

Sexuality and Sexual Labour

Sexuality has long been a subject of academic debate. A large body of material exists, focusing mainly on variations of the sexual act, sexual norms and ethical standards, sexual meanings, sexual behaviour, and the organizational arrangement of sexual relations. However, since sexuality touches upon many domains of human life, to provide a complete understanding of sexuality is nearly impossible. Many aspects of sexuality are omitted from academic discussions, and it is not certain that such discussions can shed more light on a topic so essential to human existence. As Weeks writes (1987: 11):   'The more expert we become in talking about sexuality, the greater difficulties we seem to encounter in trying to understand it'.

Until recently, sexuality was discussed in a self-contained debate, which moved from psychoanalysis to the social sciences where its analysis has become located in the domain of power relations. The ongoing debate on sexuality emphasizes the role of power at the level of codification and subjectivity. In its attempt to counterbalance economic reductionism, the debate tends to disconnect sexuality from economic relations. More particularly, within the women's movement, an additional problem inherent in the debate on female sexuality is the problem of definition and the undifferentiated use of the concept of sexuality.

The concept of sexuality has been used simultaneously as an analytical, empirical and political concept. As an analytical concept, sexuality has been used to analyse the abstract process of gender formation and the fixing of sexual differences at the level of the unconscious through symbols. As an empirical concept, it has been used to describe sexual experiences as they are directed by gender. As a political concept, it has been applied in the explanation of the power relations between men and women derived from unequal control over their own bodies (reproductive capacity and sexual desire). Because the debate has been built around the male–female relation and on the premise that sexuality is the site of women's oppression, the positive aspects of sexuality are not recognized. These aspects are nevertheless essential. As Bessie Smith wrote about the sexual lives of Black women in the United States (in Russell, 1977: 183):   'In a deliberate inversion of the Puritanism of the protestant ethics . . . how fundamental sexuality was to our survival.

Where work is often death for us, sex brought us back to life. It was better than food, and sometimes a necessary substitute.' The significance of intimacy through bodily contact in human life somehow has been left out. There is a hesitation to confront the positive aspects of biological sex as a human need which includes pleasure, intimacy and social significance.

There are many gaps to be filled before the concept of sexuality can be afforded the status of a fully-fledged theoretical concept which can be used simultaneously in the analysis, description and direction of practices. The first task is to disaggregate the concept of sexuality into its main constituents, and to identify and discuss the possible interconnections among them.

Three main aspects of human sexuality may be identified: (1) the biological (physical pleasure and procreation);   (2) the social (sexual relations, social rules and forms through which biological sex is expressed); and   (3) the subjective (individual and collective consciousness as sexual subjects and desire). These aspects are elements of a wider process which may be called the organization of sexuality. The organization of sexuality does not operate in any single social structure. The structure of the organization of sexuality responds to social change. Sexuality (biological sex, forms of sexual relations, subjective sexual identity and sexual desire) may not be taken as given. The expression of biological sex, the forms of sexual relations as well as sexual consciousness are socially and historically specific and may differ along many social lines such as gender, class, ethnicity, and age.

One of the most important contributions to the understanding of sexuality as part of a historical process is made by Foucault (1980a). Foucault rejects the notion that biological sex is some kind of instinctual force, constantly needing to express itself and constantly being repressed. He proposes that the regulation of biological sex must be understood in terms of a historical conception of the human body which lies at the root of the regime of power and politics over sexuality. Rather than reducing sexuality to either of its domains, i.e. biology, or society and economy, Foucault conceptualizes sexuality as an aggregation of social relations which he calls the 'apparatus of sexuality'. As an aggregation of social relations, the 'apparatus of sexuality' is socially and historically specific, and reflects a given period of transformation of a society.

Embodied in the concept of the 'apparatus of sexuality' are   (1) discourse on biological sex;   (2) the techniques of management and control of sexual practices, i.e. rules of regulation, organization and categorization; and   (3) the domains of discourse and practice (medicine, law, religion, pedagogy) as mechanisms of knowledge and power. Figure 2.1 attempts to concretize the 'apparatus of sexuality' as conceptualized by Foucault.

Essentially, Foucault regards the 'apparatus of sexuality' as the locus from which various forms of control and resistance are generated and exercised. The data used to abstract this apparatus are derived from the Western social experience during the Industrial Revolution. Foucault argues that biological sex must be seen as an historical experience of a given society, an experience which shapes the individual and subjective domain and which cannot be reduced to the biological, social or economic. As an historical experience,

Abstract	Discourses on sexuality		
Intermediate	Regulation	Organization	Categorization
Empirical	Practices of biological sex, forms of sexual relations (conformity or defiance, insurrection of the subjugated)		

Figure 2.1   The Apparatus of Sexuality

biological sex must be understood against the background of the 'apparatus of sexuality' which can be periodized and analysed by decoding the chronology of the techniques of control, and by examining the peripheral effects of power at its point of application.

According to Foucault, during earlier periods of history there was a certain openness about sex. With the transition from feudalism to modern industrialism in Europe, biological sex became an economic and political arena, thus a target of social intervention and a subject of 'discourse' which permeated all aspects of private life. Governments no longer dealt with people but with a population as labouring capacity. 'States are not populated in accordance with the natural progression of propagation, but by virtue of their industry, their products and their different institutions' (Foucault, 1980a: 25). Thus, biological sex becomes a means of access to both the life of the human body and the life of the species. Sex became 'a pivot of the two axes along which developed the entire political technology of life. On the one hand it was tied to the discipline of the body: the harnessing, intensification and distribution of forces, the adjustment and economies of energy. On the other hand, it was applied to the regulation of populations, through all the far-reaching effects of its activity' (Foucault, 1980a: 145). The future of society becomes linked to the use of biological sex in terms of the physical energy it generates and consumes, and in terms of the people it produces. Intervention in, and supervision of civil society by state institutions (administration, law, police, hospital, prison) in matters of biological sex marked the beginning of modern industrialism. Under this system, sex as a source of immediate bodily energy (physical pleasure) and continuing energy (procreation) is central as it is transformed into labour for industry.

The articulation of the contradictions between sex as bodily energy and sex as procreation finds its clearest expression in the Victorian morality and practices of biological sex (i.e. sex is allowed only when procreation is involved and within socially recognized unions) and in governments' interest in managing and manipulating human fertility as exemplified by the population control debates prevalent at the time.[2] The regulation of sex was motivated by one basic concern, namely to ensure that the population reproduced a labouring capacity that was physically and morally healthy. Hence emerged the centrifugal move towards a regime of heterosexual conjugality, the centre of which is the bourgeoisie, the periphery the working class. Heterosexual conjugality is a form of sexual relations which is both economically useful and politically conservative.

Foucault's analysis does not elaborate on sexuality as labour, although he has rightly identified the central aspect of biological sex as a source of life embodied in individuals. He has shown how this source of life has been co-opted by discursive practices which increase the forms of control over individuals and sexual expression. He is not concerned with the productivity of sex, but with its subjectivity.

Central to Foucault's analysis of the subjectivity, and the micro power and politics of sex is the concept of 'discourse'. A discourse contains a set of ideas and arguments which is directly linked to techniques of control as well as to social practices. For him, the explosion of a multiplicity of 'discourses' on sex in the last century in Western Europe marked the transition from feudalism to modernity. Sex became a focal point in the creation of subjective identity, constructed with the heterosexual couple as a model of sexual relations. These 'discourses' have taken very specific forms: (1) religious discourse enforces the norms and codes towards a regime of heterosexual monogamy;   (2) bureaucratic discourse glorifies the conjugal family (the legitimate, procreative couple as the model by law);   (3) the scrutinization of sexual behaviour through science, law, education; and   (4) the creation of a new kind of sexual identity (the deviant or perverse) and the persecution of such peripheral sexualities. Religious sermons, scientific debates, or even dossiers and files housed in bureaucracies are all part of discourses and their practices.

As a discourse can take different forms, there is an inherent hierarchy of these forms which may be contradictory. The dominant form of discourse is always linked with institutional practices of control and discipline — legislation, organizations based on public law whose principle of articulation is the social body and the delegative status of each citizen (Foucault, 1983). The subjugated forms of discourse represent blocks of historical knowledge which are present but disguised within, or disqualified by, the dominant discourse. However, there is no clear-cut division between the different forms of discourse, such as accepted discourse versus excluded discourse, or dominant discourse versus dominated discourse. Rather, the operation of discourse must be understood as a multiplicity of discursive elements that can come into play and the power relations thus created. Power and discourse are directly related as two sides of the same process. Power relations only exist with a correlative constitution of a field of knowledge (discourse), and there is no discourse that does not simultaneously presuppose or constitute power relations.

Thus, far from seeing the dominant discourses on sexuality only in terms of the moral divisions they accompany, the ideology they represent, and the repression they execute, Foucault sees them as part of the macro and micro power structures of society, particularly with respect to 'their tactical productivity (what reciprocal effects of power and knowledge they ensure) and their strategic integration (what conjuction and what force relationship make their utilization necessary in a given episode of the various confrontations that occur)' (Foucault, 1980a: 101–2).

Inherent in the operation of forms of discourse and their related practices is the power of resistance. Discourses can be both an instrument and an effect of power, but also a hindrance, a stumbling-block, a point of resistance or a starting point for an opposing strategy. Foucault writes:

> I also believe that it is through the re-emergence of these low-ranking knowledges, these unqualified, even directly disqualified knowledges . . . which involve what I would call a popular knowledge (*le savoir des gens*) though it is far from being a general commonsense knowledge, but is on the contrary a particular, local, regional knowledge, a differential knowledge incapable of unanimity and which owes its force only to the harshness with which it is opposed by everything surrounding it — that it is through the reappearance of this knowledge, of these local popular knowledges, these disqualified knowledges, that criticism performs its work. (Foucault, 1980b: 82)

The direct effect of the discourses on sex and the 'apparatus of sexuality' is the creation of different sexual identities through which social power is exercised. At the level of human consciousness, control is exercised through religious and ideological discourses on the communal perception of sexuality. At the institutional and instrumental level, these discourses are translated into laws, and at the level of community and household these laws are observed through the establishment of social sanctions such as medicalization, ostracism and stigmatization, or through positive rewards.

But as the 'apparatus of sexuality' is nothing more than an aggregation of social relations, 'its deployment does not operate in symmetrical fashion with respect to the social classes, and consequently it does not produce the same effect in them' (Foucault, 1980a: 127). The contradictory effects of discourses on individuals and society provide counterpoint for critique and resistance. Thus, sexual practices and sexual consciousness which contradict the dominant discourse on sex may not be seen as 'perversity' or 'deviance'. They result from specific social processes which create the conditions for them to exist. Their persecution is the site of their insurrection. Here, Foucault's position comes quite close to Durkheim's thesis of repressive morality and anomie. The difference is that Foucault does not see the history of morality in a linear fashion as Durkheim did. Rather, he disaggregates this morality into different spheres in which the process of subjugation occurs in a given episode, within which there is both persecution and tolerance. The question is what is tolerated and why, and what is persecuted and why.

Foucault's major contributions to the understanding of sexuality may be discerned along the following lines:

1   the view that the human body must be understood in terms of its historical conception enables us to discern the terms of various sexual discourses and to relate them to historical change;

2   the view that biological sex is a source of life whose regulatory structures correspond to the operation of economic processes enables us to grasp the economic basis of biological sex, and to establish the relationship between forms of sexual relations and forms of economic production;

3   the view that 'discourse' is a source both of power and resistance enables us to discern what elements of a discourse on sex have been applied by whom and how, what kinds of contradiction they create, and how consciousness and resistance are developed.

Although Foucault advocates an analysis of sexuality in terms of the historical conception of the human body, he does not make a qualitative differentiation between the male and female body.[3] Furthermore, given his primary concern with the subjectivity of sex, Foucault fails to make a link between the constitution of the subject through discourse and the process of exploitation which can utilize subjective identity as its ideological basis. To the old question of how sexuality is structured and directed through ideas and practices, others must be added: how female sexuality is valorized and how it becomes incorporated into the process of surplus extraction.

Biological sex has two main elements, namely physical pleasure and procreation. The 'products' of biological sex can be both a source of oppression and a reward (nonmaterial and material). Children can be a source of joy, social significance, burdens or additional labour. Sexual intercourse can be gratifying or oppressive. What is important is the context in which biological sex takes place. Before going into these different contexts and the meanings that acccompany them, we must recognize that biological sex is first and foremost a source of life. How it becomes a source of oppression requires an explanation, and cannot be taken as given. Oppression is derived from the structure of the social organization of sex as a source of life.

As a source of life, biological sex has been subject to various forms of control and regulation which are historically and socially specific. The process of organizing sexual relations has the human body as its material basis, the body which generates and consumes.[4] The organization of sexual relations is connected with the organization of labour and productive sources. Here, von Werlhof (1980) and Mies (1986) have initiated some points for discussion which shed more light on the political economy of biological sex. Like Foucault, these authors locate the human body in social analysis. Unlike Foucault, they do not stress discursive practice regarding sex. Rather, they stress the significance of biological sex in the process of production. Mies stresses the procreative aspect of the human body, focusing her discussion on the female body in particular. Von Werlhof emphasizes the regenerative aspect of the human body and therefore emphasizes the physical conditions of the human body in general.

Von Werlhof (1980) rejects the separation between sexuality and economy as artificial. To her, this separation

makes it impossible to analyse sexual violence against women in economic terms or economic exploitation in sexual terms . . . and to perceive that labour might involve pleasure . . . and that sexuality might involve struggle and violence, all forms of impotence from the lack of possibilities for emotional development to sadistic deformations to feelings of anxiety and frustration and the loss of sensual capabilities altogether. (1980: 36)

In her view, sexuality is to be understood not only as concrete individual sexual behaviour or sexual potential, but also as part of a general and specific human need for social communication and significance (general in the sense that everybody needs sex, specific in the sense that specific forms of sexual relations have specific meanings to people). Seen as such, sexuality relates to all spheres of daily life, 'especially in the labour process; while using and spending labour power, it is the vital potential of the labourer, his or her sexuality that is used and lost' (1980: 38).

Mies (1986) elaborates the link between sexuality (as a source of life) and production by examining the procreative aspects of biological sex. She argues that the production of life is the perennial precondition of all historical forms of productive labour. 'The first means of production with which human beings act upon nature is their own body. It [the body] is also the eternal pre-condition of all future means of production . . . Human beings do not only use their bodies to produce use-value, they also keep their body alive — in its widest sense — by the consumption of their products' (Mies, 1986: 52). Out of their own bodies women produce children and the first food for them. Thus, the first form of production of new life and production for subsistence takes place through the appropriation and utilization of women's body by women themselves. The concealment of a kind of production which is so basic to the development of human society is a result of historical processes. As societies developed, ideological structures to govern the organization of biological sex as a source of life also developed. 'In each historical epoch maleness and femaleness are differently defined. This definition depends on the principal mode of production in these epochs. This means that the organic differences between men and women are differently interpreted and valued, according to the dominant form of appropriation of natural matter for the satisfaction of human needs' (Mies, 1986: 53). Ideological definitions of maleness and femaleness obfuscate women's contribution to the production of new life and to the maintenance of living humans.

Mies's point comes very close to Foucault's argument about the historical conception of the human body. The oldest conception of the human body may be found in religious discourses and rituals. In old forms of Tantra Yoga and Taoism, for example, for both men and women the act of sex was regarded as a way to give energy to, and to obtain energy from one another. Sexual union represented the model of the union between the human soul and the cosmic forces. Rather than a source of evil, female orgasm was considered as an important source of sexual energy which could be passed on to the male (Parrinder, 1980). Similarly, in cultures where the cult of fertility was prevalent, menstruation was considered a gift of life, providing the possibility to create new life (Carmody, 1979; Gross, 1980). The dominance of the female principle in such discourses is connected with the fact that paternity as a social construct was not yet significant.[5]

By contrast, despite their variations, discourses on sex in established patriarchal religions reveal two central and contradictory themes which are found cross-culturally (Paul, 1979; Parrinder, 1980; Mernissi, 1982): (1) female sexuality is a threat to culture, a source of evil to be suppressed and controlled; and   (2) the feminine is maternal, devoted, wise and compassionate. The idea that female sexuality is a threat to society correlates with a belief in the exclusive role of semen as a source of life, sometimes as life itself. Female sexuality is then redefined as functional to procreation and to male pleasure. The ideal form of the feminine depicts female sexuality in a state of equilibrium (chastity, virginity) tied to social roles such as wife, daughter and mother. This will be shown in greater detail in chapter 4 on gender relations and Buddhism in Thailand.

This suggests that interpretations of physiological differences between men and women emerged when the sexual act (coitus) became a social act. As a social act, biological sex as a source of life became dichotomized into mutually exclusive poles (sexual pleasure and procreation). Equally, sexual identities such as the virgin (as an asexual category), the mother (as a fertile category) and the prostitute (as an erotic category) have been created to maintain the exclusivity of the two poles. Subjective interpretations of the physical constituents of the human body form the basis upon which social instruments have been developed and applied in the management of sexuality. In the process, the physical attributes of male and female bodies acquired different values. Under specific historical conditions, as in predominantly agrarian societies, these attributes constituted valued resources or intangible property (virginity, chastity, fertility) connected with access to the ownership of tangible property such as land and cattle.

As with any other socially constructed values, attributes assigned to the human body change with historical and social transformation. Thus, where landed property is becoming insignificant (as in the case of countries under socialist transformation) female labour and skills become more predominantly valued than virginity (Croll, 1984). Similarly, communal perceptions about female sexuality have changed in a number of Asian countries which have undergone industrial transformation. Research conducted in Thailand indicates a shift in the attitudes of rural communities towards the value of the female sex. In a number of formerly impoverished rural communities in northeastern Thailand, many families have sent their daughters into prostitution over the last twenty years. The remittances they receive from their daughters form an important source of income which has not only saved their farms but also has substantially improved their living conditions. As a result, the value of their daughter's sexuality have taken predominance over male labour, and families actually celebrate the birth of a daughter, because she now has potentially more access to social mobility (Nakornjarupong, 1981: 47; Phongpaichit, 1982). A similar transformation may be observed in many industrialized societies where the availability of birth control technology has put an end to the separation of sexual pleasure and procreation. The result is a changing conception of the female body which glorifies it in the context of consumerism, advertising and pornography and is far removed from the traditional Puritanist prudery.

These examples show that the ideological structures shaping the values attached to the female body (or defining how female sexuality is valorized) cannot be accepted as ahistorical and unchanging. Rather, the issue is how particular values attached to the body emerged, and how they facilitate or obstruct forms of the organization of labour based on sex. The social structures which have emerged to control human sexuality are characterized by the consciousness of biological sex as a source of life. Female sexuality is not denied as often claimed. Instead, female sexuality is valorized for economic and social purposes. However, the value produced by female sexual functions is obscured by ideological discourses through categorization.

Sexual Labour, Sexual Consciousness and the Transition to Capitalism

As has been argued, there is a category of labour which is purely sexual and which is essential to human life and to society. What makes this labour available under wage relations? Traditionally, sexual activities have been confined to kinship relations. Therefore, the transformation of sexuality into sexual labour is only possible with the disruption of kinship relations through economic and social dislocation. Although such disruption predates capitalism (as does prostitution), the emergence of capitalism intensifies the utilization of sexual labour in prostitution owing to the intensity of social and economic dislocations. As has been pointed out by Weeks (1987), sexual relations between men and women are constantly affected by external economic relations. Therefore, to understand the changing form of the organization of sexuality it is important to look into the changing forms of kinship relations. Internally, sexual norms within the marriage-based household are also dynamic. They are affected by changing forms of economic production which may induce changes in the organization of activities related to sexuality within the household and community at large (Stone, 1977; Walkowitz, 1980; Weeks, 1980; Ross and Rapp, 1981).

Broadly speaking, changes in kinship and household patterns have implications for the organization of inheritance and an impact on the social constraints imposed on the sexual act. As pointed out by Stone in his study on the family, sex and marriage in England between 1500 and 1800, it was the inheritance system which structured the sexual conduct of the young as well as of particular categories of adults such as inheriting daughters or widows, who had to remain celibate to protect their property rights. However, with drastic changes in the socio-economic system induced bu industrialization, for many people wage labour took predominance over property rights and consequently the value of chastity and virginity placed on women in connection with wedlock and inheritance was shifted to the value of the labour they represented for the rural household. Their income contributed to the household and their savings formed their own dowries or inherited property for marriage.

As urbanization and labour migration intensify, kinship systems and patterns of sexual organization cannot remain exempt from change. As Stone points out (1977), English working-class youth became sexually and economically more autonomous than their middle-class peers. With the availability of wage labour, the young could marry and set up households independently, without waiting for inheritance. With employment far too unstable to permit marriage, young people nevertheless became engaged in courtship and sexual relations with the traditional expectation that marriage would take place should a pregnancy result (Ross and Rapp, 1981). In the absence of a traditional kinship support system to exercise pressure on male responsibility, many female migrants who were incorporated in domestic services or low-paid factory work in urban areas faced a new situation. In view of their low wages, these women could neither rely on their own income nor demand male support for pregnancy and childbirth. This resulted in especially high rates of illegitimacy and infanticide among the French and English working class in the 19th century, particularly among domestic servants, who lacked savings, employment opportunities and skills to support a new household. This might have led to their abandonment by men (Weeks, 1980; Ross and Rapp, 1981). In many cases, these women ended up losing their jobs and turning to prostitution (Walkowitz, 1980).

While sexual pleasure may be governed by property relations, economic and social change may induce disruptions of traditional patterns which affect men and women differently. As Ross and Rapp (1981) have pointed out, in the absence of inherited property, men and women turned to their labour power to create their own property to prepare for marriage. However, although young men and women may have continued to meet each other's sexual needs with traditional expectations, these could no longer be met due to the uncertainty of their employment; women bore the consequences and turned to providing the same services at a price. Traditional reproduction functions connected with the family and kinship system became broken and commoditized along with the commoditization of labour power.

To recapitulate, the way in which female sexuality becomes commoditized is first and foremost connected with the changing perception of the value of their sexuality. Formerly, this was perceived in terms of chastity and virginity, wedlock and property interests, which at least provided them with some material security. As new forms of production were introduced, the value of their sexuality changed and their labour became a new form of property, forcing them to use it in the ways which could meet their survival needs under the new conditions. It must noted that their reproduction functions have not changed, but only have become disintegrated. The options available to women were either to contribute to the physical maintenance of members of a wealthy household or to the sexual maintenance of single male labourers who were able to purchase these services periodically without the responsibility entailed in wedlock.

Similar dislocation of the work force and demographic changes are experienced by many developing countries today. While there are no studies on the specific systems of maintenance and renewal of the labour force at household and communal level in areas where industrialization is taking place, studies on women's casual work in adjacent areas indicate that single women and female-headed households are providing reproductive services to the single male work force, often including sexual services (Jocano, 1975; Arispez, 1977; Nelson, 1979). How far these changes have influenced social attitudes towards female sexuality is not known. But as property relations no longer determine and define the criteria used to assess female sexuality, and as landed property is no longer of great significance for a propertyless urban work force, female labour becomes valued in connection with its functions in maintenance and renewal of the labour force outside the household. These functions become separated from biological reproduction and from property interests.

In parallel to the general process which incorporates men and women into the wage-labour force, there exists also a process which incorporates some women into the labour force as reproducers using mainly sexual labour which is not recognized as productive. While men were seen as workers with sexual licence and, in Engels' term, as being 'intoxicated by the bourgeoisie', women prostitutes are ostracized as immoral and unproductive. The commoditization of sexual labour was enabled by the disruption of kinship relations and the formation of new sexual norms. These norms provide men with more choice while maintaining a double standard for women.

Although rules of sexual conduct and the value attributed to female sexuality are subject to change in accordance with newly emerged economic and social imperatives, these changes do not fundamentally alter the types of work women perform. They only alter the confines and conditions under which reproductive services are provided by women. The disintegration of reproductive activities and the commoditization of sexual labour created a class of reproducers, performing social as well as sexual tasks and receiving minimal recognition and reward. Seen in this light, reproduction forms an indispensable activity within all forms of production. The way in which the different dimensions of reproduction are defined and institutionally channelled depends on the requirements of a given form of production and on communal and state interests.

It would be misleading to think that sexual rules are passively followed. There is evidence to suggest that such rules are also challenged, sometimes in the form of conscious resistance, sometimes as tacit expressions of preferences enabled by changing socio-economic conditions. Acquired consciousness about sexual identity is a reflection of the specific social relations under which biological sex is organized and fulfilled.

For example, the emergence of homosexual networks in Western Europe and in China in the last century coincided with the emergence of wage work and sex-segregated working conditions. Wage work rendered kinship lineages less relevant among the working class and opened new avenues for homosexual expression and alternative forms of personal bonding. Such expression took the form of a suppressed and reviled identity in Europe, where surveillance and control were more severe (Adam, 1985). It could, however, have combined elements of workers' organization with affirmation of an identity stigmatized by society. In China at the turn of the century, groups of rural women who entered wage work in the silk industry around Shanghai achieved economic independence, rejected patriarchal relations, despised marriage and formed their own lesbian communities known as 'same sex unions' (McGough, 1981). They shared households and formed self-supporting networks such as the 'Mutual Admiration Society' or 'Golden Orchid Society' and other types of workmate societies. They even selected descendants, instituting 'daughters' to enter these compacts and to succeed them.

Social, political and cultural contexts also affect the perceptions of prostitutes and their kin about their position in society and the relations which oppress them. In her study of marriage and alternative strategies of Hausa women in Northern Nigeria, Pittin (1979: 354–6) shows how women who practise prostitution with a certain degree of success can keep their freedom and secure an independent life. In due course, earlier disapproval by their kin becomes muffled, overtaken by acceptance and sometimes open respect. Similarly, several researchers have reported that rural women who entered the sex industry in Southeast Asia perceive themselves as breadwinners for their families rather than as immoral (Phongpaichit, 1982, Wihtol, 1982). Some identify themselves in terms of how much they are able to get the customers to pay. There is a source of pride derived purely from their level of income, with women calling themselves '25-dollar girls' or the '100-dollar girls'. This pride seems mainly designed to counterbalance the hypocritical morality of society and their maltreatment by pimps and clients. They see men as exploitative and manipulative, and therefore they value cunningly, handling men in such a way that they maximize every transaction (Moselina, 1981; Cohen, 1982). They do not see a differentiation in the structure of oppression. Without a long-term perspective, and given the competitiveness of the business as well as the absence of a political arena, prostitutes in many Third World countries have not been able to develop effective networks of support and organization. Therefore, they can be easily used by any group with sufficient motivation or political forces as scapegoats for a variety of social problems such as drought (Pittin, 1979: 284–9), epidemic, drug abuse and other problems related to the sphere of criminality.

By contrast, prostitutes in industrialized countries have formed unions, although these are not yet recognized. This has been made possible by the political space created by the feminist movement on sexuality, and to the active support of some sections of the women's movement, e.g. the International Wages-for-Housework Campaign, and the International Network Against the Traffic in Women. Prostitutes in industrialized countries see themselves as sex-trade workers rather than as victims of sexual violence (Bell, 1987). They differentiate the structure of oppression into elements imposed by the state, the law, sexual enterprises and individual men. The contradictions which emerge between prostitutes' organizations and some segments of the women's movement, e.g. the International Network Against the Traffic in Women, are between the immediate needs of prostitutes and the broader goals of the women's movement. These contradictions also arise from their different perceptions of sexuality.

Sexual consciousness does not exist in any single form that can be detached from social and economic relations. The material base of the structures of sexual relations is sex as a source of life (bodily pleasure and procreation). These structures operate in the sphere of economic processes and therefore they also reflect the differentiation entailed there. Their operation also conditions the emergence of forms of consciousness which exist in parallel to, or in opposition to dominant forms. Sexual identities are not only created by moral and ideological discourses on sexual behaviour, but are also formed by processes of production which affect the context in which human sexuality is expressed and experienced.

Thus, the nature of sexual oppression is not purely ideological. Instead, it must be assessed against the specific context in which biological sex is expressed, the derived social construction of sexual identities, and the implications these identities have for access to productive resources for the maintenance of one's own existence. Transformation rests upon acquired consciousness and the struggle for the recognition of the diverse effects of power relations. In this sense, it is important that feminist consciousness does not reproduce the traditional bias about prostitution or allow biases to be circulated within its acquired knowledge.

Reproduction, Sexual Labour and Social Control

While the lack of data does not allow for generalization, there is evidence suggesting that the recognition of sex as a source of life is a universal feature. So too is its management, although the techniques of management may be different owing to differences in historical context. It is now a well-established fact that all societies exhibit some forms of management of sexual pleasure and procreation. Population control is related to ecological imperatives or to economic development (Harris and Ross, 1987). Control of pleasure through social rules on mating and marriage is often related to property interests (and sometimes to eugenic interests). Although the most dominant form of organization of sexuality is marriage and kinship, there are various forms, methods and purposes of control which depend on the specific social formation. In spite of the variation in forms, a separation between sexual pleasure and procreation prevails. This separation can be further emphasized on racial lines as exemplified by the colonial and post-colonial experience.

Recent studies on colonial social histories and labour histories reveal that procreation and sexual pleasure constitute a dimension of particular concern for colonial administrations. Sexual pleasure and procreation are often separated to serve the needs of particular economic or political operations. The form and extent of colonial management of biological sex depend on the specific type of colonial operation, such as military camp, plantation, mining industry or light industry in urban areas, as will be illustrated as follows.

As Reddock (1984) has shown, in the case of plantation economy based on slave labour, colonial policies towards marriage and procreation among slaves were based on cost-benefit calculations. During the initial period, small-holders depended on the 'natural' reproduction of the slave population. The expansion of production boosted the slave trade, since planters found it cheaper to buy new slaves than to have them reproduce 'naturally'. The costs of pregnancy and nurturing of babies were higher than the market prices of slaves. Consequently, marriage and cohabitation among slaves were prohibited. Pregnant women were cursed and ill-treated. When the slave trade became stagnant, incentives were given to female slaves to increase their breeding. Female slaves who were used as reproducers developed anti-maternal feelings owing to the suffering of child-bearing and childbirth, and to the alienated character of motherhood under slavery. Protest and resistance took the form of 'birth strikes' (abortion induced with herbs), and infanticide (Reddock, 1984: 108). The procreative role of women was crucial. Not only was women's fertility manipulated according to the labour supply and demand, but also this manipulation clearly disconnected biological sex from conjugality and the human need for intimacy and social significance through social roles such as motherhood and fatherhood.

Organized prostitution as a site of the maintenance of the male labour force shows the importance of the other dimension of sexuality, namely sexual pleasure and social significance. Here, social significance through sexual intercourse is recognized only for men, while the significance of social roles such as wife and mother is denied for women.

In Indonesia from the mid-1890s to about 1913, prostitution was regulated by the colonial administration for the Netherlands Indies Army to enable soldiers to satisfy their sexual needs in a 'natural' way, given the prevailing scornful attitudes towards masturbation and homosexuality. Regulated prostitution was advocated in the belief that prostitution was necessary to satisfy men's natural sexual needs and to keep them 'manly'. Furthermore, it was argued that in the colonies the male sexual urge was increased by the hot climate, spicy food and a set of other factors. Even prisons had official arrangements allowing prisoners with satisfactory conduct to be visited by prostitutes (Hesselink, 1987). In Bombay between 1793 and 1905 the British military authorities officially regularized the provision of Indian women as prostitutes to serve British soldiers. Prostitutes were seen as necessary to help maintain the soldiers' 'manliness' while at the same time soldiers were discouraged from marrying 'native wives' (Ballhatchet, 1980). Medical services were provided to prostitutes to keep them healthy and fit for utilization. Spatial segregation between soldiers and prostitutes was maintained to prevent cohabitation or marriage.

For the civilian male work force, the organization of biological sex tended to combine sexual pleasure with physical maintenance through basic services such as food, water and bed. Prostitution and cohabitation were allowed in order to facilitate cheaper reproduction of the labouring capacity of urban male workers who could not afford to encourage their wives to abandon rural production and join them in town. For example, in Nairobi during the mid-1930s, 'vice centres' were tolerated by the state as sites for the reproduction of the urban wage labourers. These centres provided sexual as well as domestic services such as beds, cooked food, bath water, beverages, etc. in short, 'the support work that enables the male labour force to return to work at least slightly replenished . . . the work of personal and social maintenance' (White, 1983b). 'Vice centres' also saved money for the municipality on 'proper housing' for native labourers because 'the needs of eight men may be served by the provision of two rooms for the men and one for the prostitute' (Davis in White, 1986: 256).

Another example is the case of plantations in several colonial territories in Southeast Asia. In Sumatra in the 19th century, the expansion of plantations created a demand for wage labourers met by male migration from Java. Prostitutes were recruited to keep male coolies at the depot during the long wait. On plantations, female contract labourers were brought in to attract male labourers and to keep them under contract (Hesselink, 1987: 218). Female coolies served as cooks and 'bed-servants' to unmarried male labourers who were kept in debt and indentured. Payment for female services made a large dent in their meagre wages. According to one source, as late as the 1930s only about 20 to 40 per cent of plantation workers in Sumatra were men acompanied by their wives, while the rest were serviced by female coolies and prostitutes (Commission of Enquiry, 1933: 243). The wages of female coolies were kept so low that occasional prostitution with male coolies became a way to earn extra income. If a male coolie wished to take a female coolie to himself for the purpose of cohabitation and therefore to reduce the costs of services, the company had to be compensated for all expenses incurred in bringing the female coolie to the plantation. Compensation could be made on an instalment basis (Hesselink, 1987: 210). As Stoler has shown (1985) the traffic in female coolies by Dutch managers, foremen and indigenous male workers was highly profitable and well established in Sumatra at the turn of the century.

The traffic in women to work as prostitutes for plantation labourers seemed to be part of a more generalized situation in which women from a particular ethnic group were trafficked to be offered to men of the same ethnic group, i.e. between Tamil Nadu and British Malaya where there was a large contingency of Tamil labourers, between China and the large centres of immigration in Southeast Asia, between the Dutch East Indies and British Malaya. The largest group of victims of traffic among Asian countries and Asian colonial territories were Chinese women, because of the large number of contract male labourers from China in these areas and the impoverished conditions in China (Commission of Enquiry, 1933: 21–2; Eng, 1986).

More recent examples of direct state involvement in the provision of prostitutes to serve foreign military personnel have been the case of Japan during the American occupation, the Republic of South Vietnam (before 1975), Thailand, Hongkong, and the Philippines during the Indochina conflict in which over one million soldiers from the United States were involved. These countries signed agreements to provide their services as 'Rest and Recreation' centres for United States military and aid personnel (Enloe, 1983). Their presence contributed to the proliferation of forms of commoditized sexual intercourse which will be discussed in detail in the case study in Part II. Less direct intervention is exemplified by the Oriental Province of Ecuador (in the Amazon) where oil and lumber industries have emerged in recent decades as the two major economic operations led by the state and multinational companies. Here, brothels are set up along the oil pipelines and highways through the agency of the *colonos* (settlers) with the tacit tolerance of provincial authorities and involving both Quechua and transient urban women (Garzon-Zapata, 1985).

These examples show that the management of biological sex as a source of life is conducted through the manipulation of female sexuality. Sexual norms are selectively applied to increase the labour supply or to cut the costs of its maintenance. Selective emphasis is given to the different dimensions of reproduction (i.e. biological sex, procreation, maintenance through domestic work). On the basis of race and class, these dimensions are consciously kept separate rather than allowed to coalesce into conjugality. Not only are women deprived of intimacy and social significance through social roles such as marriage and motherhood, the significance of their labour is also denied. This deprivation and denial take place through ideological mechanisms which classify female sexual labourers as immoral as in the case of prostitutes, and as non-human as in the case of female slaves. Such categorization obfuscates the social relations that extract surplus from their sexual labour and inhumane treatment. This aspect will be elaborated further in chapter 5 under the section on power and production in prostitution in Thailand.

To sum up, it is argued that social intervention and control in the organization of sexuality does not necessarily take the specific form of the nuclear family. Intervention can also produce other forms of organization through which services related to the maintenance of the labour force (prostitution and domestic services) are provided. Intervention need not imply negative sanctions, but may involve measures to facilitate economic and military operations. As such, prostitution may be seen as a collective strategy for the purpose of meeting social needs of reproduction at two levels. At one level, prostitution can be seen in terms of the strategy adopted by different social agents such as the community, the state and the enterprise to ensure the maintenance and renewal of the working capacity of functionally single workers without social responsibility towards prostitutes as a subordinated category of workers. At another level, prostitution can be seen as a household's strategy from which prostitutes originate to provide additional income for the maintenance of household members who may or may not be engaged in different forms of production.

Prostitution, Traffic in Women and International Sexual Politics: The Contradiction between Race and Class

Although there exists a diversity in sexual consciousness and diverse forms of intervention in the area of reproduction, one form of consciousness dominates with its effects extending far beyond its initial boundaries. The centrifugal move towards a regime of monogamous conjugality, its categorization of the promiscuous and the deviant (products of 18th and 19th century European sexual politics) had its effects on the cognitive and institutional structures of the colonies at the beginning of the 20th century and thereafter.

Originally a peripheral subject, the prostitute moved to the centre stage of international sexual politics with the emergence of the movement against licensed brothels and 'white slave traffic'. Branching out from the social purity movement which was born at the end of the last century in the West (Victorian England, the Netherlands, Imperial Germany and the United States), the movement against white slavery became formalized at a global level as the International Agreement for the Suppression of the White Slave Traffic of 1904, and the International Convention for the Suppression of the White Slave Traffic of 1910.

This movement framed the issue of prostitution in terms of the evils of traffic, promiscuity and emotional indifference (Chauvin, 1982). Initially, the movement was concerned with Western women who were trafficked between Western European countries and the United States, and from these countries to the colonies. However, the focus on the situation in the colonies inevitably brought the tolerance of prostitution and licensed brothels in the colonies by colonial administrators under attack.

The attack on prostitution in the colonies also provided a basis for the critique of the sexual norms prevailing in the colonized cultures, and the issue of prostitution became tied to local movements for social reform in the 1920s and 1930s (Marr, 1976; Ballhatchet, 1980; Srinivasan, 1985; Hesselink, 1987). The intricacies of the contradictory discourses on sexuality and the women's question which emerged in the colonies during this period are beyond the scope of this chapter. One important product of these discourses is the transposed view of prostitution as promiscuity and emotional indifference, and the traffic in women and children as the evil product of backward customs.

Thus, despite the realities of prostitution as a collective strategy of meeting the social needs of reproduction painfully experienced by colonial societies, this transposed view subsumed the issue of prostitution under the notion of deviance, leaving out the role of the state and of clients. As such, the understanding of power relations in prostitution became simplified and reduced to the institution of the licensed brothel, regarded as a thorn in the public side. Attention turned away from the relationship between prostitution and the social needs of reproduction, and focused on the preservation of 'good morals' and the eradication of prostitution as a social disease.

However, several signatories of the International Convention for the Suppression of the Traffic in Women and Children retained an interest in maintaining licensed houses in the colonies. This was reflected in the resistance of colonial administrators to international enquiries into the local situation. As pointed out by the Commission of Enquiry into the Traffic of Women and Children in the Far East, the Assembly and the Council of the League of

Nations had laid considerable stress on the necessity of confining the enquiry to the international aspect of the problem. This meant that the existence of licensed brothels was considered a matter of internal social conditions which did not come within the competence of the enquiry (Commission of Enquiry, 1933: 14).

While member states who signed the International Convention for the Suppression of the Traffic in Women and Children of 1921 were aware of the relationship between the traffic and licensed brothels, they did not unanimously pursue the abolitionist line. They agreed on the 'evil' of the traffic in women as a means of supplying sexual labour in prostitution, but their positions regarding the practice of prostitution and licensed brothels varied. Some member states followed the abolitionist principle and closed down licensed brothels in their colonies. The prohibition of prostitution took the form of legal measures providing for punishment of those who kept brothels or houses of rendez-vous under the crime of immoral earning, and of those who solicited in the street under the crime of vagrancy. Other member states regulated through licensed brothels and the registration of prostitutes, while imposing penalties on traffickers (Commission of Enquiry, 1933).

To some extent, the positions adopted by member states as regards to prostitution must be placed in the context of the individual history of each colony as well as of the political strength of the social purity movement. In the United Kingdom and the Netherlands for example, this movement was quite influential and succeeded in mobilizing considerable public opinion on the issue of licensed brothels domestically, which later had an effect on their colonies (Ballhatchet, 1980; Walkowitz, 1980; Barry, 1981b; Hesselink, 1987). The United Kingdom and the Netherlands ratified the international conventions for the suppression of the traffic in women and children on behalf of their colonies and began an abolitionist policy in the late 1920s and early 1930s.

Japan, which did not share colonial ties with the West and was an imperialist power, ratified the Conventions of 1910 and 1921 in so far as 'Japan Proper' was concerned, excluding its overseas dependencies such as Formosa and other Leased Territories. Japan agreed only to observe and monitor the traffic in women to and from 'Japan Proper'. Even so, the absence of colonial ties meant that the political space for activism on the abolition of licensed brothels within 'Japan Proper' was considerably greater than in colonized Asian countries. There were two active and organized bodies — the Purity Society and the Association for Good Morals — which pressured the government to close down brothels, although initially without effect. These organizations focused attention on local politics, aiming at fighting for abolition at the level of a single prefecture with a spread effect to other prefectures. Induced actions at the local political level successfully forced local governments to close down all licensed brothels in ten prefectures by 1930. Meanwhile, in Japan's Kwantung Leased Territory (China), Chinese prostitutes were licensed and were deported if found to have conducted clandestine prostitution (Commission of Enquiry, 1933: 107–9).

The Philippines is another case in point. The Philippines, which shared a colonial tie with the United States until 1946, did not succeed in closing down its licensed brothels. The United States acceded to the International Agreement for the Suppression of the White Slave Traffic on behalf of the Philippines' government. It did not accede to the International Convention for the Suppression of the White Slave Traffic of 1910 or to the International Convention for the Suppression of the Traffic in Women and Children of 1921 'on the ground that these Conventions related to matters which were exclusively under the control of several states of the Union and not of the Federal Government, which makes and ratifies treaties' (Commission of Enquiry, 1933: 188). Thus, the United States left the local enforcement of the law regarding prostitution to the local government in the Philippines, yet it was powerful enough to organize prostitution to facilitate its military operation in spite of the Philippines' abolitionist orientation. In 1918, the Philippines' government issued an order prohibiting the existence of houses of prostitution within ten miles of any military or naval station. American prostitutes were repatriated at the expense of the Philippines' government in Otober 1918. As late as 1930, there existed in the neighbourhood of a military encampment of both American and Filipino soldiers a number of brothels supervised jointly by a number of civilian authorities and Army medical officers (Commission of Enquiry, 1933: 191). This situation persists around US military bases such as Olongapo and Clark Air Force Base (Moselina, 1981).

In the case of Indochina, France adhered on behalf of her colonies — excluding her protectorates — to the International Convention for the Suppression of the White Slave Traffic of 1910, but did not accede on their behalf to the International Convention for the Suppression of the Traffic in Women and Children of 1921. The general policy pursued by the French government in Indochina was regulation, i.e. control through registration and supervision of brothels and women who were already prostitutes, and safeguarding women and girls from being induced by force or deceit into prostitution. The control of prostitution was entrusted to municipal and provincial authorities. The age of consent for registered prostitution was established at 18 years for Asiatics and 21 years for Europeans. The police registered a prostitute if she was found soliciting in the streets or if a person complained of having been 'contaminated' by her (Commission of Enquiry, 1933: 213-14).

As regards the issue of traffic, a 1929 report of the police prosecutor at the Court of Appeal in Saigon stated the following:

> It may be that the supervision exercised, the severe sentences by the courts and the administrative measures taken against foreign Asiatics sentenced for offences of this nature, have warned delinquent people against the consequences of this shameful commerce; it may be that the mental attitude modified through French influence and through contact with our civilization, so respectful of the rights of women and children, has brought about an almost complete change of the native customs (Commission of Enquiry, 1933: 218).

While traffic in women was considered by the French colonial administration to be a shameful commerce connected with Asiatic traditions and customs, licensed brothels were considered as a more humane and civilized treatment of prostitutes who were assumed to have entered the profession by consent. Few French prostitutes were registered in Indochina. They stayed in the best hotels and sent money to pimps in France. If they complained in court of having been exploited by *souteneurs* (pimps) of French nationality, the men were invariably punished and expelled (Commission of Enquiry, 1933: 215–17). Vietnamese prostitutes on the other hand worked in licensed houses under highly exploitative conditions. Medical officers sometimes sent girls to hospital not because of venereal disease, but because they were in a state of 'very great exhaustion, having been obliged by the keepers of the houses to receive an excessive number of customers' (Commission of Enquiry, 1933: 217).

These examples show that the legal interpretation of promiscuity and age of consent differed along ethnic lines and with the status of being colonizer or colonized. Protective measures against the exploitation of women in prostitution and against the traffic in women differed along the same lines. The refusal to recognize the relationship between the traffic in women and children and the licensed brothel as a secure market for traffickers meant that Asiatic women were less protected by colonial laws. State control of the traffic was directed at *souteneurs* who brought European women to the colonies to practise prostitution, but not at traffic within the colonies. The equating of prostitution with promiscuity by consent meant that only the woman was controlled. The client was left out as a non-party, and the state 'supervised' the practice of prostitution together with other vices such as gambling and opium-smoking. The persecution of women soliciting on the street drove women into brothels where they were controlled by pimps and the colonial state.

The situation remains largely the same today. In 1950, the United Nations passed an International Convention for the Suppression of the Traffic in Persons. Post-colonial signatories to the Convention revised their domestic laws on prostitution to maintain conformity with the Convention, which rests mainly at the conceptual level, i.e. that prostitution is a form of promiscuity which offends public morality, the family and the community. However, there remain many areas of legal ambiguity which permit prostitution to continue to be practised. This issue will be taken up in detail in chapters 4 and 5. Here, it is important to point out that the focus on prostitution as an offence to public morality has meant that prostitution is strictly forbidden in public places. Legal formulations leave non-public places undefined and ambiguous. Legal and social measures focus on the prostitutes mainly. In a transaction which involves a seller and a buyer, only the one who sells and the one who facilitates the transaction are liable to legal charges. The buyer continues to be a non-party (Fox, 1960; Moselina, 1981; D'Cunha, 1987).

The focus on abolishing licensed brothels meant that once these were outlawed, no further public attention was given to the traffic in women and children, nor to newly formed social relations of prostitution disguised behind a wide range of entertainment activities. As pointed out by Barry (1984), the traffic in women and children has been virtually dropped from discussion by international bodies in the post-colonial era, except for a few efforts by individuals and non-governmental organizations. International attention to the traffic in women and children revived only in the beginning of the 1980s in connection with sex tourism and the mail-order bride phenomenon. Prostitution re-entered international discussions in terms of slavery, sexual abuse and exploitation (Fernand-Laurent, 1983).

To recapitulate, the national and international impact of the Social Purity movement was that it brought the prostitute as a peripheral subject into the centre stage of international sexual politics at the turn of the century. The main concern of the social purity movement was to preserve good morals and to fight against prostitution as a social evil. It associated the prostitute with evil itself, reinforcing the existing notion of the prostitute as culprit of her action. This notion continues to disconnect the prostitute from the broader social environment in which she acts. Combating prostitution has focused on the criminalization of prostitution and pimping, the rehabilitation of prostitutes, and the foiling of new forms of prostitution as they emerge and operate under the guise of legally sanctioned business. While the recent attempt to re-establish discussions on the relationship of traffic in women and children to the practice of prostitution is important, it should be kept in mind that the broader environment in which prostitution takes place is not uniform. It is necessary to avoid the reduction of prostitution to any single manifestation. Rather, power relations in prostitution must be disaggregated to enable a more precise understanding of the patterns of subjugation and their relationship to patterns of accumulation.

Power Relations in Prostitution

Power relations in prostitution can be examined through the details of the operation of its subjective (the categorization of the sexual) and objective elements (the control over the services provided, the structure of the law, and the distribution of rewards). Rather than adopt a linear view of sexual morality (i.e. the more progressive a society is the less social evil there is), it seems more useful to question how power relations in prostitution operate as an ongoing process of subjugation on the basis of class, gender, race and age, and how commercial relations extract surplus from sexual labour in prostitution.

The nature of subjective power in sexual relations has been discussed based on Foucault's approach, showing the diffusion of power through discourse and its techniques in the constitution of the sexual subject. The categorization of the sexual subject is disaggregated by Foucault from the broad notions of male and female into more specific categories: the normal, the deviant, the perverse and the offensive. This disaggregation is related to wider social transformation (e.g. kinship relations, relations of production and ideological change). Only through such a disaggregation and through the location of sexual categories in their historical configurations can one arrive at a nuanced understanding of the complexity of sexual relations and the process of subjugation.

However, Foucault's approach to power does not establish the link between the constitution of the subject through discourse and the process of exploitation. Such a process can utilize a socially constructed sexual identity as its ideological basis. To establish this link, the notion of power has to be tied to production, something Foucault has avoided.

In this respect, Harrod (1987) has developed an alternative approach to power in production which is useful in bridging the subjective and objective aspects of power in prostitution. Like Foucault, Harrod begins with an inductive approach to power. However, his conceptualization of power is essentially located at the level of productivity, i.e. the details of the social relations of production and the diversity of social consciousness (1987: 8), in contrast to Foucault's focus on power over the body and the details of sexual relations and sexual consciousness.

For Harrod (1987: 8), the objective of power surrounding production is control over what is produced, the structure of authority within production and the distribution of its rewards. The exercise of such power is facilitated by subjective elements such as religion, culture, ideology, etc. Forms of relations of production contain both objective (institutional) and subjective aspects of power. To understand the operation of power in production, Harrod calls for a multiple social relations approach, i.e. 'an approach that identifies the fundamental sources of differences between groups and classes; in so doing it provides the tools for analysis which can be used either in amplifying such differences, as in a divide-and-rule strategy, or in overcoming such differences, as in a solidarity for change strategy, which are two of the major strategies for power both among dominant groups and between dominant and subordinate groups' (1987: 26). Thus, resistance rests upon the ability to locate and understand power at its site of expression.

Harrod shares with Foucault an ascending approach to power and social relations. Foucault provides the necessary tools for the analysis of the subjective and discursive nature of power, while Harrod provides the tools for the analysis of material power arising from social relations. A material analysis of power in prostitution would provide the current and concrete use of the 'socially constructed sexual identity' and its reinforcement through application and practice. Such an analysis would take into account the structure of subjugation, namely the legal framework governing prostitution, and the framework governing commercial enterprises providing sex-related services.

With few exceptions, national legal frameworks governing prostitution view prostitution as promiscuity and an offence to public morality. Legally prostitution is defined as the act and the encouragement of the act of earning from sexual services, both of which are criminal offences. In some countries the act is not illegal but the encouragement is. However, the legal definition of encouragement is extremely narrow, limited to one individual encouraging another and ignoring direct and indirect encouragement by commercial enterprises such as the entertainment industry, the media and the tourist industry which are subject to state control. The sanction of some segments of the service industry which provide sexual services simultaneously with the criminalization of prostitution means that prostitutes are legally and morally isolated, while entertainment establishments are able to operate profitably on the edge of legal ambiguity.

The artificial isolation of prostitution by the present legal and moral system is a reflection of the power of subjectivity inherent in the categorization of prostitutes as morally deviant, sexually perverse and a source of public disturbance. The power of subjectivity contributes to the concealment of the economic basis in sexuality and prostitution, and of the process of extraction from prostitutes' labour. As pointed out above, far from being a moral issue, commercialized sex forms one of the fundamental aspects of the organization of production and reproduction. The degree of interaction between prostitution and the economy depends on how far this artificial isolation has allowed entrepreneurs engaged in the different activities of the service sector (media, hotels, entertainment and health establishments) to co-ordinate among themselves in order to create a highly organized trade, i.e. to gain control over material power or the means of production and to amplify the differences between prostitutes.

Within this general trend, there are more specific forms of operation of power relations in prostitution which can be distinguished according to the nature of services and their site of operation. As the nature of services produced in prostitution varies to include only sexual services or a combination of sexual and social services, the sites of operation vary considerably. They include a wide range of institutions in the personal service sector. The particular socially constructed sexual identity and its relationship with specific institutions condition particular relations of dominance and control.

For example, the social construct of street prostitutes as morally deviant and criminal means that the power relations surrounding street prostitution are directly related to the police, who enforce laws against indecent behaviour and public disturbance. In the absence of an employment relationship, the struggle of street prostitutes is not related to an employer (except when being controlled by pimps). It is related to the police and to the control of market rates and quality of services (competition with other street prostitutes). To avoid arrest, bribes in cash or services are paid to police officers. Unable to control market rates, street prostitutes are in a disadvantaged position *vis-à-vis* their clients. Not only are they subject to the fickle enforcement of the law, their control over earning capacity is minimized by market uncertainty.

By contrast, women who work in institutions providing sex-related entertainment such as massage parlours, night-clubs and escort agencies have a sexual identity which is defined not as sexually deviant, but as personal service. The nature of this identity is related to the social construct of the institutions in which they work. They are largely protected from the power of police, the law and the court. The legal framework under which these commercial institutions operate does not view prostitutes as criminal offenders, but as wage-workers. Prostitution law affects them only when it can be proven that they have engaged in sexual intercourse for money. As will be shown in the case study and elsewhere it is very difficult to prove legally that a commercial institution hosts prostitution. Often the police co-operate with owners and take bribes from them. Raids only take place when there is a disagreement between the police and brothel keepers (McLeod, 1982; D'Cunha, 1987).

In established institutions sanctioned by law, the forms of social relations may be confinement, or enterprise labour relations. Relations of confinement involve abducted, forced or indentured labour, while enterprise labour relations involve so-called 'free choice' prostitutes. The social origins of entrants into prostitution and their physical assets (age, physical appearance, skills etc.) have a bearing on the forms of dominance and control.

Physical coercion, abduction and debt bondage deprive a woman of her civil and human rights and are employed in order to turn her into an object of slave labour (*Human Rights in Thailand*, 1983). Whatever physical assets she may possess are used to produce pleasure for the clients while she derives no material rewards, except maintenance provided by the brothel owner who collects all the benefits. In cases of socio-economic coercion, women must compete with each other and expose their assets to attract clients. They must also invest in their assets in order to keep their market value (clothing, cosmetics, beautifying efforts, other skills), to ensure a certain degree of mobility within the hierarchy of the sex industry. Such mobility is conditioned by the sustainability of their physical appearance and by fluctuations in the market. Downward mobility from well-paid forms of prostitution to street soliciting on the basis of barter for survival may occur as early as the age of twenty-six (Generoso, 1980). Upward mobility is also possible for women who use their experience in different institutions to acquire knowledge about the market and its contacts in order to operate independently, as in the case of escort services in Bangkok to be discussed in the case study.

The institutionalization of criminality in prostitution weakens the position of prostitutes *vis-à-vis* their employers and clients, and enhances the already existing relation of patronage. The criminalization of prostitution renders prostitutes more vulnerable to control by employers of their physical mobility, their labour and earnings. The effects of the wage system as a redistributive measure, and of bargaining as a political instrument are thereby minimized.

Beyond objective factors such as the sustainability of physical strength, experience and skills, mobility within prostitution also depends on the social construct of sexual subjectivity outside prostitution. For example, the media construction of the 'exotic' on the basis of racial and ethnic elements can enhance the productivity of a prostitute who bears such elements, and therefore can contribute to her earning power. It is therefore important to bear in mind the dialectical relationship between the subjective, discursive nature of power and the material nature of power in prostitution.

Power relations in prostitution must be examined from their specific sites of expression, taking into account their subjective and objective dimensions. It should be noted that the characteristics of social relations in prostitution are not always clear-cut and separable. They often converge and sustain each other. However, I hope that by delineating them, it may be possible to arrive at a more precise understanding of the heterogeneity of the institution and the effects of power relations on sexual labour and capital accumulation from prostitution. Given the nature of subjective and objective power relations in prostitution, the view that prostitution can be placed in a linear continuum of historical progress must be rejected. Instead, it is important to recognize how prostitution is part of a series of subjugation (gender, class, race) whose manifestation must be understood in the specific terms of a particular historical configuration.

Conclusion

In bridging sexuality and the economy, this chapter shows that there is a category of labour derived from the utilization of the body — its sexual elements — as an instrument of labour. This category of sexual labour is historically specific and may encompass class and race dimensions. To understand the dynamics of this category of labour, biological issues must be recognized as part of social processes and the human body must be understood in terms of its historical conception. Using Foucault's concepts of discourse and power, I argue that biology must not be treated as an ahistorical and unchanging variable. Surrounding biology are social interpretations of biological differences. Like other ideological constructs, these subjective interpretations can be traced to very concrete processes of material transformation of society. The effect of such ideological constructs is the concealment of the value of specific types of sexual labour which in turn facilitates the process of accumulation from such labour. Given this background, an adequate analysis of prostitution must begin with an examination of the structure of the social organization of sex as a source of life. Next, the processes which disrupt traditional forms of the organization of sex must be delineated and analysed in relation to the emergence of wage work and the organization of production. Finally, the utilization of sex as labour must be placed under the diverse social relations which organize it at its sites of expression. The process of accumulation may then be assessed against the specific forms of utilization of labour, wage systems and the disposal of labour which is no longer productive.

Notes

1. One example of women's exclusion from socially valued resources is the witch hunt which raged through Europe from the 12th to the 17th centuries. Victims of this hunt were women who possessed knowledge about various sciences, particularly medicine, crafts and other useful skills. The witch hunt coincided with

the rise of male-dominated science and the whole thrust towards the domination of nature. According to Bacon, nature had to be 'hounded in her wanderings', 'bound into service' and made a 'slave'. She was to be 'put in constraint', and the aim of the scientist was to torture nature's secrets from her (quoted in Capra, 1982: 40–1). For information on the witch hunt see: Kieckhefer (1976). For information on the rise of male-dominated paradigms see also Easlea (1981).

2. The mechanistic view of fertility and population originated in 18th-century Europe, and still prevails. The following is an example of the crudest expressions of such a view: 'The government must control its population, and must possess all the means necessary to exterminate them when afraid of them, or to increase their numbers when that seems desirable' (*Histoire de Julliette*, quoted in Adorno and Horkheimer, 1979: 89). More recent examples can be found in the literature on population and development which uses highly dramatic terms such as 'the population bomb', 'the population explosion', etc.

3. The differentiated conception of the male and female body found in nearly all cultures has long been an area of inquiry for feminists who try to explore the origins of the devaluation of the female sex. For example, Leacock (1980) raised the following question, which she considers central to the understanding of women's subordination: 'When does the shift take place from "female" as symbolic of positive "fertility" to "female" as temptation and evil?' Leukert, quoted in Mies (1986: 48) expresses the same concern: 'The beginning of human history is primarily not a problem of fixing a certain date, but rather that of finding a materialist conception of man and history'.

4. This view has been advocated by Reich, in Brake (1982). Reich's work concerns mainly sexual pleasure and potency. The view of sex as a source of life is also advocated by Firestone (1971) who focuses on the reproductive capacity of the female body. These two authors have been criticized for proposing arguments which are biologically reductionist, mainly because they reduce their conceptualization of sexuality to the level of instinct in the case of Reich, or physiological construct in the case of Firestone.

5. Malinowski (1932) has shown that Trobriand Islanders were not conscious of the connection between sexual intercourse and procreation, and the concept of paternity was absent in their culture.

Part II

International Tourism and Prostitution in Southeast Asia

In this part, the structure and dynamics of international sex tourism in Southeast Asia will be analysed with particular emphasis on Thailand. The first chapter of this part, chapter 3, analyses the formation of international tourism, i.e. its genesis and expansion on a global scale, showing how prostitution and sex tourism are part of this expansion. A substantial investigation of the genesis of international tourism is necessary to show the interplay between political, social and economic forces which condition the integration of Thailand and other Southeast Asian countries into the global production of leisure services.

The choice of Thailand as a case study was determined pragmatically on the basis of available data, access to women's groups and researchers, possibilities of field research and familiarity with Buddhism. While much can be revealed from individual paths of integration into the tourism industry by a comparative study, it was decided that an in-depth example would more clearly show the workings of the industry at the international and national levels, and the interplay between discourse, culture and economy which is so crucial to the development of the industry and the exploitation of women workers in it. On this basis, Thailand was chosen as an example of a process which could be observed in other Southeast Asian countries.

In chapter 4, the character of gender relations in Thailand will be analysed showing the main power structures between the sexes: discourse (religion as a field of knowledge); its instrument of power (law); and its application in the male–female social relation. This discussion provides a background for an understanding of the formation of social relations in prostitution today which will be dealt with in chapter 5. Here, contemporary practices of prostitution within the tourist industry are discussed, highlighting the following: (1) policy measures adopted by various Thai administrations in the 1960s, 1970s, and early 1980s; (2) the effects of such measures on investment patterns and business practices; and (3) the place of prostitutes' labour in the entire structure of the tourist industry.

3. The Political Economy of International Tourism

> That was in the days when it was socially necessary to divert wealth from consumption to the uses of capital. That is no longer necessary. With our present rate of productivity, in fact it has become foolish and is no longer good business. Continuing in that course would destroy capitalism; for there can be no adequate saving unless there is adequate spending, and spending on a scale which only the masses, with mass leisure can achieve.
>
> *The Consumer Dollar*, in Goldman 1983–84: 84

> I first hoisted my sails in a world of seafaring crooks, and now I spread my wings in a world of airborne crooks. We're selling a product which is not stockable. It's as if a car dealer were told that all his cars would be worth nothing tomorrow morning. Naturally he would rush to sell them — even for a dollar each.
>
> Umberto Nordio of Alitalia, in Sampson, 1985: 22

This chapter places leisure within the relationship between production and reproduction. Like sexuality, leisure contains an existential domain, a social domain and an economic domain. Just as sexual intimacy and social significance are historically specific indicators of the quality of human life, so too is leisure. Just as sexuality has been analysed in terms of the changing forms of production and reproduction, so too leisure should be. Within the range of leisure activities and the production of leisure services, the main concern of this chapter is the emergence and expansion of international tourism as an industry within the service sector. This emergence reflects profound transformations in the global relations of production and reproduction so far neglected in academic discussions.

Leisure and Production

The relationship between leisure and production has been discussed in the existing body of literature from three main angles: social time, individual consumption (time, products, services), and leisure policy (state provision of resources for leisure activities). So far, the analysis of leisure has tended to be ahistorical and has failed to make sufficient linkages between the historical forms of leisure and production. However, forms of leisure emerge from specific political, economic and ideological contexts, and, as such, they must be understood in relation to labour and production.

Leisure: social necessity, social time, and consumption

Traditionally, leisure was discussed in philosophical debates on human existence. Most philosophical traditions (including Taoism in ancient China and Epicureanism in ancient Europe) have touched upon leisure as a quality of human existence. In the Renaissance period, Montaigne in particular provided a psychological analysis of entertainment as a means of meeting the universal human need for spiritual and emotional well-being, a condition which he considered to be essential to individual cultural and creative effort.

In contemporary social science, discussions on leisure emerged in the context of industrialization and the changing utilization of social time. Leisure is conceptualized as a creation of industrial societies where workers and democratic movements of the 19th and 20th centuries asserted their right to rest and free time. Thus, the issue of leisure is brought into the dimension of social time or the temporary patterns created by social groups and their division of labour. Here, the concept of leisure is used mainly to analyse 'free time', i.e. the block of unoccupied time during which the individual is free from work and can do what he/she wants. Leisure is placed in binary opposition with work to mean non-work, and is essentially regarded as non-productive time.

Although regarded as non-productive time, leisure is nevertheless social and has particular functions in terms of physical and mental health, e.g. rest, entertainment, and personal and cultural development (Dumazedier, 1968). Leisure studies have placed considerable emphasis on leisure activities and behaviour, time budgets and leisure policy. This emphasis is based on a conception of the relationship between leisure and production in normative terms (the home versus the workplace), and a separation of leisure studies from labour studies. The home is associated with non-work, rest, psychological fulfilment, and recuperation of human energy, while the workplace is associated with expenditure of this energy in exchange for income.

The limits of the conceptualization of leisure in terms of 'free time' and non-work in a linear continuum of historical development is revealed by the changing trends in production and organization of social time in contemporary industrial societies. Thus, notwithstanding doubts concerning the applicability of the traditional definition of leisure to non-Western and non-industrialized societies (Parker, 1975), recent social trends in industrialized societies show that the definition of leisure as 'free' and unproductive time cannot be generalized across historical periods.

For example, with the increasing rates of unemployment and forced 'free time' experienced by many societies in the last two decades, it is no longer possible to use the concepts of leisure, 'free time' and non-work interchangeably. Although they all refer to social time outside the institution of work, they are analytically separable. 'Free time' as an outcome of unemployment cannot be considered as being won by workers' struggle but rather as being imposed upon workers by industry. 'Free time' does not necessarily imply engagement in leisure and non-work activities. The growing informal economy in industrialized countries shows the obsolescence of the dualistic model upon which leisure and free time studies have been built. To understand the dynamics of leisure and production in contemporary societies, it is necessary to go beyond this dualistic framework and to place leisure within the domain of reproduction, given its functionality to human existence.

In this respect, studies which touch upon the subject of leisure from the angle of the social division of labour and stratification are more useful, because they provide guidelines for an analysis of leisure in terms of the historical specificities of production and reproduction. Such an analysis would postulate that the appearance of surplus introduces a social division of labour which provokes changing patterns in the use of social time. New patterns of social time either provide more leisure time for one part of society at the expense of the remainder, or more time for all producers to use in extra-economic activities (Mandel, 1977: 39). While the element of social time is maintained here, new questions may be raised: (1) who has access to leisure and 'free time'?; (2) to what extent 'free time' can be considered unproductive; (3) whether 'free time' has a liberating effect, or provides new pastures for industrial investment in the production of goods and services consumed during free or leisure time.

As regards the first two questions, the debate on domestic work and reproduction initiated by the women's movement in the last two decades clearly shows that the separation of work and leisure, private and public domains, conceals a socio-sexual order which is one of the main sources of social stratification between the sexes. The practice of associating women's labour in the home with non-production and 'free time' has implications for women's economic conditions, since women's work in the home is poorly rewarded or unrewarded by society. As economic conditions have a bearing on access to leisure time, sexual differentiation in the use of social time cannot be ignored. 'Free time' as time spent at home, and 'free time' as leisure time spent in consumption of products and services have different meanings for men and women. Firstly, the time spent at home by women is time spent working in reproduction, which is socially necessary and therefore cannot be considered as non-productive 'free time'. Secondly, 'free time' as leisure time spent in the consumption of products and services is determined by income levels and therefore remains a privilege of the established wage worker rather than of the wageless housewife. Such consumption often takes place outside the household.

Thus, leisure must be placed within the relationship between reproduction and production and analysed in historically specific terms, taking into account social differentials on the basis of class, sex, race and age. Within this relationship, a distinction must be made between four levels:

- leisure as a personal activity with existential meaning (personal fulfilment, satisfaction and creativity);

- leisure as social time — time outside the institution of work determined by the organization of production and reproduction;

- leisure services produced by industries;

● leisure policy as part of the provision of welfare and labour control.

Through the interplay between leisure policy and leisure industry social space and time have become political. The penetration of large-scale capitalism into the domain of leisure has transformed the elements of social practices of leisure which preceded it, in time and content. In this process, not only have new sectors of production been created, but also such sectors utilize social space (environment) where the relations of production are actively being reproduced. As Lefèbvre has pointed out, space for leisure activities has been the object of massive speculation controlled and often assisted by the state, rigidly heirarchized along class lines. 'Thus, leisure enters into the division of social labour — not simply because leisure permits labour power to recuperate, but also because there is a leisure industry, a large-scale commercialization of specialized space, a division of labour which is projected "on the ground" and enters into global planning' (Lefèbvre, 1976: 84). In the following sections, the interplay between leisure policy and the leisure industry and the latter's penetration into developing countries through innovations in the field of air transport and information technologies will be discussed.

Leisure policy and leisure industry

The emergence of leisure policy and leisure industry in industrialized countries is an outcome of changing social time and patterns of production and consumption. State involvement in the organization of leisure activities as a form of labour control emerged first in the United States during the Great Depression. This intervention simultaneously aimed to solve unemployment problems by creating new jobs in the state sector (park management, creation and maintenance of public recreation facilities), and to ensure the psychological welfare and 'cultural development' of citizens who were unemployed or underemployed (Zuzanek, 1981).

During the 1950s and 1960s, there was an upsurge in the provision of leisure services in industrialized countries. This upsurge resulted from: (1) higher income and social legislation governing holiday time;   (2) state intervention in the domain of social life outside the work place to ensure social welfare; and   (3) capital's absorption of surplus income that emerged with higher wages. Concern over the welfare and mental health of workers, coupled with higher wages and increased holiday time opened new pastures for industrial investment. Subsequently, the economic value of leisure and 'free time' as unoccupied time was incorporated into the logic of production and consumption (Goldman, 1983–84). Hence new leisure markets emerged such as sports, tourism, and the entertainment industry.

By contrast, the upsurge in the production of leisure services in the 1970s and 1980s in many developing countries may not be considered as an outcome of social progress (higher income, more leisure time, improved conditions of work and welfare). In the post-colonial era, many developing countries were predominantly concerned about employment creation, food production and economic growth. There was no leisure policy as such. The sudden interest in tourism and leisure policies which emerged in the 1970s could not have been directed at the welfare of workers, as the element of domestic tourism was absent. Only in recent years have some developing countries begun to pay some attention to this element (WTO, 1983: 40). In general, tourism and leisure policies in developing countries are investment policies intended to capture some of the flow of the tourism market from industrial countries. However, such policies did not arise from the initiative of developing countries. There has been a high degree of external influence on the formulation and implementation of tourism and leisure policies. As will be shown, this external influence is closely connected with international capital with interests in air transport, hotel accommodation and tour operation.

In East and Southeast Asia, tourism and leisure policies are also closely related to the geo-political situation. Tourism and leisure policies were initially aimed at capturing the 'Rest and Recreation' market of US military personnel during the Indochina conflict, particularly in the case of Thailand, the Philippines and to a lesser extent Hongkong and Japan (Okinawa). After the withdrawal of US troops, policies were reoriented towards the wider international market emerging from the increasing geographical mobility of corporate professionals in the region.

The geographical mobility of corporate professionals and technicians in the region is highly biased towards the male sex. Depending on the category of mobility (corporate professionals and technicians, military servicemen), intervention in the area of leisure services may be based on a bilateral agreement between two governments, as in the case of 'Rest and Recreation' for US military servicemen (Enloe, 1983), or through contractual agreements between corporations and their employees.

As certain corporate activities require mainly male labour utilized within specific patterns of labour time, the model of 'Rest and Recreation' used by the US military is increasingly adopted by corporations, to ensure the maintenance and renewal of the working capacity of their employees. For example, off-shore oil exploration is entirely dominated by men who are functionally single and who live and work in male communities on rigs for fixed periods. These workers are allowed to have intervals of 'Rest and Recreation' outside that community, in urban centres of Southeast Asia where they are psychologically, emotionally and sexually serviced. There is also a high concentration of foreign labour in the oil-producing countries of the Middle East where there are close to 4 million foreign workers (from poorer countries in the Arab World, from South and Southeast Asia, and from Europe and the US) most of whom are engaged in construction and services (Beauge, 1985). Because of the seclusion of women on the basis of religious belief, these countries pursue rather strict policies to seal off social contact between foreign workers and local women. As a result, the highly paid male workers are flown every fortnight to destinations such as Bangkok to be sexually and emotionally serviced (Mies, 1986). In some cases, 'Rest and Recreation' services in the form of sex package tours are also purchased by firms for their employees as work incentives and fringe benefits (Association of Anti-prostitution Activities, 1984).

Given this background, I would argue that the upsurge of tourism and its interconnection with prostitution in Southeast Asia are outcomes of policies skewed towards investment in personal services which contribute to the maintenance of the working capacity of the US military, and of a newly emerged international working class and managerial class. In contrast to the case of industrialized countries where leisure policy contains some elements of welfare and quality of life for their workers, in the Southeast Asian context such policies aim at creating a new industrial base. This industrial base creates new forms of leisure activities and absorbs new categories of wage work in the production of highly valued and exchangeable personal services geared towards the maintenance of the foreign workers' welfare and quality of life. The interplay between leisure industry, leisure policy and the changing organization of social time on a global scale has influenced the organization of reproduction and sexuality.

A quantification of this influence is nearly impossible for many reasons, although it has been tried (van de Velden, 1981). For reasons pertaining to the quality of data, it is not possible to distinguish accurately between travel for leisure and travel for business. Data on international tourist arrivals are usually collected on the basis of the following definition established by the United Nations: 'a tourist is a temporary visitor staying at least 24 hours in the country visited and the purpose of whose journey can be classified under one of the following headings: leisure (recreation, holiday, health, study, religion, sport), business, family, mission, meeting' (Cleverdon, 1979: 135). Such a definition only differentiates an international tourist from a foreign resident and a national of a country. The data homogenize international visitors rather than differentiate them according to the purpose of their visits. In recent years, attempts have been made by Asian governments to make this differentiation. From the differentiated data recently available, it may be observed that about 70 per cent of visitors come to the region for leisure purposes (WTO, 1983: 21). The rest are divided among business, convention and official travel.

Furthermore, it is not possible to use the reason for travel to distinguish the content of the activities of travellers. For example, a visit classified as for the purpose of official mission or business can include or exclude an extension for holiday purposes. Even without this extension, an official visit can include entertainment organized by the host of the mission (Heyzer, 1986: 61). Equally, visits to entertainment places can be 'incidental' to sight-seeing, or included in the pre-paid tour package. Finally, being a foreign resident does not exclude the utilization of local entertainment services. Thus, a correlation cannot be established between form of travel, purpose of travel and the activities undertaken in the visited country.

It seems more useful to look at the process through which developing countries become integrated into the international division of labour through the provision of leisure services, and how sexual labour becomes integral to this process. In the following sections, the background of the emergence of the international tourism industry and of the propagation of tourism as an alternative development strategy for the Third World will be analysed and discussed, showing how the interplay between the discourse on development and the interests of capital has initiated the process of integration.

Air Travel and Tourism: Genesis of an Industrial Complex

Since the beginning of the 1950s, air travel and tourism has experienced spectacular growth, to become one of the largest world trade items after petroleum. In 1955, international airline passenger traffic amounted to less than 20 billion revenue-passenger-miles;[1] 20 years later it passed the 200 billion mark (Dunning and McQueen, 1982). Although travelling is largely concentrated in OECD countries, since the 1960s there are clear indications of an increase in international tourist arrivals in the Third World. According to the World Tourism Organization, the proportion of international tourist arrivals in developing countries rose from 6 million in 1962 to 40.2 million in 1978 or from 7.3 per cent to 15.3 per cent of total arrivals. In spite of the economic recession, figures for the 1980s indicate that the growth of this share is steady (Theuns, 1985). For many countries in the Third World, including Newly Industrialized Countries (NICs), international travel and tourism constitute a significant item of trade. Tourism is the major foreign exchange earner for small-island countries with limited alternatives for diversification (Fiji, Jamaica, Seychelles and Cyprus). Countries endowed with varied resources and where tourism holds first or second place in foreign exchange earnings include Thailand, South Korea, Colombia, Kenya, Lesotho and Tanzania (*South*, April 1985: 57).

The production of tourism as a wage good initially emerged in the 1950s, as a function of the growth of disposable income in the industrialized countries and the attempts of corporations and capital holders to find ways to absorb such income. Subsequently, social and economic aspects of international tourism gained significance and were promoted via international organizations and governments under the guise of educational and internationalist values. From the standpoint of corporate capital in the industrialized countries, the civil aviation industry can be seen as the main motor generating the development of international tourism. It was interest in the profitability of capital investment in the civil aviation industry which spurred the dramatic growth of international tourism and its related sub-branches, and subsequently the provision of local leisure services. The possibility of high returns on an available supply could be realized in two ways: the promotion of international tourism to absorb the disposable income of industrialized countries, and the creation of infrastructure and services at the destination. This process has been facilitated by the involvement of international organizations which incorporate the economic logic of leisure and tourism in the development discourse and its related policy practices.

Two major phases of the development of international tourism (air travel) may be distinguished. The formative phase began during the period of post-war growth, and the consolidation and expansion phase began in the 1970s. The formative phase was marked by the politics of air transport and civil aviation, while the consolidation phase was marked by an increasing trend towards vertical integration among various producers. In what follows, the main forces behind the rise of the international tourism industry and the subsequent formation of conglomerates will be delineated and discussed, paying particular attention to the role of new technology and international financial capital involvement.

During the years immediately following the World War Two, international civil aviation was relatively immature. In the industrialized world, notably Western Europe and the United States, civil aviation was faced with a combination of large capital outlays and an unpredictable level of demand. The aircraft industry suffered from a drastic setback as demand for airplanes for the war effort collapsed. According to Sampson (1985), leaders of the aircraft and airline industry were heavily dependent on government support. There was an over-capacity generated by second-hand military airplanes and all the aircraft manufacturers were painfully feeling their dependence on war. Sampson (1985: 96) notes that the Douglas company, which had produced 29,000 aircraft during World War Two, produced only 127 in 1946.

The responses to this effect by the Western European powers and the United States differ, mainly for reasons pertaining to their histories and economic approaches. Former colonial ties enabled Western European powers to build on existing international air routes with newly independent nations to enhance their political and economic influence through various schemes of aid and support to newly set-up national airlines. As Western European economic policies are governed by the principle of 'participatory enterprise' according to which airlines are owned in part or in full by governments, losses incurred by the operations of economically non-profitable but strategically important routes are covered by government funds. From the Western European standpoint, the extension of the network of air routes posed few fundamental problems. Meanwhile, military aircraft were put to use in chartered services for tourists to the Mediterranean region, starting as early as the beginning of the 1950s.

By contrast, the United States had limited colonial ties, and was still involved in humanitarian and military overseas expeditions, e.g. the Berlin airlift, the Korean War, and (later) the Indochina disaster. Thus, rather than being used in chartered tourism, military planes were initially absorbed by these activities (Jonsson, 1981). On the commercial side, combined with the US doctrine of 'regulated enterprise' (according to which private firms are allowed to operate and compete freely under government regulations which aim at ensuring that such freedom of operation will not disturb the market function), the lack of colonial ties implied that US airlines not only had to compete with Western European airlines for international routes, but also faced competition among themselves.

Apart from the competition for air routes, there has been a fierce competition among both Western European and US aircraft producers to come up with new technology and aircraft. In view of the large capital outlays required by research and development in the aerospace industry, until recently competition among Western European nations has been one of the major factors which has impeded their advance in this area. By contrast, demand from the US defence sector combined with a skilfully designed air policy has enabled the US to attain a hegemonic position in the aerospace industry.

As early as the 1950s, attempts to overcome Western European competition and to establish a hegemonic position in the field of international civil aviation were promoted in the US through large government subsidy programmes,[2] and through the design of an air policy which encouraged and fostered the development of civil aeronautics and air commerce inside and outside the US.[3]

From both the defence and commercial perspectives, the implementation of US international air policy was executed through the channel of aid. The design of this policy involved the three important organs of US international policy-making, namely the US Office of the Assistant Secretary of Defense (International Security Affairs), the Bureau of the Budget, and the Agency for International Development. A former associate of these three policy-making organs clusters the purpose of US aid in civil aviation as follows (Heymann, 1964):

- to further the cause of US civil aviation;

- to promote the export of US aviation equipment;

- to achieve certain short-run political effects;

- to foster social and economic development of aided countries.

Heymann also points out the overriding concerns prevailing in the US as regards civil aviation:

- a pervasive desire to further the cause of international civil aviation and particularly US participation in it;

- an acute awareness of the commercial advantage of having US equipment, aeronautical procedures, and the English language accepted as the world standard; and

- a desire that the leading position of the US industry in the aviation field continues to make a positive contribution to the US balance of payments (Heymann, 1964: 17).

In this connection the venues of financing institutions such as the Export–Import Bank have been used to promote US civil aviation exports. Consequently, the bulk of US aid has been devoted to improving the international aspects of civil aviation — construction and enlargement of international airports, improvement in long-haul navigation, and financing of the development of US long-range aircraft — rather than to the development of internal air transport systems within these areas. US aircraft sales abroad during the period 1955–61 amounted to US$ 1.7 billion and constituted the largest single export item in some of those years (Heymann, 1964: 18–19).

Aircraft sales were accompanied by the concepts guiding their use in economic, political and social development. According to Heymann (1964: 42), aviation has at least three main functions which are worthwhile to consider against the background of the objectives of development assistance:

- its role as a transport mode;

- its uses for economic development; and

- its potential contribution to political cohesion and internal security.

Pointing to the lack of coherence of US foreign aid policy in civil aviation in the past (it tended to be used as a tool in Cold War politics), Heymann advocates a more comprehensive approach to aid in civil aviation. He stresses particularly its significance in economic development and suggests the incorporation of aid to civil aviation in the economic plan of the aided country through multilateral institutions and US aid agencies. The direction of this development is by no means determined in a social, political and economic vacuum. On the contrary, it is conceptualized as being closely related to the goals of free enterprise, for which tactical and strategic flexibility are prescribed.[4]

The advocated tactical and strategic flexibility in the execution of civil aviation policy has been translated into the use of multilateral aid channels to cover US interests, and overt intervention in international aviation and tourism. The promotion of tourism itself mirrored the awareness of the relation between air transport and economic development. This intervention has two main advantages for the US. From a commercial perspective, such intervention contributes to the strengthening of the US position as a manufacturer and exporter of aircraft and navigation equipment. From a political perspective, it helps to consolidate the direction of social and economic development in the Third World, which benefits US interests under a screen of peaceful understanding.

As noted by Lowenfeld (1975), in the field of civil aviation this intervention takes the following forms:

- technical assistance of various kinds;

- domination of the technical committees of the International Civil Aviation Organization (ICAO);

- low interest loans from the Export–Import Bank for the purchase of US-made aircraft and equipment.

The crucial role of the Export–Import Bank in promoting the sale of US aircraft and navigation equipment has been documented by Eyer (1979). According to him, the Bank authorized during 1977 approximately US$ 1.2 billion in long-term credits and financial guarantees; more than 36 per cent was for commercial jet aircraft. During the period from 1968 to 1977, the Bank participated in approximately US$ 6.7 billion or 66 per cent of Boeing's commercial export sales of aircraft and related equipment and services. The Bank's support is not limited to the export of new aircraft. During the period from 1970 to September 1977, it participated in the financing of 130 used aircraft with a total value of over US$ 636 million sold by US carriers. For commercial aircraft exports, the Bank provides two major forms of financing support: direct loans to foreign carriers and guarantees of loans made by commercial lenders. In each case, the Bank's policy is to encourage participation by other banks and commercial lenders in export financing and to make its own participation available as a supplement to financing provided by private sources (Eyer, 1979: 248–9).

Combined with domestic demand and demand from the defence industry, the growth of exports of aircraft and navigation equipment has enabled the US aerospace industry to gain a leading position. Today, the vast majority of aircraft — something like 85 per cent of all airliners — and a comparable proportion of navigation equipment, ground controls and the like are of US manufacture (Lowenfeld, 1975).

Figure 3.1 shows US aerospace exports, imports and the trade balance between 1968 and 1983. As indicated in the figure, despite the fact that a large proportion of exports consists of military exports, civil exports remain more significant.

The new generation of aircraft increased carrying capacity and decreased operating costs, creating a downward pressure on fares as the purchasers of new aircraft sought to fill excess capacity. Between 1956 and 1959, operating costs per ton/km decreased by 35 per cent, and between 1962 and 1970 they came down by 55 per cent at 1968 constant prices (Theuns, 1985). However, operating costs only decline if the load factor is high enough. According to Elzinga (1978: 57), during the 1960s and the beginning of the 1970s, the annual passenger load factor was never above 60 per cent on scheduled international services. So, while the commercialization of a new generation of aircraft, including wide-bodied aircraft such as the jumbo jet, substantially increased carrying capacity both in terms of size and frequency of traffic, traffic did not increase at the rate that had been predicted and assumed within the industry at the time the decision was made to introduce the jumbo jet (Lowenfeld, 1975).

Carriers which were members of the International Air Transport Association (IATA) were forced to revise their pricing and investment policies, taking into account three main factors: (1) the need for return on invested capital; (2) the need to increase the passenger load factor in order to increase this return; and (3) the competition with non-IATA carriers and 'supplementary carriers', i.e. charters marketing the Inclusive Tour, a package of services including air transport and accommodation sold at prices lower than IATA rates for transport only (Wolf, 1967: 130; Peters, 1969: 78).

The response of IATA carriers can be clustered around four major trends: (1) fostering a close link with intermediaries such as travel agents and tour operators for sales and promotion purposes, for example, by offering the

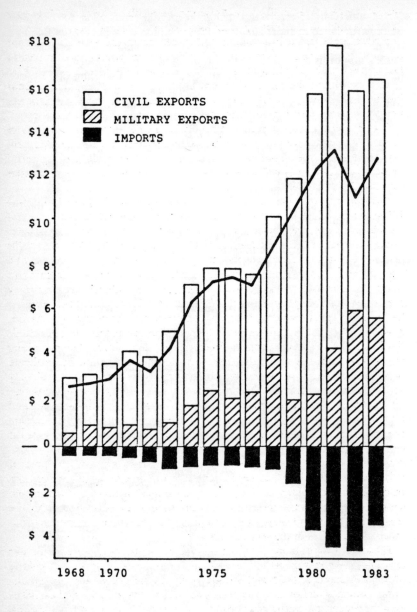

Figure 3.1   US Aerospace Exports, Imports and Trade Balance (billions of current dollars)
(Sampson, 1985: 222).

special low IXT fares at 40 per cent discount on regular rates available to tour operators only; (2) setting up their own charters; (3) moving from a basic two-class fare structure to a complicated schedule of fares designed to cater for different demand elasticities; and (4) moving into the accommodation sector (Lowenfeld, 1975; Haanappel, 1978; Dunning and McQueen, 1982). These responses opened the market for long-haul tourism to the Inclusive Tour business, which had formerly worked only within limited travelling distances using 'supplementary carriers' who chartered the whole plane for the purpose.

Coupled with airline deregulation policies, the development of computer technology enabled the process of integration in all respects. The development and application of computer technology have been backed up by powerful financial institutions as well as government bodies in industrialized countries since the 1950s and 1960s.

According to one source, in the US alone between 1955 and 1961 some US$ 66 billion was channelled to semi-conductor research and development, and an equivalent was given through subcontracts from the Department of Defense prime contractors (Piñeda-Ofreneo, 1985). Throughout the 1960s and 1970s massive US federal funds continued to be supplied for the research and development of information technology, particularly in relation to defence and space programmes. It has been estimated that the military microcircuitry market in the US has grown from US$ 500 million in 1974 to about US$ 6 billion by the early 1980s (Schiller, 1981: 31). Military support of the industry has enabled high-technology firms and individual scientists to seize the opportunities available for private projects financed by federal funds. The prevailing trend is towards the rationalization and transnationalization of hardware production through the inclusion of small firms into divisions of already vertically integrated firms. On the software side, similar developments are taking place within the computer communication industry; rationalization and transnationalization has affected the instructions for organizing, processing and transmitting data, as well as the data themselves and prepared packages of data customized to meet individual specifications (Schiller, 1981: 33).

In the context of the civil aviation industry, innovation in the area of information technology has been decisive in the integration of production. Information technology enabled the establishment of a vast international network of computerized reservations which has allowed integration within the travel and tourist industry, as well as integration between the industry and other sub-branches of the service sector.

The airlines were among the first to capitalize on the advantage of computer technology in reservations and to use spare computer capacity for the booking of other elements of the travel product such as hotel rooms and car rentals. Transnational data flow is a crucial element in civil aviation since flight services entirely depend on traffic reservation information. According to Hamelink (1984: 57), the pioneer in transnational flows has been SITA (Société Internationale des Télécommunications Aéronautiques). Set up in 1949 by eleven airlines as a reservation system using a low-speed teleprinter system, by the 1980s SITA had grown to include over 200 airlines from 118 countries. Its network is built around nine switching computers in the major capitals of the world and includes over 10,000 teleprinter stations, 2,000 reservation terminals and 20 airline reservation systems (Hamelink, 1984: 57). In the 1980s SITA network carried some 100,000 million characters of traffic a year (Schiller, 1981).

In addition to the pooling of transnational data for airline reservations, an integrated reservation system linking air transport with accommodation, sea cruises and car hire also emerged. Pan Am was among the first airline companies to develop an integrated reservation system — the Panamac system — followed by other airlines such as BOAC with the BOADICEA system. Hotel chains also developed their own reservation systems, the first and biggest (launched in 1965) the Holiday Inns' Holidex, using two IBM computers (Hudson, 1972: 60). This was followed by the emergence of an international electronic reservation system for hotel rooms — the Compagnie Internationale de Téléinformatiques (CITEL) — set up in 1969 with the backing of major financial institutions as well as the computer know-how of four airlines — Air France, Alitalia, BOAC and UTA. In 1971, American Express bought some 10 per cent of CITEL's shares with the agreement that the American Express Space Bank and CITEL would jointly provide a reservation service covering half a million rooms and some 5,000 car hire agencies in 50 countries throughout the world (Hudson, 1972: 61). Tour operators also quickly followed the trend, applying computer techniques in their production of tours, assembling travel and accommodation and ground services, and selling the result as a single unit.

As pointed out by Hudson (1972) and Hunziker (1968), the computer has been revolutionizing the basic mechanical process of the travel trade at the same time as vertical integration has been modifying its financial structure. The acquisition of computer technology required substantial investment and only large groups could consider computerizing; this encouraged horizontal links between tour operators and airlines. These electronic links are sometimes complementary to financial links in the industry, but often the scope is much wider, as the computer is also an essential tool for instant booking and thus crucial in providing customers with a total product. This encourages the trend in vertical integration.

From a financial perspective, within the service sector of industrialized countries, the participation of non-tourist companies in tourist activities has also been significant. According to Baretje (1969) and Hudson (1972), apart from the financial participation of the major banks, other branches in the service sector have also made substantial investments in tourism. These include brewing, food processing and distribution, gambling, media, telecommunications, shipping and real estate, as well as public services. The degree of participation varies and can include 100 per cent ownership (as in the case of the International Telephone and Telegraph company which bought the Sheraton Hotel chain in 1968). Other examples of participation include the Midland Bank which bought 78 per cent of Thomas Cook's shareholdings in 1972, and the Rothschild Group which bought a large share of the Club

Méditerranée in 1951. Involvement has also been directly initiated by the banks, as in the case of the Banque de Paris et des Pays-Bas which created the hotel chain SOFITEL in 1963, and, together with half a dozen other financial institutions, created CITEL.

Financial participation of non-tourist branches of the service sector in tourism may also be diversified, i.e. limited participation in sub-branches such as air transport, hotels, tour operation, travel agency and computerized reservation services. For example, American Express activities are traditionally in banking, i.e. travellers' cheques. In the 1960s American Express also bought shares in tour operating, tourism financing companies and computerized reservation systems. A diversified group of banks and service companies may also participate together in creating a hotel chain, as in the case of the Relais Aériens Français, founded in 1950 and by 1966 backed by a consortium of financing sources including the most diverse bodies (Air France, Caisse Centrale de Coopération Économique, Société Équatoriale de l'Énergie Électrique, Société de l'Énergie Électrique du Cameroun, Compagnie Transafricaine, Compagnie des Chargeurs Réunis, Caisse des Dépôts et Consignations, Caisse Centrale de Crédit Hôtelier, Commercial et Industriel). In 1972, the chain merged with Hotel France International, a wholly owned subsidiary of Air France, to become the Méridien chain.

Following the same course, many airlines sought to interlock their capital with other tourist sub-branches in order to diversify products and reduce investment risks. The character of tourist-related services requires investors to develop close financial ties as well as relationships of co-operation. The underlying strategy follows directly from the policy statements of corporate leaders made in the 1970s (see Hudson, 1972: 14–26):

> To be a tour operator without a brotherly arrangement with an airline is dangerous. To be a charter airline without a brotherly deal with a tour operator would appear suicidal. (*Financial Times*, 22 January 1971)
> For some time we have been seeking some means whereby we can participate in the development of holiday travel and bring under our direct control all the ingredients that are necessary to make up a tour package. (*BOAC Annual Report* 1970/71)
> In fact, I would go so far as to say that any airline which does not offer this sort of total package is unlikely to remain in the big league. (BEA General Manager of Supplies and Services, W. R. Collingwood,, *Service World*, January 1971)

Apart from the economic reasons for integration between the air transport, hotels and tour operation branches, there are a number of specialized hoteliers such as the Inter-Continental, Hilton and Holiday Inns, who were among the first to invest abroad in the 1950s, prior to any significant relationship with air carriers. According to Grossman (1981: 13), in the 1950s the founder of the Hilton chain already boasted that 'no new nation has got it going until it has a seat in the United Nations, a national airline and a Hilton Hotel'. This claim is by no means an expression of sheer corporate arrogance and aggressiveness. The expansion of the hotel industry in Third World countries appears to have received support even from aircraft manufacturers, notably the Boeing Company, which commissioned surveys and forecasts on the demand for hotels of international standard (United Nations/ECAFE, 1973). Aircraft manufacturers also owned shares in some hotel chains (Dunning and McQueen, 1981).

To recapitulate, the growth of the international travel and tourist industry has been facilitated by two major technological innovations, namely widebodied aircraft and microelectronics. Both technological innovations were achieved with substantial government funding in research and development, with the US government playing an important initial role. Such innovations and the adoption of mass-production techniques have revolutionized the organization of production within the industry. In addition, capital integration has also facilitated mass production. The interlock of interests in tourism led to the formation of new conglomerates specializing in the production of packages of services including transport, accommodation and various personal services at the destinations. International travel and tourism organized and marketed by tour operators — some of which are transnationals vertically and horizontally integrated with other industrial branches — now constitutes 85 per cent of total world air travel (Guldimann, 1981). Thus, the production of international travel and tourism as a consumer service is now standardized and sectioned into leisure, convention, and business travel for which inclusive group packages are available. There is a wide range of available services, varying in price and quality.

Travel and Tourism Conglomerates and Developing Countries

The international structure of travel and tourism production is marked by two main features: (1) industrialized countries are primarily tourist-generators while Third World countries are receivers; and (2) there exists a high degree of integration among the different operators in industrialized countries in terms of finance, management, research and development as well as marketing and advertising. This implies that by and large the producers and users of these services are primarily from industrialized countries. Users from developing countries are mainly constitutents of the newly emerged class of multinational professionals and managerial personnel associated with the process of internationalization of production.

The general trend in integration in international tourism is that firms from industrialized countries tend to dominate the market through control of knowledge about the market, control of the means of distribution (travel agents, banks, department stores, business travel centres, etc.), and control over the advertising industry which, to a large extent, shapes and determines demand. This entails a division of labour according to which Third World countries, with few exceptions, merely provide the social infrastructure and facilities with little or no control over the process of production and distribution of the tourist-related services at an international level.

Among the four main economic agents in international tourism (airlines, hotels, tour operators and travel agents), the trends in integration in the industry have given the tour operators a significant role as producers and retailers of travel and tourist products. As has been noted, airlines tend to rely heavily on retail trade and cannot therefore afford to bypass tour operators and travel agents. The bulk of retail trade is now package tourism, with one sector of the retail trade concentrating on business travel to the extent that there is now a separate trade association and a movement towards co-operative research. Business travel houses are becoming popular with the major travel consumers mainly because of the efficiency of services offered when compared with do-it-yourself in-house systems (*International Tourism Quarterly*, 1974 (2)).

According to Comisky (1977), an independent tour operator canvasses the consumer demand and assembles a package comprised of airline seats, hotel rooms, restaurant services, motorbus transportation and related ground services. Here, the dual responsibility of the tour operator must be noted. On the one hand, a tour operator is essentially a wholesaler who arranges the ground components of a tour for a particular travel agent, who then promotes the tour under the agency name and arranges airspace. On the other hand, a tour operator also designs and contracts for a tour programme with a sponsoring air carrier which is promoted jointly by the operator and the airline concerned, and marketed by the travel agent and airline ticket offices. In both functions, the tour operator is essentially a 'processing manufacturer' who does not deal directly with the consumers but distributes products via the travel agents or other distribution channels such as banks, department stores, etc. Distribution links depend on the relations of integration of the tour operating business with other sub-branches within tourism, or with other branches of the service sector. Travel agents may also retail air travel alone, either directly on behalf of airlines or through tour operators. The chain of distribution of tourism services is illustrated in Figure 3.2.

The international tour-operating sector is almost entirely dominated by wholesalers in the tourist-generating countries rather than by those in the tourist-receiving countries — even though part of the tour package may be assembled in the former by, or in conjunction with, wholesalers in the latter. This can be explained by certain comparative advantages enjoyed by tour operators in tourist-generating countries, most of which can be traced to their knowledge of the tastes and needs of customers, their economy of scale in serving many markets, and their connection with airlines and hotel chains headquartered in the same countries.

The prevailing trend of integration is predominantly vertical, with many phases of the production process joined under one corporate logic and a single organizational unit — from the sourcing of productive factors to the marketing of the final product. By integrating vertically, a corporation can create the conditions under which it may assert differentiated forms of control over the production process (Caspero, 1987: 196). In vertically integrated international

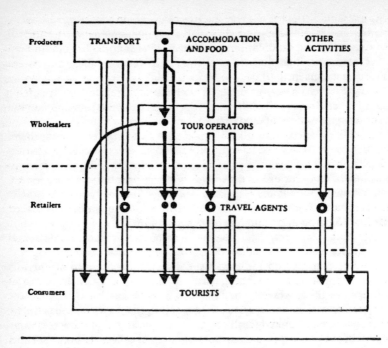

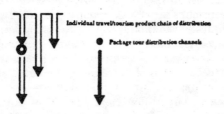

Figure 3.2 Chain of Distribution of Tourism Services
(Cleverdon, 1979: 21)

travel and tourism, tour operators are affiliates of an air carrier, sometimes via partial or total ownership.

Comisky (1977) pointed out a number of important advantages of vertical integration. Affiliation with an air carrier provides the tour operator with the benefit of airline financial resources for the production and marketing of tours. Therefore, the volume and geographical diversity of tours that can be produced and marketed tend to be greater. In addition, the tour operator can benefit from the established advertising programme of the air carrier and thus can get exposure far beyond what an independent tour operator could afford. Other advantages of vertical integration include preferential treatment in a wide variety of practices such as allocating scarce peak-season capacity to affiliates, to the exclusion of independents, and preferential treatment in terms of scheduling, rates and cancellation policies whereby the affiliate can be offered the most desirable flight time or may be relieved from cancellation charges while independents have to pay the full penalty. Where the air carrier is also involved in hotel chains either through ownership (partial or total), or management contract, similar preference can be given for hotel accommodation in terms of space, rates and cancellation.

Vertical integration also allows the air carrier to gain a competitive advantage *vis-à-vis* any competitor operating through independent tour producers. Affiliation with a tour operator will enable the air carrier to capture a market for its excess capacity and to increase traffic over its routes. Once an airline institutes a system that places it at a competitive advantage, the competitors are compelled to diversify as well. Most airlines have now moved firmly into tour operation and hotels (Comisky, 1977).

The trend towards integration in tourism has enabled two fundamental characteristics of international tourism to become structural to the industry. Integration has forged an international travel and tourist market which is dominated by inclusive tours. Independent purchase of the means of transport and accommodation directly through the suppliers or their agents now constitutes only a minor segment of the travel and tourism market. The market is now dominated by inclusive tours (or package tours) purchased by individuals, and inclusive tours purchased by organizations such as large firms (for their employees) or common interest groups (symposia, congresses, conventions, assemblies, etc.) which may include business and non-business groups. The element of leisure may constitute the group's sole purpose, or may be combined with other purposes. The striking feature here is the significance of the inclusive tour. Originally conceived for leisure travel, the inclusive tour concept now is applied in other segments of the travel market. This significance is reflected not only in the diversity of forms the inclusive tour now takes, but also in its share in the total volume of international travel.

From the standpoint of production of travel and tourism-related services, as Dunning and McQueen (1982) have pointed out, the most important aspect is knowledge. Knowledge of the market enables transnational corporations (TNCs) to design a product suited to the requirements of an international clientèle and to differentiate their product from those of their competitors, while catering generally for the upper end of the market. Through this process they also establish the standards of services. In the case of international hotels, this knowledge is embodied in human capital with enforceable property rights being largely limited to the brand name and trademark of the hotel chain. Another aspect of knowledge is the control over the data bank on potential travellers and on the world-wide availability of services. This is also considered 'proprietary knowledge'. Here, computer technology forms the essential facilitating factor which enables firms to apply this knowledge to the design, production and marketing of services. Access to such knowledge is a necessary condition for successful operation since it enables effective co-ordination of supply and demand in large-scale and long-term planning. Due to this control of knowledge and to consumer preference for brand names when purchasing services in an unfamiliar environment, the knowledge TNCs offer to local entrepreneurs is channelled through a system of specialized services charged as management and trade mark fees, etc.

From the standpoint of local investors, affiliation with international chains gives hotels a competitive edge over indigenous firms for the following reasons. Firstly, where a TNC is already involved in the hotel business, it has built up a set of intangible assets and logistical skills, making market entry for small hotels difficult. Secondly, a TNC can have access to supplies of goods and services at lower marginal costs and with better quality and design. Thirdly, it possesses superior methods of production in day-to-day operation as investment in training will enable the firm to maintain the distinctiveness of its brand image and, hence, its market share (Dunning and McQueen, 1982; McQueen, 1983).

With respect to the expansion of TNCs' involvement in the Third World, as Curry (1978) has noted, to some extent this process may be seen both as part of the export of surplus capital from the West and as the result of competition among firms within the industry, attracted by low wages in developing countries. At the end of the 1970s some 81 corporations were active in the world hotel industry and associated with over 1,000 hotels outside their home countries, a total of nearly 300,000 rooms. Some 52 per cent of all rooms were located in 35 developed market economies and the remainder in 93 developing countries (United Nations/ECOSOC, 1980).

Foreign capital participation in the hotel industry usually takes the form of minor equity participation. However, as pointed out by McQueen (1983), prior to the mid-1970s, one quarter of the TNC-associated hotels in developing countries were fully or partially owned and managed by hotel chains, with a further 20 per cent associated under leasing arrangements. From 1975 onwards, the form of involvement shifted strongly towards management contracts. In many cases, management contracts embrace the development, design and construction of a hotel and its day-to-day operation. Thus, although a management contract is a form of non-equity participation, it still gives a TNC *de facto* control over the business. Given the general vulnerability of the tourist industry, the fact that most capital investment in hotels is fixed, and that rooms and services cannot be stored for resale, non-equity participation in about half of all the affiliated hotels, and only 2 per cent of form of involvement has also occurred in the industrialized countries, but the percentages are in no way comparable. In Western Europe, TNCs have equity participation in about half of all the affiliated hotels, and only two per cent of Western European hotels are associated through management contracts. By contrast, the proportion of hotels under management contracts in developing countries is quite remarkable: 75 per cent in the Middle East, 72 per cent in Africa, 60 per cent in Asia and 47 per cent in Latin America (McQueen, 1983: 143).

In general, the control period of the management contract runs for 10 to 15 years. Sometimes the TNC has the right to renew the agreement for a similar period on the same terms and conditions (McQueen, 1983: 149). Management fee structures vary considerably among TNCs and individual hotels. In general, the structure of the fees is based on room sales, gross operating profits and total revenue. In the case of state-owned hotels the major concern is the transfer of technology and knowledge. The usual formula demanded by the TNC is a substantial basic fee, or a combination of basic fees in addition to an incentive fee based on hotel profits. In the case of private ownership the main concern is profitability, and the fee may be wholly based on gross operating profits. How such profits are accounted is another question of negotiation (McQueen, 1983; Dunning and McQueen, 1982). The structure of management fees cannot be generalized as it depends on many considerations pertaining to the nature of the contribution of the TNC and whether the same expertise is available locally.

There is a remarkable difference in rates of fees between industrialized and developing countries. In industrialized countries, management fees vary between 6 to 15 per cent of gross operating profits (GOP), with an average of 12 per cent. In developing countries, management fees vary considerably, averaging 17 per cent of GOP but in some cases reaching 23 per cent. In addition to a management fee, the TNC will extract further charges for advertising and sales promotion services, computerized reservation facilities, non-routine technical and financial services, and routine visits to the hotel for inspection and consultation (Dunning and McQueen, 1981; 1982; McQueen, 1983).

Because international tourism must rely on external economies of scale (air transport, hotel chains and tour operation) and given the dependence of Third World countries on information technology, brand names and marketing services (all of which are controlled by TNCs) those sections of the tourist industry in developing countries serving international visitors will have to be operated by the same standard (Jenkins, 1982). Therefore, it is safe to say that developing countries which have not yet developed their own stock of knowledge must remain largely dependent on TNCs to ensure the inflow of tourists. They thus occupy a weak position in the bargaining process with these corporations. As noted by Turner (1976), even if the host government is trying to gain control over the industry, its employment structure will change only slowly and the international hotel chains may well be retained on service contracts which can give them an even better return than when they actually owned the facilities in question.

Given their weak position, many developing countries have not been able to retain a very large proportion of the foreign exchange earned from tourism. At the same time, many countries rely greatly on material imports and on TNC participation in the hotel and tour operation sectors. Therefore, their expenditure in foreign currency to run the industry is quite considerable. For a small economy (for example that of Fiji) where the tourist sector is dominated by foreign hotels and tour operation, the proportion of purchases in foreign currency can reach between 50 and 93 per cent depending on the sector, e.g. hotels, tourist shops (Britton, 1980: 246). In addition, foreign currency leaves the country through profit repatriation, management fees, etc. The total percentage of outflow of foreign currency can be as high as 70 to 90 per cent of total tourist expenditures in small-island countries (Britton, 1980: 246; Turner, 1976). For a country like Thailand, expenditures in foreign currency by the tourist industry can fluctuate between 23 per cent in 1982, 31.5 per cent in 1983 and 21 per cent in 1986 (Tourism Authority of Thailand, 1986: 59). This appears consistent with UNCTAD's estimate that on average 78 per cent of tourist receipts in developing countries represent net foreign exchange earnings (*South*, April 1985: 56).

To recapitulate, the rise of conglomerates producing air travel and tourism services since the 1960s has forged the tourist industry into a large-scale operation. When expanding into developing countries, the industry has required mass production and the standardization of services and quality. Given their late entry into the field, many developing countries have limited possibilities to develop their own stock of knowledge and control over the business. They have had to adopt the established standards and therefore must rely on foreign firms to run major sectors of the industry (e.g. hotel and tour operation). Many developing countries have not had a chance of the gradual growth needed to establish a base of knowledge, experience and skills. Large-scale production asserted over them by powerful international institutions under the guise of an alternative development strategy, has eclipsed them. In the section which follows, the underlying motives for this will be analysed and discussed.

Tourism and Development: The Politics of a Development Strategy

Origins and development

Interest in the development of the tourist industry in the Third World first became apparent in the United States in 1958 when the Department of Commerce commissioned a study on the prospects for tourism in Asia. This was followed by the late president John F. Kennedy's attempt to bring these interests into the framework of world development, seen as a non-military instrument to contain political tension and insecurity. The idea was officially introduced when the International Travel Act was signed in 1961 on the basis of which the first federal travel office, the United States Travel Service, was established. At its inauguration, Kennedy declared that:

> Travel has become one of the great forces for peace and understanding in our time. As people move throughout the world and learn to know each other, to understand each other's customs and to appreciate the qualities of individuals of each nation, we are building a level of international understanding which can sharply improve the atmosphere for world peace. (Sutton, 1967: 218)

The view that tourism is educational and fosters international understanding initially emerged in Western Europe after the destructive effects of the two World Wars. When applied to Third World development, the promotion of tourism culminated in an international campaign, initiated by the United Nations declaration of 1967 as 'The Year of the Tourist'. Ten years later tourism became incorporated into the doctrine of the New International Economic Order, as a means of redistributing wealth by encouraging the rich to spend in poor countries (Lanfant, 1980). Meanwhile, the attention afforded to tourism by the United States took a new turn and became tied to the general model of development for the Third World as manifested in a stream of writings which tie tourism to development economics.

In 1969, in the Senior Seminar series on Foreign Policy held by the US State Department, the theme of tourism as a resource for development was addressed. Tourism became an issue of US foreign policy and development because of pressure from banking houses which were already providing financial support for the manufacture of wide-bodied aircraft for international travel (Lockheed, Boeing, McDonnell Douglas). The banks and manufacturers also have helped to sell aircraft by financing airline purchases and by setting up subsidiaries to buy aircraft and lease them to airlines (Tragen, 1969: 4). Banks and airlines were preoccupied by 'where to house the passengers when the Boeings 747 start to disgorge some 450 passengers at a time hour after hour, day after day' (Tragen, 1969: 2). To ensure adequate accommodation facilities in developing countries, large capital commitments had also to be ensured, as in many developing countries local capital to be diverted into hotel construction was limited. As international private capital was hesitant to invest in an unpredictable new economic venture, tourism had to be tied to development issues so as to tap the financial resources available for development purposes.

Woven into development issues, the macro benefits of tourism were singled out as its contribution to the balance of payments and its direct and indirect domestic income and employment effects. Cultural demonstration effects were also suggested as follows:

> The increased contact with foreign societies, new ideas and different cultures can facilitate and support modernization and change. The psychological effects of showing off one's country and culture have also been often cited as good medicine for overcoming chronic inferiority complexes which technological lag has inflicted on many LDCs. New hotels and motels provide the front parlours for countries to meet foreign visitors and appropriate environments for doing business as a member of modern society. (Tragen, 1969: 6)

In general, the attention afforded to the tourist industry in the Third World by the US Department of Commerce and State Department operates at two levels: the level of the potential of international tourism to absorb surplus income and capital from the West, and the level of tourism's infrastructural requisite, which could facilitate the integration of Third World countries into the world system of production. These interests have been translated into concerted actions by the private sector as well as by national and international agencies. These actions are geared towards the development of the tourist industry in the Third World, which requires substantial capital investment, particularly in the acquisition of aircraft,[5] hotel construction, infrastructural development and information technology.

The claim that tourism is educational and fosters international understanding conceals the economic and political dimensions of the tourism industry and the powerful influence of corporate and governmental interests in this field. The effects of this concealment is manifested in the fact that in spite of the economically and politically transnational context of tourism, little academic attention has been given to tourism as a domain of international relations.[6] With the exception of the few recent analyses of tourism in the context of international trade (Gray, 1970; Peters, 1969), transnational corporate practices (Dunning and McQueen, 1982), and North–South issues (Philip-English, 1986), the subject remains largely a domain of micro-studies in behavioural science and development economics, while the dynamics of state and capital interests and the process of accumulation are virtually ignored.

The Checchi Report and international decision-making

One of the major early studies in which the significance of tourism was brought to the attention of policy-makers in the Third World and in international development agencies was made by Checchi and Company, a US-based private firm specializing in tourism and regional development. The report entitled *The Future of Tourism in the Far East and Pacific* (Clement, 1961) was commissioned by the United States Department of Commerce and sponsored by the Pacific and Asia Travel Association (PATA), a private trade association. A similar report, *The Future of Tourism in the Eastern Caribbean*, was produced in 1969, contracted by the Agency for International Development and executed by Zinder and Associates, Inc. In view of the context of this study and the pioneering effect of the Checchi Report, the discussion will only deal with the Checchi Report.

According to the Checchi Report, the undertaking of this reconnaissance study on tourism in the region was prompted by 'a desire to assist the countries in the Pacific and Far East region . . . in building up a basis for prosperous tourist business as an element of their economic development' (Clement, 1961: iii). The rationale for exploring the possibilities of tourism development in the region is based on the argument that for many countries this development is a major factor in building international understanding. At the same time, such development provides a significant source of income for those nations that encourage and foster it. Checchi and Company estimated the income effects of an increase of the tourism sector in 17 countries in the region and made recommendations on investment accordingly. The major flaws in terms of the concepts and methodologies used by the report have been discussed and analysed by Gray (1970). The main attempt here is to show the significance of the impact of the report on international decision-making.

Checchi and Company began working on this project in September 1958. Fieldwork began in January 1959 and was completed in May 1960. It included three separate trips requiring almost 400 person-days, covering 17 countries and thus averaging around 23 person-days per country, assuming that field-work was conducted by a one-person team. Although produced within such a short period of research, the report claims to be a blueprint for action. In the context of this study, the interesting feature of this blueprint lies not so much in its economic formula, but in the guidelines it provides on how to claim resources, something which seems to indicate the underlying motive of the report itself.

The report states that 'throughout the Pacific and the Far East there is a widespread ignorance or misunderstanding about what international tourism really is' (Clement, 1961: 88). The examples provided by the report to illustrate this misunderstanding consist mainly of comments by 'persons of some standing and importance' cited as follows: 'why should we spend money to help tourists? We should help our own people first!'; 'if tourists come here they will sweep us into the sea. Our way of life will disappear'; and 'why should we encourage tourists to come here, and eat up the best food and monopolize local services, when our own people don't have enough to eat' (Clement, 1961: 88). The author claims that these charges could be refuted with facts and figures. That the validity of the facts and figures presented in the report was subjected to criticism only after large capital commitments had been made on the part of various international institutions and governments in the region indicates the strength of PATA's sales ability and the US government's overriding interest in the field. As will be shown in what follows, the impact of the Checchi Report was by no means limited to the Pacific and the Far East.

Conscious of the fact that unawareness of the potential of the new tourism market could lead to blocking at the different levels of the administrations of the various governments involved, the Checchi Report called for 'a long-term internal promotional programme ... to foster understanding within each country and to create a consistently favourable atmosphere for tourism in both governments and in communities' (Clement, 1961: 58). It drew attention to the fact that the development of tourism needs top-level government support:

> This report is heavily weighted with statistical and financial data, presented as evidence that as a foreign exchange earner, as a job creator, and as a booster of national income, and as an increaser of tax revenues, international tourism is or can become an important economic tool. This is essentially a 'money argument' ... pointed directly at top government officials who are interested in money arguments ... The purpose in compiling the financial material and other data in this report is to place in the hands of tourism officials and people in the travel business the 'ammunition' needed to obtain top-level governmental support. Once this support is obtained, action on many of the recommendations made elsewhere in this report will follow automatically. (Clement, 1961: 67)

The idea of obtaining government support was related to broader aims made elsewhere in the report, namely the incorporation of international tourism development as an important part of the long-term development plans of various countries, and the inclusion of international tourism as a desirable programme objective for international organizations such as the United Nations, and the US International Cooperative Administration, the former US Agency for International Development. The realization of these aims was first channelled through the US administration and later on through the administrations of international agencies.

The Checchi Report became widely cited — including two submissions as evidence given by the US Congressional Committees — (Gray, 1970: 148), and its specific recommendations have been applied at the various levels of the United Nations system. Among these, the most important are the following:

- tourism requires and deserves the kind of attraction given to trade development;

- most of the financing needed to run long-term tourism programmes should come from government sources, supplemented by a maximum contribution from private sources;

- raising private capital for hotel financing is inextricably involved in creating adequate concessions or incentives such as the abolition or reduction of taxes, duties and various regulatory hindrances;

- since local financing for hotel construction is usually a prerequisite for international financing, the participation of development banks and government lending institutions with their own resources in the financing of sound hotel projects is necessary;

- the establishment of special funds to finance hotel loans;

- where private funds are not available, feasibility or pre-investment studies for new hotels should be financed in part by the UN Technical Assistance Administration, the UN Special Fund or the US International Cooperation Administration. (Clement, 1961: 67–9)

The report also indicated potential lending sources, including the Export–Import Bank, IDA, IFC, recommending that the Export–Import Bank's approach to hotel financing should be used as a model. The report's aim was to mobilize both national and international agencies to deploy policies facilitating the operation of international civil aviation and tourism. The ideas promoted in this report have evolved into a social and economic doctrine propagated by the international decision-making institutions and incorporated in the field of development economics in the 1970s.

The argument supporting the promotion of tourism propounded in the report is, however, double-edged. Obviously, the promotion of tourism as an effort to build world understanding and peace is directed at potential travellers from high-income countries. In so far as governments of high-income countries are concerned, the main issue rests with the impact of expenditures in foreign currency by citizens travelling abroad on the countries' balance of payments. Thus, governments prefer to maintain some control over such expenditures. Such a control may hurt the travel business and therefore lobbyists for the travel business must take this into account. One example is the case of US travel policy under the Johnson Administration during which the concern over US deficits and balance of payments prompted attempts by the Administration to impose stricter regulation over US citizens travelling abroad. However, pressure from the travel industry, which advanced the argument that deficits would be compensated by the export of aircraft and navigation equipment, blocked such attempts (Matthews, 1978; Lowenfeld, 1975).

As regards Third World governments, obviously the concern over balance of payments is hardly connected to expenses incurred in foreign currencies by their citizens travelling abroad. Rather, the overriding issue of lack of foreign exchange is tied to development issues. The foreign-exchange earning potential of tourism thus became heavily emphasized.

With respect to international agencies, the promotion of tourism as an item of export was initiated by the United Nations Conference on International Travel and Tourism (1963). The conference advocated guidelines which conspicuously reflected those advocated by Checchi and Company, particularly as regards the provision of utmost support to the industry as shown in the following recommendations:

> The conference was of the opinion that it was necessary, especially in developing countries, that the government should leave the organization for tourism — whether a governmental or semi-governmental organization or a government agency — complete autonomy in the exercise of its functions (UN, 1963: 24);

> Governments should be recommended to adopt special measures (financial, fiscal, customs, by-laws) in favour of that industry, as described in this publication . . . The recognition of the industry's importance should result in the inclusion of credits in the tourist development plans, and in some cases in awarding priority to those credits in such plans (UN, 1963: 31);

> The conference recommends that governments should, whenever possible, avoid any kind of activity hostile to tourism and based on arguments of a religious, racial or political nature. The conference asked that its opinion on that point be communicated to the United Nations Commission on Human Rights (UN, 1963: 29).

In addition, the conference recommended that the United Nations regional economic commissions, and the regional development banks affiliated with the United Nations system should take tourism into account. These recommendations have been translated into numerous hotel and infrastructural projects, financed by a wide range of sources both multilateral and bilateral.

To recapitulate, the motor behind the formulation of tourism policy as an alternative development strategy may be located in the interests of large financial institutions involved in aircraft production as well as the travel and tourism conglomerates which sought new pastures for the expansion of their business and the diversification of their products. In this expansion and diversification, a spatial division of labour is crucial. To facilitate their activities in different sovereign territories, considerable influence was placed on governments and international agencies to propagate an alternative development strategy which would qualify tourism for access to development funds.

Financing the development of tourist infrastructure

Among the international institutions involved in tourist-related projects, the World Bank stands out as most significant. The World Bank's interest in the tourist sector was first expressed in 1968 based on the argument that world demand for international travel is growing faster than that for merchandise exports (David Davis, 1968). This interest became institutionalized with the establishment of a special department in 1970, the Tourism Projects Department, in charge of the financing of self-contained tourism projects which are sometimes referred to as tourist plants. Besides such projects, the Bank also funded the construction and renovation of airports; such projects often fall into the category of overall infrastructural development, sometimes referred to as specifically tourist-related.

During the 1970s the Bank lent direct support to 24 such tourist projects in 18 developing countries, with loans and International Development Association (IDA) credits totalling about US$ 450 million. Total investment in these projects was approximately US$ 1.5 billion (David Davis and Simmons, 1982). Some additional US$ 250 million in loans and credits for airport projects costing a total of nearly US$ 1,000 million were also provided (Schwartz, 1981). However, mounting criticism of the social, cultural and economic impacts of tourism on Third World societies (de Kadt, 1979; Noronha, 1979) coupled with implementation problems regarding a number of large-scale tourist development projects led the Bank to scale down its activities in this area. The Bank has now phased out the tourism department and returned to its original method of financing, which is to channel loans to development banks in its member countries, a number of which utilize the Bank's funds partly to help finance hotel and other tourism projects (David Davis and Simmons, 1982). Direct allocation to the tourist sector was thus only made to projects which were in an advanced stage of preparation as of 1979 and were completed by 1983.

Apart from the World Bank as a major financing source, bilateral technical and financial co-operation in the construction of hotels and resorts also occurs (United Nations/ESCAP, 1980). The patterns of involvement of other multilateral and bilateral organizations in the promotion of tourism which led to the centralization of tourist policies were traced by Lanfant (1980). She identifies the following indices of the emergence of tourism planning from a sectoral to a global phenomenon:

- centralization of information, research and consultancy services that are subsidized or contracted;

- preparation of master plans for tourism within the framework of co-operation and development aid schemes;

- recommendations and guidelines sent to the government of receiving countries and regions concerning investment codes, tax guarantees, establishment of balance of payments, and setting up an administrative corps;

- training of personnel, particularly high level personnel for the tourist industry in internationally reputed schools sponsored by international organizations;

- active involvement of consultancy services and international experts in the most varied contexts.

International tourism thus became part of an overall economic and political plan with a specific underlying doctrine consolidated by the transformation of the formerly private trade association, the IUTO (International Union of Travel Association) to a semi-governmental organization, the World Tourism Organization (WTO) whose members include governments as well as private enterprises. WTO has a unique relationship with the United Nations and its specialized agencies and acts as a centre of documentation, information and consultation on activities related to tourism and development for governments as well as intergovernmental agencies.

Given the factors conditioning the growth of the tourist industry on an international scale, the development of international tourism as a leisure activity and package tours as a leisure product should be seen as a synthesis of capital, state and international interests, and not simply as the outcome of the functioning of market forces. Without a substantial degree of involvement by state and international agencies as facilitators for the deployment of private capital interests, international travel and tourism would not have reached today's magnitude.

Serving the Tourist Market: Female Labour in International Tourism

Traditionally, the term 'labour process' refers to the ways in which a work force is created and utilized. This process involves two main aspects, namely the technical and the social. As shown in the previous section, the main process of production in international travel and tourism involves aircraft and information technologies, both of which are controlled by TNCs. The social aspect of the labour process involves the ways in which specific types of labour are mobilized for the production of tourism and tourism-related services.

To understand how specific types of labour are mobilized to serve the tourist industry, the characteristics of the tourist product itself must be taken into account. There are three central characteristics of tourism which affect the organization of production and the mobilization of labour: (1) tourism as 'an experience commodity';   (2) the symbiotic relationship between tourism and advertising; and   (3) the unpredictable nature of tourism demand.

The first characteristic of tourism is the combination of services (transport, accommodation, local services) whose quality is experienced essentially at the tourist destinations rather than at the place of purchase, i.e. travel agency bureaux. The salient feature of this 'experience commodity' is the replication in a commercial context of household-based services (hospitality, personal services, accommodation, personal and psychological fulfilment). This feature entails an inherent contradiction in tourism services between the personal and the commercial. The quality of household-based services provided without charge through personal relations is generally of a durable nature and usually linked with the quality of such relations. By contrast, services in tourism are offered under commercial relations in a non-durable context and through a variety of sites. The quality of such services is assessed by the consumer according to how 'personal' these relations are.

Thus, beyond standardized requirements such as the safety of means of travel and the comfort of accommodation, the expectation of quality tends to be focused on the personal attention given to the tourist in a wide range of services. Not only must the tourist be attracted by the standard of services offered, he/she must also be entertained and pampered. As noted by several researchers, in some cases, concern over the quality of the tourist experience extends even to the manner in which local citizens treat tourists. This concern can be translated into a public campaign, such as the 'smile' campaign in Jamaica (Turner, 1976; Matthews, 1978), and 'help the tourist' and 'hospitality campaign' initiatives in several other countries. The 'hospitality campaign' is itself a recommendation of the 1963 United Nations Conference on International Travel and Tourism, and since then it has been incorporated into many policy documents. Local cultures are transformed to suit the needs of tourists. In the process, a new homogenized tourist culture has emerged and become highly commercialized. This transformation has been the subject of numerous anthropological studies which have concluded that tourism is a new form of cultural domination (Smith, 1977; Wood, 1980; 1984). The potential of tourism as cultural exchange and communication remains by and large minimal (Mowlana, 1986).

The second characteristic of tourism is its symbiotic relationship with advertising. As has been pointed out, the tourist market is essentially a 'symbiotic market', which unites under a single concept (conveyed through the medium of advertising) factors that by nature are not directly related to tourism, but become tourist attractions once they are processed into goods (Krippendorf, 1971). As such, without advertising, the tourist product means little else than household-related services (food, accommodation, rest) provided to the traveller away from home, or landscape and cultural traits, products of nature and human history. With advertising, all these aspects become incorporated into 'the tourist market basket of goods and services'. In this connection, the significance of the ideological constructs of the advertising industry cannot be separated from tourism itself.

Like some other markets of consumer goods, the tourist market is one in which not only supply determines demand, but also one in which the ideological constructs mediated through advertising play a significant role in shaping the demand itself. Notwithstanding the growing importance of the advertising industry as an integral part of corporate capital, (Ewan, 1976; Peet, 1982, Anderson, n.d.), analyses of advertising in tourism pointed out that this area must be considered significant by virtue of the symbiotic relationship between the tourist products and the images advertised (Uzzell, 1984; Thurot and Thurot, 1983).

Advertising in the tourist industry is a form of discourse. As Uzzell has shown (1984) holiday companies attempt to attract holiday makers not through the overt and superficial attributes of holiday destinations portrayed in the brochure photographs, but by utilizing the discourse of advertising to provide the reader with a range of cultural tools with which fantasy, meaning and identity can be created and constructed. In this connection, the ways in which promotional campaigns focus on aspects of hospitality, such as female submissiveness, caring and nurturing as well as sexual temptation, may be considered as part of this discourse sustained by governments and enterprises.

As has been noted by a number of authors, the development of tourism is closely connected with the rise of a playground culture in which sand, sun, sea, sex and servility are the main elements (Smith, 1977; Matthews, 1978; Turner and Ash, 1975). Images associated with brand names of tour operators and destinations have been developed and quickly propagated through various media. For example, Uzzell (1984: 85) notes the advertisements of Club Méditerranée which suggest that a holiday 'may be a chance for you to discover yourself . . . and meet someone special and when the mixing and mingling is done . . . get away somewhere quiet and discover each other'. An image has developed of the Club Méditerranée that it is the place to go for uninhibited sex, lots of food, drink and group recreation, all with little or no contact with the local population except for brief sexual encounters with the native club staff (Matthews, 1978). As *Playboy* describes it: 'for sex, it is Club Méditerranée, hands down. As for Club Méditerranée, most of what you've heard about is probably true, the good along with the bad. There are three club villages in the Caribbean . . . And yes, two of them are sex factories' (Matthews, 1978: 83). Other examples of such advertisements is the case of sex tour operators who offer trips to Thailand and other destinations with detailed descriptions of the kinds of sexual services available and their costs (Barry, 1984).

Concurrent with this development is the emergence of semi-pornographic motion pictures or pornographic video films, stressing the sexual and exotic characteristics of these cultures, showing how foreign visitors to these countries can enjoy uninhibited sex (Stol, 1979).[7] Thus, to understand why personalized services, including sexual services are often included in tourist-related services with varying degrees of explicitness, it is essential to bear in mind the power of ideas surrounding the industry itself. This realm cannot be easily separated from material forces which condition different practices of prostitution related to tourism. Particularly in the context of tourism services, the intangible nature of their constitution implies that the effect of advertising is necessarily diffuse while its instrumentality remains central.

The present international information order is such that the Third World has virtually no control over the information produced about its societies, or in Foucault's terms, no control over 'the tactical productivity' of knowledge and power and their 'strategic integration'. As Foucault has pointed out, the power of information is not just a question of ideology. 'It is the production of effective instruments for the formation and accumulation of knowledge . . . power, when it is exercised through these subtle mechanisms, cannot but evolve, organize and put into circulation a knowledge, or rather apparatuses of knowledge, which are not ideological constructs' (Foucault, 1986: 237), as they are integrated into practice. Many countries which promote sex tourism have allowed segments of their societies to be incorporated into the power–knowledge apparatus of advertising to produce information (with examples of practices) about the trade in sexual services involving the women of these countries.

A third significant aspect of tourism is the unpredictable nature of the demand side. Unpredictability is derived from aspects which are external to the industry such as political and economic instability (e.g. effects of recession on discretionary spending; social and political upheavals at destination areas; the effect of changes in fashion and taste on tourist arrivals). Therefore, on an international scale, business has tended to favour the creation of big groups with sufficient resources to invest in a variety of activities, hedging against a setback in any one branch or geographical area. As a result, there is a constant movement within the industry as regards to 'pooling arrangements' between and diversification among the different producers in terms of finance, production and marketing.

By contrast, in the peripheral tourist-receiving countries and particularly in low-income and small-island countries, tourist resorts and hotels tend not to be well-integrated into the local economy. With the exception of those cases where the industry is fairly well developed (India, Singapore, Hong Kong, Mexico), the degree of intersectoral backward and forward linkages remains limited. By and large the tourist industry remains an enclave-like and footloose sector in less developed countries. Thus, on a local scale, enterprises engaged in the entertainment business, ground tours or other local services generally are not linked financially with other sub-branches of the service sector, as are those originating from industrialized countries. Capital investments of local enterprises are less liquid with few possibilities for diversification. Due to the need for return on capital investment, the perishable nature of services (i.e. rooms and local transportation services which cannot be stored for resale), and the standardization of production, there is a tendency among firms to incorporate more and more services of a 'personal' nature into the travel and tourist product to increase its appeal.

In the production of tourism services, two new categories of wage labour are created. There is a labour category formally employed in the maintenance of the tourist infrastructure (air transport, accommodation, tour operation) and in the provision of services (banking and exchange, etc.), and there is a category of 'casual' labour engaged in providing personal services through the venues of the entertainment industry, which has a dynamic function in attracting tourists. The demarcation between formal and casual occupations only exists in legal terms. In practice, such occupations form a part of a unified economic operation.

The established worker shares a direct relationship with the tourist industry which is determined by wages and other regulations whereas the casual worker shares an indirect relationship through which income is determined by shares of profits, commissions, or other forms of unregulated payment. Female workers may be engaged simultaneously in formal and casual occupations. Under the guise of formal occupations such as hostess, waitress, bartender, masseuse, go-go dancer, etc., female workers may also be engaged in prostitution on their own account. The 'personal' nature of their services means that their work is seen as non-productive. Therefore it can be paid irregularly and is easier to control. The relationship between formal and 'casual' work will be discussed in detail in chapter 5.

The character of the organizational link between prostitution, sex-related entertainment and tourism depends on the forms of prostitution involved. Sex package tours represent an extreme form of the merging of tourism and prostitution. They involve three main industrial branches, namely the airlines, hotels and entertainment establishments, and require a high degree of co-ordination between the branches. Besides sex package tours, there are other forms of prostitution catering to foreign visitors with a different type of linkage to accommodation, entertainment and services (bars, night-clubs, massage parlours). In these cases, services are purchased locally and are not incorporated in the package tours. Sex tourism is then carried out by individual purchase of the means of transport and accommodation, or individual purchase of a package tour. Prostitutes' services are then purchased locally through the agency of various enterprises, for example those providing the services of a 'hired-wife' who comes with a furnished flat for visitors staying for long periods, or, in the case of some hotels, providing information on prostitutes' services available in local entertainment and personal service establishments (Korean Church Women United, 1984; Senftleben, 1986). Some hotels also provide a selection of sexual services upon guests' arrival as part of their internal commercial practice. In this context, there is no concrete link between tourism and prostitution, except by way of supplying information on prices, locations, and the forms of sexual services available at the destination.

The combined existence of established and casual workers in the sex-related entertainment industry is an outcome of the contradiction between the moral and economic aspects of the industry. Moral concerns impose limits on the degree of public tolerance of forms of entertainment, while economic concerns force governments either to turn a blind eye, or to stimulate the organization of prostitution directly or indirectly. Owing to the composition of vested interests (national, international, and private capital), the mobilization of female labour in the entertainment industry can become integral to government policies as well as to business practices.

For example, in Japan during the period of post-war reconstruction, the government officially praised the *geishas* who served US servicemen as patriotic, for bringing in the foreign exchange needed to rebuild the country. The same happened in South Korea in the 1970s when the *Kisaeng* servicing Japanese businessmen were instructed to 'make sacrifices to get foreign money, and [to see that] this self-sacrifice is a matter of pride for them and for the nation' (Lenz, 1978; *Asian Women's Liberation*, 1980; Korean Church Women United, 1984). Expressed differently, the same logic is found in Thailand and the Philippines, where government officials (under the Marcos regime) publicly made explicit that female sexuality was to be regarded as an economic asset in their tourist ventures for national development.

It is important to point out here that newly emerged ideological mechanisms have enabled the moral justification of the mobilization of female labour for the entertainment industry on a wide scale. To be applicable, these mechanisms combine traits of the female role which are familiar to the traditional society while at the same time reflecting the vision established for the society under transformation. Thus, the ideology of hospitality, servitude and self-sacrifice inherent in the traditional female role is used in combination with the ideology of nationalism and development. The ambiguous nature of ideological mechanisms enables the mobilization of female labour on a large scale while ensuring effective labour control. The glorification of self-sacrifice for the household and nation justifies the act of prostitution, while the criminalization of prostitutes makes labour organization in this area impossible.

Against this background, services which fall into the category of 'personal' and 'informal' but which are nevertheless crucial to the maintenance and development of the travel and tourism industry are to be considered as belonging to an ongoing process of accumulation which takes place mainly from sexual labour. Unprotected by legislation, yet highly integrated in business practices, commoditized sexual services benefit governments and firms from a variety of angles.

For corporations employing a highly mobile male work force, the availability of sexual and household-related services helps reduce the costs of maintenance of needed labour power traditionally provided through family relations. For enterprises such as bars, clubs, and other entertainment establishments, disguised prostitution stimulates clients' expenditure and ensures high profits from sales as well as low or irregular wages. For the international tourism conglomerates, the availability of sexual services as an exotic commodity functions as a source of tourist attraction and helps to fill airplane seats and hotel rooms. National accounts benefit from taxes on accommodation, food, drinks and services. Unlike their flesh, the contribution of prostitutes' labour to this process of accumulation remains invisible.

To recapitulate, it may be observed that the nature of tourism services and their production is such that there is an unequal technical as well as social division of labour. Technology and production remain by and large in the hands of large corporations that transport tourists and manage their accommodation. Tourism TNCs enjoy numerous sorts of preferential treatment as compared to local firms that mainly enter the tourism sector through the small-scale production of personal services. From a social point of view, there is a division of labour between the established workers in large firms and the unprotected workers affiliated with the industry through a proliferation of social relationships. They nevertheless all work within a unified economic operation. The services provided are of a non-durable nature yet highly valuable in a context where similar services (generally provided within the household) are absent.

Conclusion

This chapter has shown that the intersection of prostitution and tourism cannot be understood as a patchwork of discontinuous events resulting from individual behaviour, or simply as a synchronic expression of sexism or racism. Instead, it must be placed in the context of the operation of relations of power and production in the field of air travel which preceded its development. The emergence of tourism and sex-related entertainment is an articulation of a series of unequal social relations, including North–South relations, and relations between capital and labour, male and female, production and reproduction. This articulation has been induced by capital and state interests and therefore cannot be considered as an outcome of a policy mistake, or an effect of uncontrollable poverty. Rather, it is evoked by an interplay between external and internal economic and political forces. To bring this articulation to the fore, a detailed examination of the internal power structure governing the male–female relationship and its interaction with broader processes of social change is required.

Notes

1. One revenue passenger transported one mile. The sum of such RPMs is the customary measure for total airline passenger traffic.
2. In 1950, the US Senate authorized the appropriation of US$12,500,000 for the Secretary of Commerce to promote the development of improved transport aircraft. Such assistance was deemed necessary to meet the European challenge to US leadership in international air transport (*Congress and the Nation*, Vol. I, 1945–64, Government Printing Office, Washington, DC: 539).
3. These attempts were translated into the United States Federation Act of 1958 (Public Law 85–726, 85th Congress, S. 3880, August 23 1958, Section 305).
4. In Heymann's words 'a point that is not fully understood is that aid objectives are essentially identical with and a reflection of the aims and the objectives of US

foreign policy as a whole . . . the prime objective of both has been stated somewhat grandly and immodestly as the creation of a stable community within a viable world order. The assumption that underlies this objective is that in the long run, the development of such a world community offers the best prospects for security and peace for the United States. Clearly, there must be tactical and strategic flexibility in the execution of policy, and no single grand concept or guiding principle can encompass the diverse demands and opportunities of our international relations' (Heymann, 1964: 38). Heymann further stresses that a close relationship exists between aid policy and foreign policy as a whole, and that aid is only one of a number of foreign policy instruments, which include diplomacy, military power, trade and commercial policies, information, cultural and scientific programmes. In his view, all these instruments aim at furthering the interests of the United States and, to some degree, those of its principal allies whose long-run interests and cultural traditions more or less coincide with those of the United States.

5. US\$ 50 million for a jumbo jet including spare parts and backup services compared to US\$ 10 million for a middle-range aircraft (*The Investor*, November 1977). In the 1980s such costs are likely to be much higher.

6. This is even more surprising considering the fact that in the case of major treaties of co-operation such as the Treaty of Helsinki signed in 1975 between the governments of Western Europe and the Soviet Union, the issue of tourism was dealt with in several sections. Yet the subject remains largely neglected by the field of political science (Richter, 1983; Kosters, 1984).

7. A relation exists between sexual inhibition, sexual violence and the definition of the 'Other'. This issue will be taken up in detail in chapter 5. For present purposes it suffices to note that discourse on the 'Other', power and practices over the subjugated are inseparable. For example, the pornographic film 'Snuff' was advertised by its producers as featuring the actual murder of a prostitute from South America 'where life is cheap'. The idea that the murder was not staged was meant to be a sexual turn-on (Bell, 1987: 157).

4. Gender Relations and Prostitution in Thailand

> There were poor girls whom fortune failed in need:
> They sold their charms and threw their youth away.
> Old age caught them alone and desolate —
> Unmarried, childless, where could they seek help?
> Alive, they drained the cup of bitter dregs;
> And dead, they eat rice mush in bayan leaves.
> How sorrowful is women's destiny.
> Who can explain why they are born to grief?
> *Nguyen Du, in Huynh, 1979: 28*

This chapter locates prostitution in Thailand within the broader structure of gender relations and its discursive practices rooted in religion and law. Through an examination of the relationship between the discourse on sexuality in Buddhism and gender relations, it shows how Buddhist thought and principles have served to reinforce class and gender inequality as it emerged from social forces at various historical junctures. The trade in women in Thailand arose from social conditions which were external to Buddhism as a body of thought, but has been consolidated by the biases inherent in Buddhism. The institutionalization of Buddhism and the utilization of its discursive elements as the basis for the formulation of law have enabled the transformation of the trade in women into the most overt forms of exploitation, expressed clearly today in the sex industry affiliated with the tourist industry.

Buddhist Discourse on Sexuality and the Male–Female Relationship

Throughout the history of Thailand, *Therevada* Buddhism has played a central role in shaping the law, cultural framework and social life of its people. However, the influence of Buddhism in Thailand has not been uniform. It has depended on the nature of the relationship between Buddhism as a religion, the Buddhist *Sangha* as a religious organization, and the state (Tambiah, 1976). The extent to which Buddhism ideology influenced polity, and how the Buddhist *Sangha* functioned as a political instrument of the state depends on the specific socio-economic and political situations at any given time (Keyes, 1977b; Suksamran, 1982). Given the profound influence of Buddhism on the cognitive and institutional structure of Thai society, an understanding of social relations and practices in Thailand today cannot omit the role of Buddhism as a religious institution. As a social and political institution, the Buddhist religion was a foundation of feudal law, and it still provides the people with a world-view, shapes their consciousness, and acts as a subjective form of power which provides legitimacy to social relations.

Unlike the position of women in Christianity, which has been explored by many writers to show the relationship between the power of ideas and practices (Gage, 1893; Harris, 1984; Haug, 1984) with few exceptions the question of gender has been rarely raised by scholars on Buddhism (Horner, 1930; Reynolds, C. J., 1977; Paul, 1979; Kabilsingh, 1984; Boonsue, 1986). One reason may be that Buddhism has been studied mainly from the standpoint of ethics and metaphysics rather than as a religious institution. Therefore, the focus has been placed on emancipatory principles in a metaphysical sense rather than in a social sense. However, it must be acknowledged that Buddhism is not just a metaphysical tradition but also a religious institution. Thus, a complete understanding of Buddhism must also treat it within the framework of ideological discourse and social power relations. As regards the male–female question, of particular importance are how specific constitutions of religious and social views about sexuality emerged, how elements of basic Buddhist doctrines are included and excluded from such views, how they are applied, and the consequences of their application.

As in other institutionalized religions, knowledge of essential metaphysical principles is restricted to one class, the ordained theologians or monks who belong to the Buddhist Order (*Sangha*), who have the responsibility to learn and disseminate them. Dissemination of Buddhist thought to lay people is done through tales and parables which reflect Buddhist cosmology and ethics while incorporating local folk tales. As a result, there is a profound transformation of Buddhist basic universal law and principles for emancipation (*Dhamma*). Complex formulation of Buddhist universal law such as the Four Noble Truths or the Eight-fold Path remains alien and esoteric to the majority of Buddhism's followers.

It is impossible to argue adequately whether or not misogyny is inherent in Lord Buddha's thoughts for reasons of historical data and diversity of interpretation. Buddhism emerged some 2,500 years ago in India and began to spread through the Asian continent some 300 years after Lord Buddha's death through a missionary movement initiated by King Asoka of India, who was the patron of the Third Buddhist Council. Lord Buddha himself left behind no written teachings. All components of the Buddhist canon were written some four hundred years after his death by his followers, in Pali (which is now a dead language). There are three major components of the Buddhist canon, namely the *Sutta* which contains the original dialogues between Lord Buddha and his disciples, the *Vinaya* which is the code of monastic discipline, and the *Abhidhamma* which contains the more sophisticated construction of Buddhist universal law. Interpretations of the canon differ according to the historical experience of countries and regions. For popular consciousness, the basic doctrines of Buddhism are disseminated through the *Jataka Tales*, stories about the life and birth of Lord Buddha mingled with local folk tales.

Despite the diverse interpretations of Buddhist thought, there are two major doctrines which remain consistent: the doctrine of *karma* (the embodiment of physical, verbal and cognitive actions of past lives) and *atman* (the law of the transmigration of the eternal soul). To understand *karma* and the transmigration of the soul, it is necessary to understand the Buddhist perception of the natural or phenomenal world, the spiritual world and the causal connection between *karma* and *atman*.

Buddhist cosmology and universal law are most clearly depicted in the *Sutta* (dialogues between Lord Buddha and his disciples). This cosmology rests upon the law of transmigration of the human soul (*atman*) and the distinction between the phenomenal world and the world of spiritual enlightenment. In a sermon addressed to his disciples, Lord Buddha described the phenomenal world as follows:

> The body is not the eternal soul, for it is subject to destruction. Neither feeling, nor ideation, nor disposition, nor consciousness, together or apart constitute the eternal soul, for were it so, feelings, etc., would not likewise be subject to destruction. . . . Our physical form, feeling, ideation, disposition, and consciousness are all transitory, and are therefore suffering, and not permanent and good. That which is transitory, suffering, and liable to change is not the eternal soul. So it must be said of all physical forms whatever past, present, or to be, subjective or objective, far or near, high or low: this is not mine, this I am not, this is not my eternal 'soul'. (Nakamura, 1976: 9)

The phenomenal world is a world of suffering, impermanence and transitoriness, while the world of spiritual enlightenment is the world of ultimate religious reality which depicts total detachment and the non-self. Eternity is equated with the non-self. As part of the phenomenal world, the human body and its psycho-structure are subject to the laws of impermanence and decay. The human body is only a medium for the transmigration of the eternal soul. Attachment to the cravings and desire of the body and the phenomenal world, both of which are transitory, is a source of human suffering and ignorance, and therefore the antithesis of metaphysical emancipation.

The law of transmigration of the eternal soul is built upon the notion of a chain of causation postulated in the doctrine of *karma*. The doctrine of *karma* maintains that each human act carries its own merit or demerit. Reincarnation into the phenomenal world is determined by one's *karma* and the merits and demerits accrued by one's acts in the previous life. A soul with imperfect *karma* can be reborn in the phenomenal world to learn and to purify *karma*. Virtuous practices can elevate *karma* to a higher state, and reincarnation continues until *karma* is totally purified and reaches the state of permanent enlightenment (*nirvana*). In the state of *nirvana* the soul is truly eternal. It ceases to be reincarnated into the phenomenal world. Reincarnation and *nirvana* are thus karmically conditioned.

The *Jataka Tales* contain stories about the birth and life of Lord Buddha, the transmigration of his soul and how he reached *nirvana*. The *Tales* maintain a nebulous position on women in the areas of sexuality (procreation, sexual desire) and reproduction (physical maintenance and child-rearing). This nebulous position may be the result of the translation of complex metaphysical principles into ordinary tales which could be used to disseminate Buddhist thoughts. To concretize such thoughts, existing social categories were utilized to portray the phenomenal world and extra-ordinary categories were created to portray the non-phenomenal world.

Procreation is conceptualized in the *Jataka Tales* as something necessary and functional to the law of reincarnation. Reincarnation requires birth. And birth requires conception, gestation and delivery. However, the entire physical process of birth is not reflected in Buddhist discourse. The story about the exceptional conception of Lord Buddha as the blessed one is a case in point.

In the *Jataka Tales*, Buddha's birth did not occur as a result of sexual intercourse between his parents, but as a result of a dream his mother had about a white elephant descending from heaven and entering her womb. This story clearly de-links sexual intercourse from conception. That he was born 'clean, unstained with liquid, unstained with phlegm, unstained with blood, unstained with filth . . . his male organs were enclosed in a sheath' (Parrinder, 1980: 42) de-links labour in delivery from the birth of the child. The complete physiological cycle the female body must go through in conception, childbearing and childbirth is therefore denied. The story about the birth of Buddha shows that there is a selective acknowledgement of the role of women in procreation, from which sexual intercourse and labour in childbirth are discarded. This selective acknowledgement underscores the fact that sexual intercourse as a physical moment of conception, and the social relation between women and men resulting from this physical moment, both stand in contradiction to Buddhist emancipatory principles.

There is no notion of sex as sin in Buddhist thought. Rather than defining sex as sin, sex is tied to the natural world, the world of suffering and ignorance. As a form of bodily craving, sex is a source of attachment to the phenomenal world and therefore is opposed to the basic principle of non-self and detachment. The activation of sexual desire is considered to be caused by women, and sexual relations are considered incompatible with religious attainment.

Women are to be looked upon by monks with fear and contempt since they may awaken desire for intimacy and social attachment. As pointed out by Parrinder (1980: 44) the well-known advice recorded as having been given by Lord Buddha to his disciples about the danger of women was not to look at them, not to talk to them, and in case this could not be avoided, then to 'keep wide awake'. The danger of women was located in their 'nature' as depicted in the following statement made by Lord Buddha in reply to the request of his disciple — Ananda — to allow women to be ordained:

Women are soon angered; women are full of passion; women are envious; women are stupid. That is the reason, Ananda, that is the cause, why women have no place in public assemblies, do not carry on business and do not earn their living by any profession. (Coomaraswamy, 1956, as quoted by Kabilsingh, 1984: 66)

By considering the female body as a source of sexual desire (nature),

Buddhism excludes women from the upper realm of existence (metaphysics). By acknowledging the natural role of the womb in childbearing, yet simultaneously rejecting the natural moment of childbirth as filth, Buddhism reinforces the location of the female body at a low level of the natural world. The female body is recognized for its functionality in procreation, but it is rejected for specific physiological moments of procreation, i.e., intercourse and delivery. The fragmented conception of the female body and of the process of biological reproduction may be regarded as one of the major sources of gender bias which has implications for the social position of women.

One of these implications is the relation between ordainment and enlightenment. Although there was an initial hesitation about opening the Buddhist Order to women, a tradition was established which accepted women into the Order, even as missionaries (Kabilsingh, 1984: 73–4). The fact that Buddha yielded to the request of his disciple Ananda depicts the essentially non-hierarchical approach of Buddhism to knowledge. Disciples could challenge their masters, who were obliged to change their position if they could not find an answer. However, in changing a position (i.e. the opening of the Buddhist Order to the female sex) without changing the terms of the discourse (i.e. the definition of female sexuality), the source of gender bias in Buddhist thought prevailed. The notion that the female is impure, carnal and corrupting re-emerged in the course of history and was used again to prevent women from entering the Order. This notion was particularly pronounced in cases where Buddhism became interwoven with state politics, e.g. Thailand, Sri Lanka and Burma where the tradition of ordaining female priests (*Bikkuni*) died out.

Impurity was further extended through the formation of the notion that to be born a woman is a result of imperfect *karma*. This notion was inscribed on temple walls in Thailand expressing the wish of pious women who donated to the construction of temples. For example, in the 15th century the following inscription was made on the request of a Queen Mother: 'By the power of my merit, may I be reborn a male . . .' (Reynolds, C. J., 1977: 3). This shows the powerful impact of the doctrine of *karma*, and the female collusion in rejecting the worth of their own sex. Over the centuries, this collusion has kept the gender bias in Buddhism alive, including the belief that only through rebirth as a man can a woman be ordained and therefore achieve the ultimate goal of Buddhism, namely enlightenment.

Furthermore, due to the principle of non-self and total detachment, Buddhist discourse maintained an ambivalent attitude towards the household and the male–female relationship. Mutual duties between husband and wives were defined as follows:

A husband should minister to his wife in five ways: respect, courtesy, fidelity, giving adornments, and allowing her the authority in the household. A wife should minister to and love her husband in five ways: by doing her duties well, by being hospitable to relatives of them both, by fidelity, by watching over his goods, and industry in all her business. (Parrinder, 1980: 55)

Thus, the wife must be responsible for the management of the household and common property, and love and care for the husband. Love from the husband to the wife is not mentioned.

The lack of commitment ascribed to the husband has its source in the Buddhist rejection of the household. As noted by Parrinder (1980: 43), to counteract some of the criticism made by his disciples concerning the principle of self-denial and detachment from the phenomenal world which includes social intimacy and family life, Lord Buddha said the following:

> The household life is full of hindrance, a path for the dust of passion. How difficult it is for the man who dwells at home to live the higher life in all its fullness, purity and perfection. Free as the air is the life of him who has renounced all worldly things.

The household was seen as hindering men's religious goals, yet crucial to the maintenance of the society upon which the Buddhist Order was built. The role of women in reproduction (biological reproduction and maintenance) had a clear function in Buddhist thought as confirmed by the warning of Lord Buddha upon the opening of the Buddhist Order to women. Lord Buddha warned that if permission were given to women to leave the home and to enter the homeless state under Buddhist doctrine, Buddhism could stand fast for only five hundred years instead of two thousand years (Thitsa, 1980: 17). This warning shows awareness of the significance of women's role in reproduction, without which there can be no grown men to enter the Buddhist Order. The warning also reflects the fear of female sexuality as a potentially disruptive force.

While female sexuality is regarded as a corrupting force, polygamy and prostitution are sanctioned in Buddhist discourse. The *Vinaya* gave a list of ten kinds of wives: 'Those who were bought for money, those living together voluntarily, those to be enjoyed or used occasionally, those who had given cloth, those who provided the house with water, those with a head-cushion to carry vessels, those who were slaves and wives, those who were artisans and wives, those who were prisoners of war, and those who were temporary or momentary wives' (Horner, 1930: 43). This categorization of wives reflects the recognition of the functionality of women's social roles while it simultaneously sanctions the lack of male commitment to the marital relationship.

As for prostitution, there is an insinuation that being a prostitute is a result of imperfect *karma* caused by a verbal act. The *Jataka Tales* contains a story about a woman named Ambapali in the Indian city of Paisali who, after serving her terms in hell for having cursed a monk by mistake in her previous life, was reborn as a woman of exceptional beauty. Ambapali became a courtesan. Ambapali gave birth to a son who became a disciple of Lord Buddha. After her son attained ultimate enlightenment (*nirvana*), Ambapali entered the Buddhist Order and reached a lower level of enlightenment (*arahat*) (Hantrakul, 1983: 5; Boonsue, 1986: 39). This story shows the absence of condemnation of prostitution in a social as well as a religious sense. Prostitutes and courtesans are not degraded in Buddhist thought for there is no notion of sex as sin. Rather, there is the notion that sexual cravings are part of the world of ignorance. Therefore, the status of a prostitute is not considered as a result of sexual impurity, but karmic impurity. Just as all individuals can improve their *karma* through social acts, so too can prostitutes. However, the conditions for prostitutes to improve their *karma* remain within the dominant terms of Buddhist discourse, namely to discontinue sexual relations, and to acquire the role of motherhood and reproduction.

Although Buddhist discourse exhibits some lenience towards sexual rules, there is a difference along gender lines. Polygamy is sanctioned because of the usefulness of women's work and contribution to the household, in addition to being a source for male enjoyment. Polygamy is sanctioned mainly for male benefits. In sexual terms, polygamy is essentially an expression of male rather than female lust. By placing the notion of sexual impurity and lust on women, and by sanctioning polygamy at the same time, Buddhist discourse gives the best of both worlds to men. Men can express their lust and believe that it is caused by women and not by themselves. Men can categorize women and control them, while benefiting from their social roles. Men can have many wives and at the same time reject marital relations in order to purify their *karma*.

For women, sexual misconduct is consequential to their *karma*. Unfaithful behaviour such as adultery will result in rebirth as a woman, i.e. no change in their *karma*. Womanly behaviour defined as devotion to the responsibility to procreate and to the household will result in the accumulation of merits and therefore the improvement of *karma*. Improvement of *karma* can mean rebirth in a higher social status, or rebirth as a man (Boonsue, 1986: 38–40). Women can neutralize the consequences of their offences through merit-making. But their merits remain limited in so far as the ultimate goal of spiritual attainment is concerned. In the state of eternity, there is a difference between high (*nirvana*) and low (*arahat*) and women can only attain the low state. To be able to achieve the high state, they must be reborn a man.

The position of women in Buddhist discourse depicts an ambiguity between belonging and being rejected. The major source of this ambiguity lies in the Buddhist definition of the phenomenal world and the cosmology in which this world is located. From the start, the definition of the phenomenal world is biased towards the female sex. Biological sex and household relations are portrayed in a fragmented manner, depicting both recognition and denial. Procreation, sexual desire and household relations constitute a woman's world, a world which is defined as transitory and therefore must be rejected. The world of men is more complete. Men can belong to the phenomenal world, as well as to the metaphysical world. As part of the social world, men may enter sexual relations inside or outside marriage, able to reject such relations to pursue higher spiritual causes.

Buddhist thought defines clearly the discontinuous, i.e. the phenomenal world, but remains ambiguous about the eternal, i.e. the relationship between *karma* and the eternal soul, i.e. *atman*. As a metaphysical category, *karma* is conditioned by social acts, or acts which occur in the phenomenal world. *Karma* is the bridge between the world of eternity and the world of discontinuity. But if the phenomenal world is transitory and illusionary (discontinuous), in what way are social acts real and how can they influence *karma*, the bridge to *atman*? The ambiguous relationship between the categories of the eternal and the transitory leaves Buddhist metaphysical thought vulnerable to reinterpretations which are functional to the legitimization of an existing social order.

Although originally Buddhism emerged as a salvation movement which rejected existing social hierarchy and advocated the view that all humans were born equal, the translation of Buddhist metaphysical though into practical moral lessons for lay people conveys the message that there is a hierarchy of karmically conditioned souls, i.e. there are human souls with *karma* at different stages of development. In real terms, this qualitative differentiation of human souls cannot be substantiated except by examining the social conditions of the humans such souls inhabit. When applied in a popular context, the doctrine of *karma* helps support the widely held notion that social classes and gender division originate in human deeds and not in socio-economic forces or practices. Therefore, the emancipatory principle lies in virtuous practice rather than in social struggle. This opens the possibility for the utilization of a hierarchy which is metaphysical by definition to reinforce a social hierarchy which is a product of human history.

Buddhism, Law and Gender in Feudal Thailand

It is not known exactly when Buddhism arrived in Thailand. Some scholars trace Buddhist influence to when the Buddhist missionary movement under the Third Buddhist Council reached the area (Na-Rangsi, 1984: 2). The oldest compilation of the Buddhist canons with commentaries in Siamese prose is the *Traibhumi of Phra Ruang (The Three-Worlds Cosmography)* which dates from 1345 AD. This compilation marked the beginning of the systematization of Buddhist thought and the establishment of the relationship between religion and polity (Griswold and Prasert na Nagara, 1975: 50). There is evidence that earlier texts existed but were destroyed, although elements of these might have been incorporated in the *Traibhumi of Phra Ruang* (C. J. Reynolds, 1976). Since its appearance, this body of text has served as guiding rules for Thai polity and religious practices. It was used as a basis for the formulation of Thai law until the turn of this century, was cited by Thai kings for references, and used for sermons and monastic instruction. Many of its elements have been translated into common parlance and proverbs.

As a holy text, the *Three-Worlds Cosmography* has not been exempt from change and adaptation. At various stages of Thai history the text has been revised and amended. Destruction of the text by war and pillage made revision and amendment necessary when peace was restored. Seizure of political power by new rulers of different ethnic groups and lineages also required revisions for the legitimation of their rule (Reynolds, F.E., 1977: 268-9). Therefore, revision and amendment were not just textual. They were also political as the past was re-created to legitimize the present. This was particularly relevant as regards the definition of kingship and forms of social organization.[1] As will be shown, there is a difference in the interpretation of Buddhist thought which corresponds to the change from Buddhist kingship to Brahmanistic kingship, and to changing socio-economic relations. Thus, although essential to Thai society, Buddhism cannot be treated as a uniform body of thought. Buddhism should be understood in terms of how particular discursive elements are applied, and the consequences of their application.

Tracing the impact of Buddhism on the legal framework governing the male–female relationship in Thai history is a difficult task for several reasons. Firstly, it is not possible to interpret Thai history as a uniform and linear political succession of different kingdoms from Sukhodaya to Ayudhya to Bangkok, and finally to the present form of constitutional monarchy. Modern Thailand is the embodiment of earlier power struggles among many different ethnic groups and the cultural vestiges of these groups make what is known today as Thai culture, unified at some levels by *Therevada* Buddhism. Secondly, historical records are scanty, and how particular cultural elements emerged, whether they emerged for internal reasons, or whether they were external practices which were adopted for one reason or another cannot be established with any certainty. Nevertheless, from the existing data, some general observations may be made concerning the legal position of women.

Firstly, although the feudal law was generally consistent with Buddhist principles, there have been a series of legal reforms with important consequences for women. Such reforms may be located in major changes pertaining to the organization of the relations of production and the nature of the state. Secondly, the legal position of women has varied over time according to the specific elements of marital status ascribed by law. Thus, despite the existence of the legal rights unmarried women may possess in some areas of Thailand (e.g. bilateral inheritance) when they enter a marital relation their legal position changes. To avoid over-generalization about the legal position of women, it must be borne in mind that most of the legal rights enjoyed by women in a marital relationship only apply to the wife of the first order — the principal wife. Such rights diminish as the order descends. In what follows the legal position of women will be traced in relation to the transformation of Thai polity and social relations.

Buddhist kingship, law and women

Scholars of Thai antiquity have suggested that Buddhist universal law (*Dhamma*) was already applied in social organization, civil conduct and kingship prior to the compilation of the Buddhist canon in Siamese prose in the 14th century (Griswold and Prasert na Nagara, 1975). Indications of such application were found among the small states which occupied what is now Northern Thailand and which shared some cultural, social and environmental similarities (Damrong, 1959: Kirsch, 1984; Wyatt, 1984). This period is called the Sukhothai (or Sukhodaya) period. Sukhothai polity is described as relatively simple, compared to the later periods of Ayudhya and Bangkok. Rulers of these states pursued what is often referred to as the 'personalistic and paternalistic style of leadership' (Griswold and Prasert na Nagara, 1975). The ideological role of Buddhism was limited to the control of the moral conduct of the people and the legitimation of political rule by kings whose conduct had to be cogent with the ideal kingship stated in the *Dhamma*.

Two notable sources which provide insight into the nature of early polity and the class structure are King Ram Khamhaeng's inscription of the state of Sukhodaya and the *Mangraisat* (or legal codes) of King Mangrai of the state of Lan Na. In the *Mangraisat* there was already the notion of kingship legitimized by Buddhist ideology. As pointed out by Kirsch (1984) and Wyatt (1984), the Preamble which begins the *Mangraisat* and the Peroration which concludes it locate King Mangrai's authority in the Buddhist tradition of royal decrees. The Preamble also justifies history according to Buddhist universal law (*Dhamma*) which underlies and activates the universe. As a law-giver, King Mangrai's task was to link Buddhist universal principles to the customary rules and forms of organizations of the people. Such legitimation was less clear in the case of Ram Khamhaeng's inscription. However, evidence suggests that Buddhist universal law (*Dhamma*) was cited and coupled with *Rajasastra*, or the legal codes promulgated by King Ram Khamhaeng (Griswold and Prasert na Nagara, 1975: 75).

As regards social organization, the *Mangraisat* and Ram Khamhaeng's inscription showed that there were forms of social hierarchy defined in relation to services provided to the king. The king himself was the lord of land (*Phra Caw Phaen Din*). Below him were lords (*Caw Nai, Caw Khun*) who were aides, advisers, and administrators in both military and civil affairs. The ranking of lords was done on the basis of a hierarchy of officials controlling units of citizens established on a decimal basis (i.e. groups of 10; 50; 100; 1,000; 10,000). This is an important point to bear in mind when comparing this with the ranking methods of later periods (Ayudhya and Bangkok) which were based on units of land allotted by the king.

Free citizens were required to contribute compulsory labour services, 'ten days in the King's service and ten days working at home'. Citizens had the right to borrow money from lords for investment for three years without interest. Land bought by a citizen for cultivation was also exempt from taxes for three years (Wyatt, 1984: 248). Production by citizens was thus subsidized by the lords. The welfare of citizens was the primary motive of political rule, as succinctly put in the following inscription: 'If society is morally sound and the people have a high spirit by keeping steadfast to Buddhism and adhering to *Dhamma*, the kingdom will be tranquil and prosperous' (Suksamran, 1984: 29). Out of the concern for the welfare of the citizens, slavery, although present, was not encouraged. The *Mangraisat* forbids the acceptance of debtors, thieves and deserters as slaves, although it also recognizes the existence of bankrupts who became slaves (Wyatt, 1984: 248). Slavery was regarded as an 'achieved' rather than 'inherited' status. Owing to concern over the 'achieved' status of slavery through bankruptcy, slaves were not allowed to inherit automatically, but through specially granted bequests to avoid bringing relatives into bankruptcy and subsequent slavery. Slaves were also physically protected because harming slaves was a capital crime (Kirsch, 1984: 256–261). As stated in the *Mangraisat*, citizens were rare and were not to be wasted by allowing them to become slaves (Wyatt, 1984: 248).

On the whole, the class structure during the Sukhothai period was relatively simple, based on the kinds of services rendered to the king. Although some form of social hierarchy did exist, preventive measures were adopted to ensure that social differentiation as a result of economic factors did not become widespread.[2]

The same cannot be said about gender. The law prevented women from participation in public affairs and provided for an unequal treatment in matters related to sexuality. Political participation by women was prevented by a clause which stated that 'any judgement rendered by a woman should be vacated' (Kirsch, 1984: 259). One may assume that in conformity to Buddhist principles women were denied participation in public affairs on the basis of their ignorance and imperfect *karma* which disqualified their judgement, although some exceptions may be found among women of the court who were allowed to participate in court and religious rituals (Kabilsingh, 1984: 72), or in battle (Griswold and Prasert na Nagara, 1975: 81).

Unequal legal treatment was prevalent in matters related to family and kinship. The *Rajasastra* had a clause on abduction which dealt with penalties imposed on those who abducted someone's slave or wife. The injured party was not the abducted person but the owner of the goods (i.e. the husband of the abducted wife, the father of the abducted child, or the owner of the slave), and the fine was to be equally divided between the Crown and the injured party (Griswold and Prasert na Nagara, 1975: 77). It is not known whether polygamy or the category of slave wife existed in the Sukhothai period, but the law on abduction showed that a man had the same right of alienation over his wife as he had over a slave.

Despite this, women's rights to property, to custody of children, and limited personal rights were ensured. They were allowed two-thirds of the property in case of divorce (Kabilsingh, 1984: 71–2), and could initiate divorce proceedings on very little evidence (Reynolds, C. J., 1977:10). Adultery remained within the sanctity of the family and therefore a private offence — i.e. no public judgement. A man could kill his wife and her lover without penalty if they were caught 'in secret' (Kirsch, 1984: 250), or he could demand a fine from her lover in proportion to the rank of the wife (Reynolds, C. J., 1977: 6). Adultery was punishable only when caught and therefore women were protected from physical violence without substantiated causes.

However, such rights were limited to the wife of the first order. The lower the order the less rights a woman had. Nevertheless, it appeared that slave wives who entered the household through purchase or indebtedness were uncommon because of the limits established on entry into slavery in general. The existence of the slave wife may have stemmed from the practice of giving women as objects of reward for military prowess (Kirsch, 1984: 259) or as dowry (Turton, 1980: 275). Although internal slavery was discouraged under the *Mangraisat* for reasons pertaining to the rarity of citizens and therefore women citizens were ensured more protection (Kirsch, 1984: 158), this did not stop the practice of giving captured women (external slaves) as objects of reward and dowry, reinforcing women's weak personal rights and transformed them into the symbol of male prowess, wealth and prestige. As will be shown, this practice affected women of all classes and not just slave women. The objectification of women in military and political transactions which occurred during this period established a tradition which flourished later as the nature of kingship, class structure and land-ownership changed, and as women lost more and more personal and property rights.

In summary, it may be stated that in early social organization the adherence to Buddhist principles by political rulers provided several measures which prevented the exacerbation of social differentiation by economic factors. Gender differentiation did not receive the same attention owing to the gender bias inherent in Buddhism. Women had fewer personal rights than men, although they were protected by general measures against social differentiation. Furthermore, the application of Buddhist ideological discourse on women was inconsistent. Deviation existed in the area of sexual offences such as adultery, for which the *Jataka Tales* prescribed no violence; while by law, women convicted of adultery were subject to the death penalty. Religion and the law were consistent in their definition of the intellectual capacity of women. The idea that women belonged to the low level of the phenomenal world (ignorance) disqualified their judgement, and subsequently prevented their participation in public activities.

Brahmanistic kingship, *Sakdina* and gender

The beginning of the 15th century marked the coming to power of an ethnic group who inhabited the Central Plain, and who established the Ayudhya kingdom, incorporating part of the northern territories. The Ayudhya kingdom was destroyed by the Burmese in the 18th century, but was resurrected soon after as the Kingdom of Siam with Bangkok as its capital. The polity and relations of production of the Ayudhya kingdom — which were adopted with some amendments during the Bangkok period — contrast sharply with those of the early states.

Of notable importance were the following: (1) the adoption of the Brahmanistic ideology of kingship, which asserted a tighter control over the monastic community; and   (2) the introduction of the *Sakdina* system which tied social rank with land distribution. As will be shown, the conflation of religious power and political power in this period brought about more severe forms of discipline over civil conduct, and the introduction of the *Sakdina* system created sharp class and gender differentiation. As a consequence, women lost many of the rights they had had earlier and they were brought under the severe discipline of both male and state authority.

Statesmanship in the Ayudhya period was marked by the notion of divine kingship, which did not exist during earlier periods. In addition to the use of Buddhist universal law (*Dhamma*) to legitimize political rule and social organization, the notion of divine kingship introduced the king as the counterpart of the divine figure, Lord Buddha, or as his reincarnation (Reynolds, F.E., 1977: 269–70), and emphasized the control of the state over agriculture (Kirsch, 1977: 252). Although the notion of divine kingship was essentially antithetical to Buddhism, and although Thai rulers claimed to be devout Buddhists, the introduction of Brahmanistic ideology was possible because both ideologies share the same cosmology. Furthermore, Brahmanistic ideology was restricted to political rule and administration and therefore it could co-exist with Buddhism and be seen as enhancing cultural prestige rather than the autocratic nature of kingship (Kirsch, 1977).

Three main reasons may be given to explain the introduction of the divine king into the polity of Ayudhya. From a cultural perspective the notion was applied in the Angkor Kingdom of the Khmers, who had ruled the Central Plain, and therefore the notion may be considered as a vestige of the Khmers (Griswold and Prasert na Nagara, 1975). From a political perspective, the introduction of this notion conflated religion with polity and gave the king absolute legitimacy, something which was probably necessary in view of the prevailing conflict over ethnicity and royal lineages. The monarch could establish royal supremacy over the monastic community, the Buddhist *Sangha*, and thus had the power to order recension of the text of Buddhist cosmography in order to legitimize his rule and the newly adopted social organization, and to remove monks who refused to co-operate (Reynolds, F. E., 1977:270). From an economic perspective, the notion of the divine king gave the monarch absolute control over land and labour. Rather than being merely the lord of the land, the monarch became the 'Lord of Land and Life'. The monarch's control was asserted not only over the means of production but also over civil conduct and the sphere of the personal.

The control of land and labour by the monarch was instituted by a system of ranking the population which was tied to land distribution. A law was proclaimed in 1455, *Phra Aiyakan Tamnang nai Thaharn lae Phonlaruan*, which defined social rank as an indication of a person's status and authority in the social order and his responsibility towards society and the administrative system (Suksamran, 1982: 17). As the sole owner of all land, the monarch allocated it to his subjects according to their rank. There was no private ownership per se. No beneficiary of land distribution had the right of sale and any beneficiary could lose his entitlement if the monarch considered him undeserving. This law established a relationship of mutual dependency between social rank and control over the means of production. Through this relation, the monarch could control the loyalty of his citizens, their division of labour and their acceptance of such a division.

The system of mutual dependency between social rank and land allocation was called *Sakdina. Sakdina* derived from the Hindu concept of 'Shakti' which means power in terms of resource, or energy. Literally, *Sakdina* means 'the control over the rice field'. The operationalization of the concept of *Sakdina* had two dimensions. *Sakdina* was a unit of land (rai or about 0.16 hectare). It was also a numerically hierarchical system of dignity marks which substantiated the ranking of the population through land allocation. For example, those holding *Sakdina* of 400 up to 100,000 rai were appointed directly by the king and formed the small ruling stratum (Turton, 1980: 253). Monks were allocated from 400 up to 2,400 rai and novices between 200 and 300 rai (Suksamran, 1982: 17). Serfs (*Phrai*) were alloted 25 rai for an adult married male in service to the king and lords, 20 rai to one who supervised war slaves and refugee families, and 10 to 15 rai for a common serf. Adult male slaves, beggars and destitutes had 5 rai (Poumisak, 1987: 93). Perhaps no more than 2,000 persons had *Sakdina* of 400 rai or higher in the Ayudhya period out of an estimated population of 2 million (Turton, 1980: 253).

From these data it appears that the monastic community emerged during this period as part of the ruling stratum and therefore was bound to protect its interests. According to Suksamran (1982: 17) the monastic community also enjoyed the allocation of serfs and slaves who were the main source of labour on temple estates. Ecclesiastical honorific titles were also awarded to individual monks, which contributed to their mobility within the structure of the Buddhist *Sangha*. The award of stipends encouraged the accumulation of personal wealth (Suksamran, 1982: 23). Thus, whereas the role of the monastic community in early social organization was to ensure the application of Buddhist tenets to preserve existing social structure and to avoid the exacerbation of social differentiation, under the *Sakdina* system the community was bound to defend the interests of the monarchy and its interests rather than the interests of the peasantry who formed the bulk of the population.

Serfs (*Phrai*) had to pay to their lords a tax in kind which could range from 50 to 80 per cent of their entire yield. *Thay* (freemen) rented land from the lords for a fixed price, usually 50 per cent of the produce, known as the 'half-share-of-the-field' system (Poumisak, 1987: 47). There were four categories of slaves — war slaves, temple slaves, debt slaves, and juridical slaves. War slaves were captured during raids and included males and females. They performed public or private work and could also be donated to temples. Temple slaves produced food for priests and were required to build, rebuild and maintain temples. Juridical slaves were those who had committed criminal offences and were unable to pay the heavy cash fines assessed as penalties. Unable to do so, they were condemned to servile status in the household of the plaintiff. Debt slaves were bankrupts who sold themselves into slavery. Debt slaves and juridical slaves included males and females (Turton, 1980).

The allocation of land to the peasantry may be seen as a strategy to enable them barely to reproduce themselves, but not for their own accumulation. As Poumisak (1987: 100) noted, cultivators working fewer than six rai were forced to find other sources of income to cover their expenses. Furthermore, the system of *corvée* labour which disengaged them from working on their own land did not permit production beyond subsistence, even when they had sufficient land. *Corvée* labour could be mobilized by a royal decree according to which all males from 18 to 60 years of age (except for sons of the royalty, aristocrats and monks) were required to register with the royal government agency in charge of *corvée* and serfs. There were three categories of serfs: *Phrai Luang* (king's serf); *Phrai Som* (aristocrat's serf); and *Phrai Suai* who contributed highly valued goods in lieu of service (Turton, 1980). Depending on the category, the *Phrai* class was obliged to work on royal, aristocratic and temples' estates and buildings for six months per year or longer, as compared to ten days according to the *Dhamma* (Buddhist universal law) in earlier social organization. *Phrai* could use slaves as a legal substitute for *corvée* (Turton, 1980: 281).

The extension of *corvée* to six months or more under the *Sakdina* system gave an indication of the existence of a sexual division of labour in the area of reproduction and production. According to the law, women were not obliged to contribute to the *corvée* system, except when they were family members of prisoners of war. Given the male *corvée* obligation, men's contribution in the area of agricultural subsistence production was bound to be limited. Thus, although only male serfs and slaves were entitled to land allocation, the bulk of agricultural subsistence production was done by women, responsible for household subsistence and the subsistence of their adult male relatives. Beyond subsistence, women were also in charge of the production of textiles and of intra-village trade which might have been the main source of surplus (Elliot, 1978; Skrobanek, 1983).

These data suggest that social stratification among the peasantry was based on the extent to which accumulation could take place through the productivity of the women, whether the men could delegate a slave as their legal substitute for *corvée*, and whether they could provide goods in lieu of service. This might have created a demand for women as family slaves among the better-off peasants. As pointed out by Turton (1980: 281) slave women performed domestic work (rice milling, cooking, care of children) and small-craft production. They also contributed to the increase of the slave-labour force in the household (procreation). Thus, the sexual and manual labour of female slaves contributed to surplus, much of which was extracted by the state and individual lords through taxation and sharecropping.

Under Buddhist kingship female slaves initially emerged with the practice of giving women as rewards for military prowess, in political transactions and as dowry. They were external slaves and were exchanged mainly between ruling men. Internal slaves were protected. Under the *Sakdina* system, there were mechanisms which produced slavery internally, making slaves available to commoners as well. As the monarch was the sole owner of the land, the person to whom land was allocated did not have full rights of ownership, and therefore land was not available as collateral. With the right of alienation of persons traditionally given to men, the non-availability of land as collateral led to the practice of using family members as collateral. Thus, slave women, bonded women and free women were exposed to the threat of being used as collateral. The status of a woman could change from free citizen to slave not as a result of her own actions but by the act of the person with right of alienation over her.

As pointed out by Turton (1980: 281) debt and juridical slavery may be seen as ways to mobilize internal female and child labour which might otherwise not be so directly available. As women of the *Phrai* class were obliged to provide the means of subsistence for their families, they could not be so easily disengaged from agricultural production. By allowing the right of alienation to become the right to use legal dependants as collateral or objects of sale, a certain level of mobility of female and child labour through sale and mortgage was ensured.

On the whole, it may be stated that the *Sakdina* system of land allocation and division of labour created more social and gender differentiation. Through the authority of the male citizen, the state could ensure the continuity of the cycle of reproduction and production at village level, while periodically benefiting from male labour. Several labour control practices contradicted Buddhist principles, but as the monastic order was brought under the patronage of the monarch, the legitimacy of the new order could not be challenged.

Law, sexuality and gender under the *Sakdina* system
The most comprehensive body of legal texts during this period, the *Three Seals Laws* was compiled under the reign of Rama I (1782–1809) of the Bangkok period and finalized in 1805. The *Three Seals Laws* introduced new laws as well as incorporating surviving laws of earlier periods (Wyatt, 1984: 246). Among the old laws which were incorporated was the law which ranked wives into three orders: (1) *mia klang muang* (the principal wife) whose parents consented to her marriage and who brought property into the marriage; (2) *mia klang nok* (the secondary wife); and (3) *mia klang thasi* (the slave wife) who was acquired through purchase, or indebtedness. This categorization of wives originated in a 1361 royal decree, introduced by King U-Thong who established the Ayudhya kingdom.

As has been shown in the last section, in Buddhist discourse the husband must minister to his wife with respect, courtesy, and fidelity. He was to allow her authority in the household. Adultery committed by the wife was defined as an offence consequential to her *karma* and entailed no concrete punishment. When translated into the *Mangraisat* law, the authority in the household was given to the husband who also acquired the right of alienation over his wife. Adultery committed by women had concrete penalties which entailed death, or a fine to be paid to the husband by the lover.

Under the *Three Seals Laws*, the husband's authority over the household and the penalties for sexual crimes (such as adultery), committed by women were more harsh. Through marriage the parents transferred the custody of their daughter to the husband. This custody gave the husband the traditional right of alienation over his wife. He could sell her or give her away, and administer corporal punishment, provided that the degree of punishment was in proportion to her misdeed. The husband had the right to manage the property held by both spouses. Property was differentiated between prenuptial and postnuptial. In case of divorce by mutual consent, each spouse was compensated for prenuptial property disposed of in the course of the marriage.

With regard to postnuptial property, the wife's share was one-third and the husband's share was two-thirds (Reynolds, C. J., 1977:7). In the case of desertion by the husband, the husband maintained the same rights as under divorce. An 1857 royal decree gave husbands of a certain noble rank the right to government assistance in pursuing a wife who fled the household. An adulterous wife lost all rights to property (Reynolds, C. J., 1977: 7). In addition, she was subjected to alternative forms of punishment: (1) the death penalty; or (2) public shaming, from which she could be exempted if she paid a large fine (Wedel-Pattanapongse, 1982: 359). Women without the legal protection of parents or husbands had no right of complaint against sexual molestation (Hantrakul, 1983: 3).

Changes under the *Three Seals Laws* had important juridical and economic consequences for women. First, women had fewer property rights and less right to manage common property. The right of custody and the permission given to husbands to sell their wives or to use them as collateral meant that women became vulnerable to sale and resale and subsequently to losing the supportive relations of their kin. Impoverished male serfs could now save themselves from slavery by selling their wives and children.

Second, offences pertaining to sexual relations were no longer considered as being within the sanctity of the family. Adultery and desertion committed by women were redefined as legal offences which required public intervention. The shift of the legal terms of sexual offences from the sanctity of the family to the public domain rendered women vulnerable to two kinds of authority which had been synchronized, male authority and public authority.

With less protected personal rights, ruling women as well as slave women were exposed to various forms of sexual violence which might have included forced and indentured polygamy and prostitution. The practice of giving women as awards for military prowess, initiated earlier, flourished in new forms and came to be practiced by the ruling class as well as by better-off commoners. Women of the ruling class were exchanged for reasons pertaining to pledges of loyalty between ruling families and requests for military and political protection (Reynolds, C. J., 1977: 14–15). Slave women were available for productive and reproductive services. From military prowess and social prestige, the exchange of women and the accumulation of wives later acquired the meaning of economic and sexual prowess. This symbol was legitimized in a revised version of the Buddhist cosmography text which attributed 24 million wives to the Brahmanistic God Indra whose counterpart on earth was the king of Siam (Reynolds, C. J., 1977: 12).

It seems that the emergence of the prostitute as a legal category was conditioned by this vulnerable legal and economic position of women. According to Hantrakul (1983: 6), the first record of the word prostitute — *ying nakorn sopaenee* — is found in the collection of the *Three Seals Laws* of 1805 in the section dealing with husband and wife, which referred to the parable about Ambapali (the courtesan in the *Jataka Tales*). Consistent with the parable, *ying nakorn sopaenee* was categorized as a woman publicly shared by all noblemen and their sons, subsequent to a religious offence (cursing a monk) she had committed in her previous life.

European travellers to Siam in the 17th and 18th centuries reported the existence of some forms of prostitution: their observations predate the *Three Seals Laws*. La Loubère, who visited Siam in the 17th century, noted a titled official as 'that infamous fellow who buys Women and Maids to prostitute them' and Hallet claimed that 'the prostitutes are all slaves' (as quoted by Turton, 1980: 281). Salmon noted the existence of prostitution among the nobility. According to him (Salmon, 1725: 358–9), among the aristocracy, adultery committed by royal concubines, defined as being 'unfaithful to their bed', was punishable either by death or by condemnation to some kind of prostitution house reserved for noblemen. 'If a Person of Quality's Daughter goes astray, she is sold to an Officer who has a Patent from the King for liberty to prostitute Young Women; and he has not less than Five or Six Hundred of these ladies under his care' (Salmon, 1725: 359). These observations point to the existence of a legal sanction of pimping prior to the definition of prostitution in the *Three Seals Laws*.

Poumisak (1987: 134) found that at the end of the Ayudhya period prostitution was rampant, owing to polarization of land control by the *Sakdina* class and to extreme rural poverty. The government did nothing to correct the situation; it only collected taxes. Tax collected from prostitution amounted to a sum of 50,000 baht per annum in the middle of the 18th century, compared to water taxes collected from fishing in rivers, canals, swamps and lakes which amounted to 70,000 baht in the same period. There is evidence of women trying to sell their bodies secretly outside the brothels to avoid taxes. Fearing the resultant loss of taxable profits, a royal decree was issued in 1763 which said: 'Henceforth, Thai, Mon, and Lao are forbidden to have sexual intercourse in secret with Indians, French, English, Kula [?] and Malays — who are heathens (i.e. not Buddhists) — in order to protect the people from misfortune . . . If anyone fails to heed this and secretly has sexual intercourse with heathens she is to be arrested, interrogated, and punished at the maximum by execution. Parents and kinfolk, near and far, who fail to make her obey and prevent this are to be punished' (Poumisak, 1987: 134). Thus, religion was once again used to drive women back to the brothels for more effective control by the state.

The incorporation of the category of prostitute into the legal framework in 1805 formalized the social position of women who sold their bodies. This required a definition of their status and an ideological justification. This definition rested upon the combination of what was formerly regarded as a result of a religious offence (prostitution) with what was formerly regarded as a private crime (adultery). Henceforth, the legal definition of prostitution in the *Three Seals Laws* conflated the private with the public, the religious with the secular. This meant that entry into prostitution was legitimized by the violation of social norms of chastity and the religious ideology governing transmigration of the soul and multiple rebirth. Furthermore, the incorporation of this category in the legal texts formalized prostitution and pimping on different terms. Being a prostitute was an acquired status resulting from having committed a sexual offence caused by previous deeds. Being a pimp was an acquired status by royal decree.

In summary, the following remarks may be made regarding the relationship between religion and the law in Thailand. First, in feudal Thailand, the symbiotic relation between religion and the law has produced a socio-cultural parameter which is heavily biased against women. The legitimation of the weak social and legal position of women falls within the general application of Buddhist universal law in Thai polity. The notion that gender is karmically conditioned was translated into various forms of legal categorization, regulation and control over the female sex. The assertion of political control over the Buddhist *Sangha* by the monarchy, and the adoption of the notion of the divine kingship, made women much more vulnerable in legal terms. Buddhist principles — however biased in their origins — no longer protect women as the monarch had the authority over the *Sangha* in the finality, the interpretation and application of such principles.

Second, interwoven into social relations, religious discourse forms part of the process of the constitution of the female subject within the Thai socio-cultural framework. The psycho-structure of female subjects in feudal Thailand was marked by the acceptance of their social conditions as a result of *karma*. Religious discourse is constructed in such a way that the application of its dominant elements provided limited counterpoint for critique and resistance. The doctrine of *karma* provides the hope for rebirth in better conditions or cessation of rebirth altogether. It does not provide the notion of social struggle and therefore social inequality was accepted as a result of human deeds and not of socio-economic forces. This rendered countercritique and resistance for women pointless. As will be shown in the section that follows, critique was initiated by external forces whose main interest was to forge a restructuring of the Thai social order which would be conducive to Westernization and trade rather than defending women's interests. Therefore, the impact on legislation was minimal. The monarchy sought to preserve the old order concerning the male–female relationship.

Polygamy and Prostitution under Democratic Law

At the dawn of the 19th century, Thailand was exposed to considerable pressure to open up to Western trade and communication. Reforms between the second half of the 19th century and the first half of the 20th century replaced the absolute monarchy with a constitutional monarchy. The issues of slavery and polygamy became incorporated into the discourse on modernization and capitalist development together with the issue of private property. In what follows, laws concerning slavery, polygamy and prostitution will be examined as part of a process of legal liberalization. Attention is also paid to the self-invalidating elements contained in these new laws showing how the state and the ruling class today have found new ways to secure their interests in controlling and profiting from female sexual labour as in the past.

Most of the foundations for reform which led Thailand to a constitutional monarchy may be attributed to the initiatives of King Mongkut, who remains a controversial figure. He spent some 27 years as a Buddhist monk before his ascension to the throne, had travelled to the West and was exposed to Western morality and customs prevalent at the time. According to C. J. Reynolds, (1977: 12–17), he had six hundred wives and concubines and was sensitive to Western criticism of his excessively polygamous behaviour. As his reign saw the decay of the *Sakdina* system, the advance of the West and the emergence of a new commercial community, Mongkut first sought to revert to the old forms of Buddhist kingship and to abandon Brahmanistic ideologies and rituals. Later he moved to foster ties with the West and the new commercial community, as he clearly saw them replacing the *Sakdina* class in terms of their economic power.

In the discourse on modernization, Western missionaries and traders criticized polygamy as a 'pernicious custom' (Reynolds, C. J., 1977: 16) and slavery as 'a canker which saps the manhood of a people, encourages them in indolence, prevents them from enriching themselves and the State' (Turton, 1980: 283). In a newspaper article published in 1863, an American missionary wrote that 'virtue can never have much sway in Siam, or any true prosperity until polygamy is made a crime by the government' (Reynolds, C. J., 1977: 16). Attacks on slavery and polygamy as social systems were based on capitalist ethics and on the argument that both systems hampered the prosperity of the country. The response of the monarchy and the nobility was initially defensive. They sought a legitimate basis in the Buddhist religion and were reluctant to change social systems which for centuries had provided them with capital and income.

In response to Western criticism, King Mongkut published a rebuttal, claiming he was not excessive, as his brother had more wives than he did. He then published a list of all his wives and concubines. The monarchy's formal response in defence of polygamy as a social system and not just as an excessive behaviour of the monarch was published in the *Kitchanukit* (A Book Explaining Various Things) written in 1867 by the Minister of Foreign Affairs under King Mongkut. As shown by C. J. Reynolds (1976: 214–20; 1977: 24–30), the book set out differences between male and female nature and sexuality, cross-culturally compared these differences, and concluded that polygamy in Thailand was functional to male sexual convenience and for male need for merit-making. Polygamy enabled a man to alternate among his wives so as not to force himself on anyone against her will, and thereby lose merit.

Having used the Buddhist religion to defend polygamy, the monarch was forced to re-examine the validity of old laws, to invalidate laws which emerged during the *Sakdina* system and to introduce new laws which combined Buddhist law with some elements of liberal democracy. The monarch reassured the European community living in Bangkok at the time of the possibility that monogamy for the monarch would be written into the 1856 trade treaty with America (Reynolds, C. J., 1977: 17).

Action to pare down his own polygamous household was initiated in 1854 when a royal decree was introduced to allow palace women of all ranks to resign from royal service if dissatisfied. The monarch declared that he had so many wives that anybody could have them for the picking (Pramoj, 1959: 218). In his lengthy decree, the following was stated:

> Should any of the ladies, having long served His Majesty, suffer discomfort and desire to resign from the Service in order to reside with a prince or noble or to return home to live with her parents, or to dispel such discomfort by the company of a private husband and children, let her suffer no qualms . . . her wishes will be graciously granted, provided always that whilst still in the Service and before submitting such a resignation the lady shall refrain from the act of associating herself with love agents, secret lovers or clandestine husbands by any means or artifice whatsoever . . . His Majesty harbours no possessive desire in regards to the ladies, nor does he intend to detain them by any means whatsoever. (Pramoj, 1959: 219–20)

In spite of its liberal appearance, this decree maintained a firm position on the issue of chastity. Although the king permitted the ladies of the Court to marry nobles and princes, a distinction was made between those who were chaste and those who were not. Adulterous court women were detained and denied the right to resign. Given the large number of concubines and their isolation, some form of friendship or love relations must have developed between them and the men or women of the Court.[3] By granting them the right to resign while stipulating chastity, the monarch simultaneously invalidated this right for the majority of his concubines. Only twelve ladies submitted their resignations, three of whom were above the age of 37 and nine others between the ages of 15 and 23. This was interpreted as the sanctioning of polygamy by the women themselves (Pramoj, 1959: 217–21).

For King Mongkut, this decree was a sign of his willingness to adopt the Western notion of free choice as expressed in the following statement which is worthwhile quoting at length:

> That a man should be free to choose a woman of his heart's desire as his wife is the wish of His Majesty, and so happy He will feel to know that the satisfaction of any such man is shared by any of the ladies who recently resigned. In fact, His Majesty might have gone one step further by graciously giving the said ladies in marriage; but He was restrained by the consideration that he might have erred in his choice to the dismay of the parties concerned. Wherefore, the present middle course has been adopted in the hope that the honour and liberality of His Majesty will be firmly established in the newly founded customs. (Pramoj, 1959: 222)

By introducing the notion of free choice and by restraining himself from deciding for others in matrimonial affairs, King Mongkut sought to express his desire for wider change, although with hesitation. Nevertheless, the newly founded customs for the nobility also provided a basis for common women to demand the same rights.

Soon after the release of the decree quoted above, a petition by a woman who complained of having been forced to marry against her will was brought to King Mongkut's attention. Upon examining the basis of the complaint, he issued another decree which stated the following:

> It gives rise to the suspicion that they [the parents] might have made a written contract selling her into bondage to the man, for which reason they were obliged to permit the use of force by the buyer. If such rule be the truth, then a decision shall be given laying down the rule that no parents own their children as if they were cattle, which can be disposed of by sale at a price . . . Parents are not permitted to plead poverty in a sale of their children. Such a sale shall always be subjected to the consent of the person being sold, and whatever the price being consented to by such a person shall be the price in the sale. (Pramoj, 1959: 232)

The sale of children by parents was declared to be a crime that violated consent. The parental right to sell children was withdrawn, but the children could now set their own price. The decree also revived the old law concerning divorce and adultery which gave women more rights to claim divorce and which imposed only a fine as penalty for adultery. The decree also stated that it was applicable only to commoners and not to the nobility. As the monarch had argued, the dignity of the nobility must be secured and therefore women of the nobility could not be allowed the same freedom (Pramoj, 1959: 236).

A decade later, in 1868, King Mongkut issued a decree which dealt comprehensively with husbands selling wives and parents selling children. This decree forbade the insertion of names of wives and children into sales deeds. It also added that the husband could only put the name of his wife in a sales deed if she gave her consent by putting her 'mark' (signature) to the deed. The sale of slave wives, and children under 15 years of age was, however, permitted without their consent (Nartsupha and Prasartset, 1976: 371–74).

Towards the end of his reign, King Mongkut decided to apply the law on adultery to the nobility as well, to show his willingness to liberalize the country's cultural framework. He set an example by applying this law to the case of one of his concubines who was abducted from a royal boat, demanding only a small fine for compensation from the abducter (Pramoj, 1959: 214). Reforms introduced under King Mongkut's rule show a gradual influence of liberal notions of free choice and consent. Nevertheless, the changes were partial and still maintained elements which could invalidate the rights of women and children.

The reluctance to grant full rights to women must be seen against the background of the prevailing power structure. The nobility who benefited from slaves and wives as a source of capital and labour were initially not prepared to accept reforms. However, towards the end of the 18th century under the reign of King Chulalongkorn, the cash economy began to gain in significance and new forms of production and consumption made slaves and slave wives less economical. The slave-owning élite had a greater need for cash than personal services, and for investment capital than slave labour. The monarchy also had an interest in freeing slaves in general because the slave-owning élite had acquired considerable wealth and social power, which reduced the monarchy's control over *corvée* labour. Male *corvée* labour had been reduced to eight days for slaves and three months for free men (Tei Bunnag, quoted by Turton, 1980: 283). The successful introduction of anti-slavery laws must be seen as part of changes in the relations of production and in power relations between the monarchy and the slave-owning élite.

In so far as slaves were concerned, the introduction of legislation abolishing slavery meant that new labour relations were introduced (wage labour) in a formal sense, while the ideology of slavery prevailed. Legislation abolishing slavery was fragmented and provided too many loopholes. For example, in 1899 a law was introduced which allowed the sale of labour in advance (indentured labour). Breaking this labour contract was considered a criminal offence with penalties of up to three years imprisonment (this law was in force until 1931). The Lasker Act in 1900 prohibited the use of forced labour except by the central government and when wage labour was not available. Juridical prisoners continued to be used for public works (Turton, 1980: 284).

As regards women, the freeing of female slave labour and the abolition of polygamy did not put an end to the buying and selling of female sexual labour, nor to the accumulation of wives as a symbol of social prestige and sexual prowess. The nobility and the newly emerged ruling class (bourgeoisie and military) continued to defend their interests with the introduction of new laws and practices which prevented the enactment of anti-slavery, anti-polygamy and anti-prostitution laws.

In 1909, as soon as the final act abolishing slavery was introduced freeing a large number of slave wives, the new Venereal Disease Control Act required brothels and prostitutes to register for health and fiscal purposes. The abolition of slavery led to the rapid increase in the number of prostitutes — who were newly freed slaves without land or other means of subsistence and who were absorbed by brothels (Hantrakul, 1983: 6), many of which probably operated outside the law. Disguised behind the issue of health, the sanctioning of prostitution was mainly based on its profitability as the influx of Chinese migrants (traders, miners and port labourers who were mainly single males) created new demands for prostitutes' services. The increasing exchange relations with the West further diversified the ethnic composition of prostitutes. In the 1930s a small number of American, English, French, Russian and Vietnamese prostitutes were trafficked into Thailand (Commission of Enquiry, 1933: 316). Thus, while anti-slavery laws should in principle free women from bondage, this possibility was immediately curtailed by the continued legal sanction of prostitution owing to its lucrativeness. Rather than being bonded to a slave owner, newly freed women became bonded to pimps and brothel owners who became their new masters.

According to the Venereal Disease Control Act, anyone who wanted to operate a prostitution business needed approval from the government and a licence. The operator was obliged at all times to maintain a list of prostitutes employed in his business and could not employ a prostitute without a licence. The women had to be at least 15 years of age, and could not be forced into prostitution. To get a licence (which was valid for three months and non-transferable) a fee was paid to the government (Fox, 1960). Through this system, the government could continue to collect direct taxes from the operator of the brothel as well as from the prostitutes. The Act allowed any prostitute who wished to reform and give up her practices the right to apply for the cancellation of her licence and registration. While such applications were in practice always granted, about half of those prostitutes who were 'liberated' through cancellation eventually went back to the brothels, as 'sly' prostitution was forbidden. A prostitute was also allowed to marry provided that the husband-to-be paid a sum corresponding to her worth to the brothel keeper (Commission of Enquiry, 1933: 313). Through the Venereal Disease Control Act, the control of female sexuality could be maintained either by the state, the pimp or the husband-to-be.

As regards the issue of free choice and consent, under the Penal Code of 1908, the seduction of minors under 12 years of age and the abduction of any child under 10 years of age was punishable by law. However the Code also specified that for children between 10 and 14 years of age inclusive, penalties were applied only when the child did not consent to the abduction, or to the motive of abduction such as lucre or any immoral purpose (Commission of Enquiry, 1933: 311). This maintained the barrier on the prostitution of children above 10 years of age, but made it removable open to consent.

With respect to polygamy, the loss of its legal sanction was immediately replaced by the sanction of an alternative system, the system of 'minor wives'. Polygamy formally disappeared with the promulgation of the Civil Code in 1935. Under the Civil Code a husband can obtain a divorce on the grounds of adultery, while a wife must 'prove that the husband has maintained or treated another woman as his wife' (Plukspongsawalee, 1982: 151). Thus, the wife must show that the husband has formalized his adulterous relationship, while no such requirement is applied to the husband. This Code transformed polygamy into the system of 'minor wives' which prevails today, particularly among the ruling class. The prevalence of disguised polygamy may have been a result of the combination of the ideology of social prestige and prowess with the law regarding adultery. Indirectly, the Civil Code of 1935 still sanctions polygamy by defining adultery for men in terms of the formalization of an adulterous relationship, rather than the act of entering into extra-marital relationships. In these terms polygamy did not entirely lose its legal sanction. A man can still have many mistresses without any formalization.

As a consequence of considerable external pressure, the Thai government subsequently moved from the sanction of prostitution to its criminalization as a form of promiscuity. Thailand's adherence to and ratification of three international agreements on the traffic in women and prostitution has pressurized the application of new legal norms established by the international community. These agreements are:

- the International Agreement for the Suppression of the White Slave Traffic of 1904;

- the International Convention for the Suppression of the Traffic in Women and Children of 1922;

- the International Convention for the Suppression of the Traffic in Persons and of the Exploitation of the Prostitution of Others of 1950.

The convention of 1950 included two main clauses, namely the punishment of any person who exploits another person, even with the consent of that person, and the abolition of laws and regulations by which prostitutes are subject to special registration or exceptional requirements for supervision (Plukspongsawalee, 1982: 255).

As a party to these international agreements, Thailand revoked the Venereal Disease Control Act of 1908 which sanctioned prostitution, as late as 1960. The influence of the discourse on prostitution at the international level could be seen in the terms of the newly formulated laws. Yet, some elements which were essentially part of Thai male-dominated culture were retained.

According to Plukspongsawalee (1982: 156), in 1956, the Penal Code was revised to increase the age of consent on sexual offences. According to the revised code, penalties were imposed on any man for the seduction or abduction of a girl or woman for the sexual pleasure of others, and on anyone above 16 years of age for subsisting on the earnings of a female prostitute, *except children and dependants of the prostitute* (author's emphasis). The Prostitution Suppression Act introduced in 1960 and still in force today defines prostitution as a crime of promiscuity — the act of 'promiscuously rendering sexual services for remuneration' — a definition adopted by the United Nations Convention of 1950. Every party involved in prostitution is subject to penalties *except the customer*. Promiscuity is located in the one who sells and not the one who buys. The act further imposes penalties on the seduction and abduction of minors (under the age of consent of 18 years), and on owners, caretakers and managers of entertainment places who allow prostitution to take place in their establishments.

The terms of the laws on sexual offences and prostitution indicate the recognition of sexual seduction of minors as a crime, yet the interests of the dependants of prostitutes were protected according to the traditional breadwinning role of women. The Prostitution Suppression Act protects the customer according to the tradition which recognizes men as having a legitimate right to buy sexual satisfaction. The penalizing of employers remains only at the formal level. In practice, a new field of investment was opened in 1966 by an act that allows the employment of 'special service girls' and grants a new legal status to prostitutes.

The Service Establishments Act of 1966 legitimized entertainment as an industry and sought to control its operation and effects on the public order and morals (Plukspongsawalee, 1982: 158). Legally, women working in this industry are expected to provide only 'special services', a known euphemism for prostitutes' services.[4] In practice, 'special services' are left open to the customers' request and customers are exempt from penalty. Thus, while the existence of prostitution is legally suppressed and deformalized, entertainment places (pimping) became formalized to protect owners and customers. This shift of emphasis made it impossible to enact anti-prostitution legislation, except in the case of street soliciting. It also drove women into entertainment places. The existence of three separate acts indicates that the seduction of minors, prostitution and entertainment are seen as three separate issues rather than as part of a connected whole.

The coexistence of the Prostitution Suppression Act with the Service Establishments Act has led to an enormous increase in investment in entertainment places over the last two decades because of their lucrativeness. Owners of such places can now employ prostitutes as 'special service girls' under the conditions of the labour code governing service establishments. Because owners maintain an irregular wage system, rarely verified by labour inspectors, 'special service girls' often turn to prostitution to supplement their incomes, with the encouragement of the owners. As prostitution is illegal, 'special service girls' must seek protection from their employers, who bail them out or bribe the police for them to be allowed to return to work. The interests of the state and investors in maintaining the entertainment industry as a structural component of the tourist industry has turned prostitution into an element of local folklore to be experienced by visitors of many nationalities and professional backgrounds.

Conclusion

Throughout history, religious, legal and social practices in Thailand have accorded men the right to control and use female sexuality for their own ends. Since the feudal period, the symbiotic relationship between religion and polity has produced a gender-biased socio-cultural parameter, periodically used against women by the state and male representatives of the household. The use of religious doctrines against women must be understood in the context of the assertion of state control over the religious community, whereas women's socio-economic vulnerability must be placed against changing relations of production. Women's legal vulnerability has been an outcome of a combination of material and ideological forces.

In spite of the gradual influence of liberal democratic ideals, legislative reforms since the beginning of this century concerning polygamy and prostitution still leave considerable space to men to continue such practices. The focus on female promiscuity penalizes women and leaves men out as non-parties. The introduction of the liberal notion of consent remains an adornment of a legal framework whose terms have been conditioned for centuries by a deeply rooted ideological bias regarding the male–female relationship and an equally deeply rooted state interest in sanctioning prostitution. The defence of polygamy in the middle of the last century has been replaced by a defence of prostitution led by some segments of the ruling bureaucracy and the commercial community. This has accelerated the intensification of the utilization and disposal of female sexual labour, given the derived financial gains.

Notes

1. For more information on how the Buddhist religion was used to legitimize the introduction of new forms of social organization, see: Poumisak, 1987. Rulers created titles for themselves as 'a Buddha seated above the head of a subject of population, as a Holy Man, or as Buddha's reincarnation'.

2. On the basis of findings on land distribution, Poumisak (1987) argues that the *Sakdina* system was founded during the Sukhothai period. As this study is more concerned with the Buddhist law regarding women, it is more important to maintain the focus on the legal system, rather than to probe into the question of the origins of *Sakdina*.

3. Poumisak (1987:57) notes that lesbianism was prevalent among women in the inner quarters of the Court and in the households of the nobility as a result of their confinement.

4. The term 'special services' was devised by the Police Department (Tongudai, 1982: 8).

5. Foreign Exchange, Prostitution and Tourism in Thailand

> This is my rifle
> This is my gun
> One is for killing
> The other is for fun
> *Training exercise used US Army during the Indochina conflict, quoted in*
> *Bergman, 1974: 62*

This chapter deals with the economic and political forces shaping prostitution into sex tourism in Thailand in the last three decades. These forces include the expansion of tourism and entertainment as part of the global process of internationalization of tourism production, and inducements of a geo-political nature which further skewed this expansion in a particular direction, so that sexual services are provided in a highly organized fashion. The interplay between these two forces has been facilitated by an alliance between two powerful local factions, namely the military and the commercial community who are making use of existing ideological constructs as well as a legal framework which reinforces male domination and ensures limited protection for women in the area of sexuality. Here, the relationship between class alliance, policy choices and the diversified forms of control over female sexual labour is most clearly expressed.

Tourism as an Export-led Growth Strategy in Thailand

A political economic prelude

Thailand's tourism development fell into the general 'open economy' strategy pursued by the country since 1960. Prior to that date, Thailand's economy went through different phases of liberalization and inwardly-oriented industrial policies. Apart from external factors related to changes in the world economy in general, the choice of policy measures was also related to internal change, particularly in the nature of class alliances and control over the state apparatus.

Without formal colonization, Thailand's economy was prised open by the British in 1855 with the Bowring Treaty, which set the conditions for trade similar to those in British colonies and allowed Thailand virtually no control over trade and capital movement. In the early 1930s, with the demise of the Bowring Treaty, the country regained some control over its trade and fiscal policies. This control was regained through a change in the political system and a shift in the traditional power structure.

The conversion of the absolute monarchy into a constitutional monarchy separated the *Sakdina* class from its traditional direct control over the state apparatus. This conversion was achieved by a successful coup d'état in 1932, led by a faction composed of military officers, Western-educated intellectuals and bureaucrats. Influenced by the prevailing ideology of economic nationalism, the new ruling group sought to cope with external and internal forces by assigning an entrepreneurial role to the state, providing more opportunities for state participation in capitalist production. The expansion of state enterprises was geared towards the building up of local industries (import-substitution) to counter the effects of external economic and political forces, and towards control over local commerce and industry predominantly owned by ethnic Chinese (Elliot, 1978; Phongpaichit, 1980a; 1980b).

However, from the 1950s onwards the fervour of economic nationalism was undermined by the consolidation of economic power within the local business community (Phongpaichit, 1980a; 1980b). Despite state control over local commerce and industry between the 1930s and 1950s, the business community became prosperous through its external trading with the Japanese during World War Two, and was further stimulated by revived international trade after the Korean War.

Throughout the 1950s this community sought to consolidate its ties with prominent bureaucrats and military figures by enticing them to enter into partnerships in the commercial sector. According to Phongpaichit (1980a; 1980b), in the mid-1950s members of the military and administrative élites were included on the board of directors of 20 of the 33 major insurance companies in Bangkok. The same applied to eight of the ten major non-Western banks and trust companies and to 17 of the 20 major non-Western import–export and shipping companies. Leading officials also had shared ownership in the leisure sector (cinema, theatres) and rice trading. A new power bloc was formed linking financial and industrial capital with the state apparatus.

This new power bloc sought to achieve a dual economic objective which stressed a long-term commitment to open Thailand's economy to foreign investment in local industry, and a commitment to maximize short-term profits by investing in new ventures in the leisure and service sector catering to the needs of the US military whose geo-political interests in the region had become more pronounced (Elliot, 1978: 123).

The USA's main geo-political interest in the region was to pursue its 'containment' policy in East and Southeast Asia after the Korean War (Gaddis, 1982). Conceptualized under the administration of John F. Kennedy and guided by Robert McNamara, this strategy sought to combine military and economic goals into a single package which would support and strengthen the US position in the area, in order to 'contain the spread of communism'. Deployed in Thailand, this strategy sought to open the economy as much as possible to trade, foreign investment, grants, loans and aid through the instrumentality of multilateral and bilateral institutions. On the military side, it aimed at strengthening Thailand's defence and counter-insurgency system as well as establishing military bases from which the US military could pursue its own goals in Vietnam (Elliot, 1978; Permtanjit, 1982).

The geo-political interests of the US Administration and the interests of Thailand's new class alliance forged the country's pattern of investment and industrial structure in the 1960s and 1970s. The Investment Act for the promotion of industries introduced in 1959 deleted many import duties on capital goods and provided many tax concessions to private business, both local and foreign. This Act was formulated along the lines recommended by a 1958 World Bank mission: (1) a reduction of government activities in industry; and (2) an attempt to maximize the level of private and foreign investment. The government was to concentrate its efforts on the construction of infrastructure with foreign loans (Choonhavan, 1984). In the 1960s, government investments were mainly channelled to the building of the infrastructure required to stimulate local and foreign investment. Initially, funds came mainly from US bilateral sources and multilateral sources such as the World Bank and the Asian Development Bank (Permtanjit, 1982).

With the US withdrawal from Indochina in the mid-1970s, the inflow of US aid, loans and military support went into a steep decline. Meanwhile, Thailand was facing unfavourable world market conditions for rice, rubber and tin, which were the major foreign exchange earners. It became necessary for the country to diversify its external sources of financing as well as its export structure. New ties were fostered with Western Europe, Japan, and commercial banks to ensure the flow of aid and loans (Permtanjit, 1982). Foreign investment was stimulated by a new Investment Promotion Act passed in 1972, which gave foreign companies free movement of capital, the right to own land and to transfer profits and full exemption from taxes and duties on machinery whether bought locally or imported. The Investment Promotion Act was part of a strategy to increase the inflow of foreign investment to fill the gap caused by the decline of aid, and to diversify the structure of exports by concentrating on the production of manufactured goods and services through joint ventures (Phongpaichit, 1980a; 1980b).

Against this background, it is necessary to locate policies which stimulate the tourist industry in two phases. The first phase was integral to the short-term strategy of maximizing profits by catering for new demands imposed from the US military forces during the Indochina conflict. The second phase was integral to the strategy of diversification of the country's export structure and financial flow.

It is important to bear in mind that during both phases army officers played leading roles in the formulation of tourism policies. As has been shown in chapter 4, the ideology which views the accumulation of women and wives as a source of military prowess, social prestige and wealth is as old as the Thai state itself. Strengthened by the gender bias in Buddhism and the relation of patronage between the state and the Buddhist *Sangha*, this ideology survived historical change and still prevails among the ruling class, particularly among the military.[1] The military emerged in the 1930s as a dominant social group, with control over the state apparatus as well as over some branches of industry, so its involvement in the formulation and execution of tourism policies must have provided some continuity to discursive and social practices which consider female sexuality as a source of male pleasure and wealth. The sanction of prostitution in the entertainment sector defined as the 'special services sector' or the 'personal services sector' is a logical outcome of such practices.

Tourism policies and performance

In 1959, the Tourist Organization of Thailand (TOT) was formed by a royal decree. This decree was followed by the 1966 Service Establishments Act (sometimes also referred to as the Entertainment Act) which regulates hotel operation and legitimizes the operation of entertainment places (massage parlours, night-clubs and bars) whose main clients were US military servicemen stationed in the country. In 1967, a treaty was signed between the Thai government and the US military to allow US soldiers stationed in Vietnam to come on 'Rest and Recreation' leave (henceforth R & R), thereby enlarging the already existing demands by US soldiers stationed in the country.

Negotiations for the R & R treaty were conducted by a general of the Thai Royal Air Force whose wife was a co-director of the first tour agency — Tommy Tours — together with a foreign Air Force officer. The monthly net income of Tommy Tours in the first year of its operation was estimated to be around US$ 150,000 (*Le Monde Diplomatique*, 4 July 1970). The lucrativeness of R & R activities was particularly significant given the large number of US soldiers stationed in Indochina. In 1967 it was estimated that the spending of US military personnel on R & R leave in Thailand came to US$ 5 million (*Bangkok Bank Monthly Review,* August 1967: 266). In 1970, this amount rose to around US$ 20 million (*Bangkok Bank Monthly Review*, October 1973: 666), or as much as one-fourth of the total value of rice exports for that year.

The response of the local business community to R & R activities was spectacular. Initial local investment in hotels and entertainment places was boosted by the incentives given to private business under the First Investment Act and by the loans provided by the Industrial Finance Corporation of Thailand (IFCT) (*Bangkok Bank Monthly Review*, April 1966: 131). IFCT is an affiliate of a consortium of international private and public financial capital, including the Bank of America Corporation, the Chase Manhattan Corporation, the International Finance Corporation, and the Deutsche Bank AG (Permtanjit, 1982: 214). Between 1960 and 1972 some 80 million baht (US$ 4 million) were lent out by the IFCT to seven companies providing 'personal services' (Permtanjit, 1982: 215).

Such substantial capital investment in a small number of companies reflects the fact that 'personal services', including massage parlours, and entertainment places and hotels, were operating on a large scale. While disaggregated information on the loans given by IFCT to the personal services sector is not available, it is worth noting that the scale of operation of a massage parlour can be as large or even larger than a hotel. There are massage parlours employing between 500 and 700 'special service girls' with a diversified structure of prices and services.

Investment in small-scale operations was also considerable. According to a 1974 nationwide survey, there were over 20,000 entertainment places including bars, night-clubs, tea-houses and brothels. In 1978, a survey conducted in Bangkok showed that there were over 1,100 entertainment places, the largest category being the massage parlours, go-go bars and tea-houses (Thai Delegation, 1985). Investment in small-scale operations also has a foreign component, which cannot be easily traced owing to investment methods. By law, 50 per cent of ownership must belong to Thai nationals. In practice, foreign investors in small-scale operations can marry Thai women and invest through them, or can use Thai nationals as owners of record. Investment, production and management may be entirely under the effective control of non-Thai nationals. Local sources indicate that there are many foreigners using this method. They have introduced new methods of operation, management and skills, such as girlie bars, go-go bars and sex floor shows in the Western tradition.

One example is the Soi Cowboy which is the nickname for a street of bars and clubs. The Cowboy bar was initially set up by a retired US Air Force officer. Over a period of time, the whole street turned into a night-life centre nicknamed after the bar and its owner (*Bangkok Post*, 28 November 1983). Another example is Pat Pong Road, where an initial major investment in entertainment places was made in 1969 by an American who transformed an existing tea-house into a luxurious night-club (*Bangkok Post*, 5 February 1984). Since then, Pat Pong has been the main sex-entertainment street of Bangkok, widely known and cited in tourist guides and brochures.

The diverse nature of services, including traditional as well as newly introduced practices, reflects a high level of foreign involvement in the entertainment sector. The 'open' economic policy and the vested interests in this sector mean that the government as well as the investors have aimed only at maximizing short-term profits, while defying legal regulations of all sorts and ignoring long-term social costs.

Apart from investment in 'personal services', short-term, high-interest loans were also provided for hotel construction by local commercial banks, while international financial institutions provided loans on more favourable terms. In a single year (1967) local investment in hotel construction went up by 80 per cent (*Bangkok Bank Monthly Review*, January 1969: 8). In the same year, the US Export–Import Bank advanced loans amounting to US\$ 3.15 million for the construction of a new 217-room hotel and an expansion of one existing hotel, both managed by US-based hotel chains, i.e. Hilton and Sheraton (*Bangkok Bank Monthly Review*, August 1967). In 1968, the Board of Investment promoted six new luxury hotels (*Bangkok Bank Monthly Review*, January 1969: 8).

In the years which followed, US military operations intensified in Indochina and the US deleted Hongkong and Sydney from the list of available destinations for R & R, further enlarging the market in Thailand. Entire hotels which were financed by short-term and high-interest loans were leased out to US military personnel (*Bangkok Bank Monthly Review*, December 1969; October 1971). The erratic nature of investment created a significant over-supply of rooms and personal services at the beginning of the 1970s.

Given the unstable geo-political situation in Indochina and the subsequent uncertainty of the R & R market, a more coherent policy was needed. In 1971, during a visit by the former president of the World Bank, Robert McNamara, a mutual agreement was reached between the Thai government and the Bank according to which the Bank would send its specialists to plan the development of Thailand's tourist industry. The World Bank's study, completed in 1975, assessed the growth potential of tourism in Thailand irrespective of R & R, and recommended more public sector investment in infrastructure, i.e. airport expansion and maintenance, development of provincial sites and resorts (*Bangkok Bank Monthly Review*, October 1972: 468–9). The same year, a National Plan on Tourist Development was commissioned by the government, to be jointly prepared by a firm based in the Netherlands and a Thai firm. The plan cost 8 million baht or around US$ 500,000 (*Business in Thailand*, December 1981: 60). The primary aim of the Plan was to provide both government and private enterprises with policy guidelines for future growth. The Plan also served as a framework for feasibility studies and the development of master plans and detailed plans for selected areas.

The Plan recommended that the Tourism Organization of Thailand (TOT) should be given more authority to guide and control the activities of the private sector, and in 1979 a Parliamentary Act established the Tourism Authority of Thailand (TAT) for this purpose, headed by an army officer who had been the Director of TOT. The act provided TAT with the power to invest in the development of infrastructure and other tourism-related facilities, as well as to declare suitable areas reserved for tourism development (Rojanasoonthon, 1982).

On the juridical side, the National Executive Council Announcement (N. 281 B.E. 2515) introduced the Tourism Promotion Law, a guarantee against nationalization, against state monopoly of the sale of products similar to those produced by a promoted person, and against price controls. It also gives foreign companies permission to bring in foreign nationals to undertake feasibility studies, and foreign technicians and experts to work on promoted projects. It permits foreign companies to own land needed to carry out promoted activities, and to take or remit abroad foreign currency. Furthermore, the law provides an exemption or reduction of import duties and business taxes on imported machinery and a reduction of import duties and business taxes up to 90 per cent on imported raw materials and components (United Nations/ESCAP, 1980: 99). With combined efforts favouring invest-ment, tourism in Thailand became an economy of scale producing a wide range of services whose contribution to national income gradually became significant.

As regards its performance, two main observations can be made. First, in absolute terms the growth of the tourist industry has been spectacular. Earnings from tourism rose from about 200 million baht in 1960 to over 37 billion baht in 1986. Second, compared to other major commodities, tourism has been since the mid-1970s the major foreign exchange earner, overtaking rice in 1982. From the second half of the 1970s, the contributions of primary products such as rice, rubber, tapioca and tin have declined while those of tourism and manufactured products have increased. Data on the performance of the tourist industry are presented in Table 5.1 for the period 1960 to 1986. Data on the comparison between tourism and other major export products are shown in Table 5.2.

Table 5.1
International Tourist Arrivals and Gross Foreign Exchange Revenues, 1960–82

Year	Visitors	Annual change (%)	Million baht (current values)	Annual change (%)
1960	81,340	–	196	–
1961	107,754	32.47	250	27.55
1962	130,809	21.40	310	24.00
1963	195,076	49.13	394	28.00
1964	211,924	8.64	430	9.14
1965	225,025	6.18	506	17.67
1966	285,117	26.70	754	49.01
1967	335,845	17.79	952	26.26
1968	377,262	12.33	1,220	28.15
1969	469,784	24.52	1,770	45.08
1970	628,671	33.82	2,175	22.88
1971	638,738	1.60	2,214	1.79
1972	820,758	28.50	2,718	22.76
1973	1,037,737	26.44	3,457	27.19
1974	1,107,392	6.71	3,852	11.43
1975	1,180,075	6.56	4,538	17.81
1976	1,098,442	–6.92	3,990	–12.08
1977	1,220,672	11.13	4,607	15.46
1978	1,453,839	19.10	8,894	93.05
1979	1,591,455	9.47	11,232	26.29
1980	1,858,801	16.80	17,765	58.16
1981	2,015,615	8.44	21,455	20.77
1982	2,218,429	10.06	23,879	11.30
1983	2,191,003	–1.24	25,025	4.80
1984	2,346,709	7.11	27,317	9.16
1985	2,438,270	3.90	31,768	16.29
1986	2,818,092	15.58	37,321	17.48

Sources: Immigration Division, Police Department and Tourism Organisation of Thailand, in: *The Investor*, September 1976; Ayudhaya et al (1982); Tourism Authority of Thailand.

Table 5.2
Gross Revenues from Tourism and Major Export Items, 1970–86
(million baht, current values)

Year	Tourism	Rice	Rubber	Tapioca	Tin	Textiles products	Integrated circuits
1970	2,175	2,516	2,252	1,223	1,618	–	–
1971	2,214	2,908	2,286	1,240	1,569	–	–
1972	2,085	4,437	2,781	1,547	1,664	–	–
1973	3,393	4,573	3,598	2,035	2,537	–	–
1974	3,852	9,778	6,078	3,757	3,836	–	–
1975	4,538	5,848	5,071	3,449	4,538	–	–
1976	3,990	8,609	5,280	7,512	5,280	–	–
1977	4,608	13,428	6,122	7,706	4,541	–	–
1978	8,894	10,425	8,030	10,892	7,229	6,800	–
1979	11,232	15,546	12,346	9,906	9,527	8,795	–
1980	17,265	19,562	12,399	14,836	11,347	4,755	6,193
1981	21,455	26,367	10,840	16,446	9,091	12,531	6,221
1982	23,879	22,504	9,496	19,869	7,773	14,049	5,930
1983	25,025	20,157	11,787	15,387	5,623	14,351	5,829
1984	27,317	25,932	13,004	16,600	5,280	19,155	7,352
1985	31,768	22,524	13,567	14,968	5,647	25,575	8,248
1986	37,321	20,315	15,116	19,086	–	31,268	11,640

Notes: 1. A comparison with the data presented in Table 5.1, column 4 shows some marginal inconsistencies due to the use of several sources;
2. (–) = not available.

Sources: Ayudhya et al (1982); Tourism Authority of Thailand.

It must be kept in mind that the data on foreign exchange earnings from tourism are obtained from the Tourism Authority of Thailand, whose method of calculation leaves much to be desired. Revenues from tourism are calculated by multiplying the average length of stay by the average expenditure per person per day. Such indicators are obtained through periodic surveys. Net revenues for 1982 to 1986 show that on average around 25 per cent must be deducted from gross revenues to be accurate (Tourism Authority of Thailand, 1986: 59). This 25 per cent covers expenditures related to material imports. In addition, there are other costs, including promotional campaigns, tourism administration and the maintenance of a tourist police force. The data presented in the tables are thus estimated of gross revenues.

On the basis of estimated gross revenues, it may be observed that growth was steady between 1960 and 1970, with the exception of 1964 and 1965 owing to the uncertainty surrounding US policies in the region after the death of John F. Kennedy. The growth trend picked up again with the decision under the Johnson Administration to escalate the war in Vietnam. From 1970 to 1975 the growth trend was irregular, probably owing to the peace negotiations between Vietnam and the US and the gradual withdrawal of US forces from the region. In 1976 the industry went into a steep decline with a negative growth rate of 12 per cent. The market picked up again in 1977. Between 1977 and 1986, there were two slow years — 1983 and 1984. In 1985 and 1986 the industry began to regain momentum. The reasons for this fluctuation will be discussed later, in combination with a disaggregate analysis of the tourist market.

As Table 5.2 shows, in contrast to revenues from other major export products, there is a major shift on the export side of the current account, showing a decline in primary products and an increase of tourism and other manufactured products, i.e. a diversified structure of export earnings. Comparative data on export earnings, presented in Table 5.2 covering the period from 1970 to 1986, were obtained from the Tourism Authority of Thailand and show only the major categories of foreign exchange earnings. As a traditional export item, earnings from rice were irregular from 1970 to 1976. They picked up again in 1977 to 1981, but have remained stagnant from 1982 onwards. The same is true of rubber and tin. By contrast, after being equal to rubber in 1970, tourism earned twice as much as rubber in 1986. As for textile products, after an irregular take-off in the late 1970s, earnings come quite close to those of tourism in 1986. Integrated circuits, which emerged in 1980 in a position half as important as tin, overtook tin in 1986. Overall, the export structure of Thailand shows an increasing trend towards diversification and a shift from primary products to manufactured goods and services, in which tourism plays a significant role.

In summary, it may be stated that during the initial phase of tourism development, emphasis on short-term objectives of profit maximizing from the R & R market led to an erratic pattern of investment and an excessive supply of accommodation and entertainment facilities. Such investment created an expansion of production and employment in the service sector which could not be easily reduced once earnings from the US military declined. Owing to the vested interests of members of the ruling class and foreign investors in entertainment and hotel facilities, there was a need to integrate tourism more firmly into a wider strategy of economic growth which would maintain the momentum of the R & R period. Hence, tourism became incorporated into the export-diversification strategy in order to achieve export-led growth, a strategy which widened the R & R market to a more international market.

Tourism Investment and Prostitution

Apart from the involvement of large-scale capital in 'personal services' and the hotel business, two additional problems internal to the tourist industry may be identified as contributing to the gradual and systematic incorporation of sexual services in tourism in Thailand: (1) the nature of hotel services as a consumer good; and (2) biased investment policy.

A classic problem for the hotel industry is the matching of supply and demand. Capital in the hotel industry is generally fixed with a long pay-back period of ten to twelve years (Bukart and Medlik, 1976: 149–50). The supply of rooms is inflexible and cannot be easily adjusted to demand. Room services are therefore perishable as they cannot be stored for resale. Furthermore, maintenance costs and depreciation continue even if rooms are not occupied. Even when supply and demand are matched, tourism is seasonal. Therefore, most hotels have to find a formula to maintain a certain rate of occupancy during low seasons in order to have a favourable rate of return on capital. The usual formula includes: (1) offering a differentiated structure of room rates which provides discounts to group services for conferences and purposes other than leisure; and (2) entering long-term contractual arrangements with tour operators by leasing out rooms at discount rates. Within this general situation, the capacity to cope with market fluctuation depends on how a hotel is financed and what kind of relationship it shares with third parties such as airlines, tour operators and travel agencies.

In the case of Thailand, investment policy in the initial phase of tourism development aimed primarily at stimulating the rapid construction of hotels to meet the demands of the R & R market. Investment policy tends to favour large-scale operations, while small-scale investors seek financial support from commercial banks. Market fluctuation thus affects hotels differently. When the market declined in the mid-1970s, hotels with short-term and high-interest commercial loans could not afford price-cutting to maintain high occupancy. They were forced to close, to lease out rooms to tour operators, or to disaggregate the unit of room service from a period of twenty-four hours to shorter periods of three to six hours. Special rates such as 'wash-up' rates are offered to clients who need the room not for accommodation as such, but for prostitution.

According to official sources, in 1978 at least 248 hotels in Bangkok hosted prostitution as a means to increase gross income (Thai Delegation, 1985). Joint-venture hotel companies have closer contact with airlines, travel agencies and tourist associations throughout the world and enjoy high rates of occupancy. For example, during 1976 when Thailand experienced a drastic decline in tourist arrivals, first-class and deluxe hotels had occupancy rates of over 70 per cent while second- and third-class hotels recorded rates of occupancy of 67.02 per cent and 47.11 per cent respectively (Ayudhya et al., 1982: 44).

Rather than finding ways to help small-scale enterprises, investment policy during the National Tourism Development Plan period favoured joint ventures and large-scale operations. Such ventures benefited from the financial support of international and national development finance institutions. These institutions provide them with equity investment and long-term loans as seed capital with favourable lending terms in addition to investment privileges which can save projects up to 20 per cent of their costs (Nananukool, 1980: 36).

The Bangkok Bank estimates the cost per room including construction, facilities and decoration as 1.2 million baht or around US$ 60,000 for a deluxe hotel, 1 million baht or US$ 50,000 for a first-class hotel in Bangkok, and US$ 40,000 in provincial resorts, and US$ 25,000 for a second-class hotel Bangkok (Nananukool, 1980: 33–41). In 1960 there were 959 rooms in Bangkok spread out in some five first-class hotels and none in provincial towns. During the 1970s, some 17 deluxe and first-class hotels were expanded or constructed in Bangkok alone. Sizes of these hotels range between 184 rooms to 816 rooms, and most are under the management of international hotel chains (*Business in Thailand*, December, 1980: 42; Rojanasoonthon, 1982). In 1981, the total of first-class and luxury rooms had increased to over 27,000 rooms; over 12,000 of which were in Bangkok and the rest in four major tourist resorts, namely Pattaya, Chiangmai, Songkhla/Hat Yai, and Phu Ket. Construction of first-class and luxury rooms continued to expand. In Bangkok, the number of first-class and deluxe rooms rose from 12,000 in 1982 to over 22,000 in 1986. At present, Thailand has a total room capacity of about 116,997 rooms, including all types of accommodation (Tourism Authority of Thailand, 1986: 66).

The Tourism Authority of Thailand (TAT) listed some ten major tourism development projects implemented during the 1970s, including the construction and expansion of some 17 deluxe hotels with a total of over 9,000 rooms (Rojanasoonthon, 1982). Compared to the total number of luxury and first-class rooms, the number of rooms classified under the category of development projects was significant. The classification of these hotels as development projects suggests that state and international public funds are involved. Notwithstanding the general profitability of the hotel business in Thailand and supportive state policies, in general local investors are also attracted to hotels to shelter income from other sources, benefiting from the appreciation of land values of adjacent property (Nananukool, 1980). There has been a race towards investment both to benefit from the appreciation of land values as well as to secure state subsidies.

As regards foreign investment, direct investment by transnational enterprises is quite small given the slow accrual of returns from hotels to developers and given the unpredictable nature of demand in tourism. As shown in Table 5.3, there was an initial participation by foreign enterprises in the Thai

Table 5.3
Transnational Hotels Foreign Exchange Inflow–Outflow (1969–79)
(million baht, current values)

Year	Inflow (+)	Outflow (−)	Net flow
1969	*	226,848	− 226,848
1970	348,121	*	+ 348,121
1971	*	102,000	− 102,000
1972	2,424,499	1,391,051	+ 1,033,448
1973	13,472,662	4,652,101	+ 8,820,561
1974	*	2,444,669	− 2,444,669
1975	*	2,705,192	− 2,705,192
1976	*	2,202,082	− 2,202,082
1977	n.a.	n.a.	n.a.
1978	n.a.	n.a.	n.a.
1979	*	14,000,000	14,000,000

Notes: 1. * = zero;
2. n.a. = not available;
3. Figure for 1979 is rounded up in original source;
4. Rate of exchange: (1969) US$1 = 20.897 baht; (1979) US$1 = 20.149 baht. The lowest rate during this period is 20.336 in 1978 and the highest is 20.9892 in 1970, 1971, 1972. (*Source: IMF International Financial Statistics*, Volume 37, 1984.)

Source: Ayudhya, et al (1982).

hotel sector. Between 1970 and 1973 the total accumulated value of foreign investment in hotels amounted to 16.2 million baht at current value (or a total share equal to some 80 luxury and first-class rooms at current costs). After 1973, capital inflow from transnational hotel chains ceased. Hotel expansion in 1977 and 1978 absorbed most of the cash outflow of international hotel chains and therefore there was no expatriation of profits during these years. Outflow resumed in 1979, totalling 14 million baht in the form of interest, dividends and management fees. It may be noted that between 1969 and 1979 there was an outflow in every year except 1970, and that outflow exceeded inflow in six out of nine years.

Between 1969 and 1979, capital invested by transnational hotel chains in the Thai hotel sector constituted less than 1 per cent of total investment in the sector. However, while direct investment is a marginal form of TNC involvement, involvement through management contract appears to have been more common. According to Ayudhya et al. (1982), there are 20 luxury/first-class hotels that are 100 per cent Thai owned while 15 hotels are joint ventures under the management of transnational hotel chains. Management fees average 17 per cent of gross operating profits and in some cases reach 23 per cent (McQueen, 1983). The fact that TNCs ceased to invest in hotel construction and began to opt for management contracts may indicate that this mode of operation is clearly much more advantageous. In view of the unpredictable nature of demand in tourism, management contracts ensure profitability without investment risks.

Given the favourable position of large-scale enterprises under TNC management contracts, small-scale enterprises must find a formula to make their operations profitable. They tend to turn to tour operators as a third party to supply guests. Tour operators bring in about 60 per cent of the total number of international visitors to Thailand and get large discounts — up to 25 per cent or more off regular prices (*Business in Thailand*, March 1979). They also play a crucial role in promoting local attractions. Small-scale hotels cannot afford to bypass tour operators, because they are dependent on the inflow of tourists and on the promotion of local entertainment (which has a dynamic function in attracting tourists). At the end of the 1970s, there were about 270 travel agents and tour operators in the Bangkok area, of which the largest 20 handle about 70 per cent of incoming overseas business (*Bangkok Bank Monthly Review*, August 1978; Ayudhya et al., 1982).

The shift in TNC involvement, from direct investment to management contracts in the hotel sector, has been accompanied by their growing involvement in tourism-related business and tour operation. Like management contracts, tour operation, which requires minimal fixed capital investment and uses mainly cheap local labour, can be highly profitable. According to Ayudhya et al. (1982) there are ten major transnational tour companies registered in Thailand, whose total revenues have increased from 2.5 million baht in 1975 to 32 million baht in 1979, a twelve-fold increase over a five-year period. It is also noted that the accuracy of registered income is open to question since tax evasion is common and much of the intakes goes unrecorded. Foreign-owned tour operators share established links with airlines and hotel reservation systems. They also benefit from the matching of cash flows and the ability to acquire sufficient working capital, and can squeeze out smaller competitors through price-cutting.

Competition among tour operators and a dearth of regulations have allowed tour operators to include more and more services of a personal nature, in particular sexual services, to give their packages particular appeal. As previously pointed out, the inclusion of sexual services in tourism initially stemmed from attempts by small hotels to compete with larger firms. However, once the practice was instituted, larger hotels were compelled to follow, particularly since the rate of accumulation by hotels accommodating prostitution is very high.

One example is the case of a first-class hotel, the Grace Hotel. With 104 rooms built in 1966 to host US visitors on R & R, the hotel was transformed in the 1970s into a 'sex farm' whose services were contracted to tour operators from Switzerland and Germany, and to visitors from the Middle East and the Asia–Pacific region (*Business in Thailand*, November 1981: 44). In 1966, the original capital of the Grace Hotel was 8 million baht, in 1982 64 million baht. Its capacity is now 350 rooms (*Bangkok Post*, 29 October 1982).

Although it is often remarked that hosting prostitution is a practice found mainly in small second-class hotels, my observations during fieldwork indicate that it can also be found in some first-class and luxury hotels, in which prostitutes are disguised as sophisticated escorts whose educational background is high and whose ethnic and national origins are very diverse. They include Europeans, Americans, Australians and non-Thai Asian nationals. The question is not whether luxury hotels host prostitution, but whom they host as prostitutes.

At present, there are about 20 legally registered escort agencies and some 50 small and illegal operations (*Thailand Development Newsletter*, Vol. 4, (1), 1986: 18). Data obtained from advertisements in a number of first-class and luxury hotels show that escorting is an established international business:

> Service by well-trained and educated escorts. Our girls are known for their beauty. European, American and Australian escorts are available on request. We have all ages for all occasions.

> Reach for the exclusive connection, the High Society, whenever the occasion arises, on any day when executive-type escorts and hostesses are desired. Academics, professionals, corporate executives, senior officials and businessmen the world over know and find the services we offer both useful and convenient. Reasonably educated, intelligently acceptable and readily communicative. And you can expect a high level of fair play, discipline and discretion, as you could from the most reliable and reputable agency in Bangkok and Singapore. We give you a combined total of fourteen years' experience and confidence. (*Look East*, Vol. 15 (8), 1984)

The rate of accumulation of escort agencies is quite high, as investment and labour requirements are limited, i.e. a small office with a telephone can be run by one person. Income is divided between the agency and the escort on a 50–50 basis and can approach US$ 300 per night for qualified escorts such as top models (*Thailand Development Newsletter*, Vol. 4 (1), 1986: 18). Declaration of income and taxation are dubious and almost impossible to control since the agency does not directly employ escorts. While it is not known how many escort agencies are linked with hotels functionally or financially, it is clear that hotels generally assume part of the responsibility of marketing for escort agencies.

As far as the provision of sexual services is concerned, the incorporation of sexual services in hotels can be either direct or indirect. Direct participation is found in the case of sex package tours which offer sexual service as part of the package. In this case,the tour operator is affiliated with an air carrier and a hotel through a two to three year contract, and possibly has limited financial investment in the hotel as well. Tour operators offer a package through which transport and accommodation are paid for in a lump sum, while sexual services are made available in the hotel. Prices for sexual services are set in advance in tour brochures. They vary according to the unit of sale (time periods of six hours) and the age of the woman. Prices decrease as more units of sale are purchased (e.g. 12 hours, 18 hours, 24 hours, or one week). According to local sources, this form of participation is limited and involves no more than five to ten first- and second-class hotels in Bangkok.

Indirect participation is found in the case of first-class and luxury hotels which only provide information to clients on sexual and personal services available in entertainment places outside the hotel. They also provide information on group visits to entertainment establishments offering sexual services (massage parlours and night-clubs), and on escort services. They charge a 'joiner fee' for visitors who bring in female guests. Indirect participation is practised by the majority of hotels.

It may be stated that the lucrativeness of the business has converted the ad-hoc method of hosting prostitution in hotels to recoup losses from market fluctuation into a systematic measure for maximizing profit involving tour operators (local and foreign) and a large number of hotels that directly or indirectly participate in hosting prostitution. All parties have a share in the business. The state benefits from a room tax of up to 16 per cent and from taxes on entertainment that can reach 16.5 per cent (*Business in Thailand*, March 1979: 44). Hotel management companies enjoy high percentages of gross-operating profits when their rooms are fully utilized. Tour operators benefit from commissions and other direct gains and the investor gets a high rate of return on the invested capital which enables reinvestment and expansion.

Against this background, the relationship between tourism and prostitution can no longer be seen only as an issue of employment alternatives available to women, but also as an issue related to the internal structure of the tourist industry and to vested interests of a financial nature.

Foreign Visitors and the Defence of Prostitution

Since the 1960s the number of foreign visitors to Thailand has grown significantly both in number and diversification. As shown in Table 5.1, the total number of tourist arrivals rose from over 80,000 in 1960 to over 2.8 million in 1986. The data include all arrivals, according to the following definition of the tourist:

Any person visiting Thailand for any reason other than to exercise remunerated activity within the country. The person must stay at least 24 hours but not longer than 60 days and the purpose of the journey can be classified under one of the following criteria: leisure (recreation, health, holiday, study, religion and sport); business, family; mission; meeting. It refers also to arrivals by sea with overnight stay at accommodation establishments ashore and excludes cruise passengers who spend overnight on board. Direct transit passengers who do not pass through immigration are not included. (Tourism Authority of Thailand, 1985: 8)

It is not possible to disaggregate the data into business travel and leisure travel. Furthermore, a precise assessment of the number of visitors who come to Thailand exclusively for sexual entertainment cannot be made for the following reasons. Visits to entertainment places which provide sexual services can be carried out in parallel with other activities, such as business, missions, conventions, etc., or can be 'incidental' to sight-seeing. Although there are tour operators who offer sexual services as an inclusive element of the package, not all tour operators do so. Tourists travelling through the agency of the tour operators are not necessarily sex tourists. Nevertheless, several indicators may be used to show the relationship between tourism and prostitution, namely the changing trends of market shares and their sex ratio, and the advertising campaigns.

Data on international tourist arrivals by region of origin are shown in Table 5.4. Looking at the major markets, it may be observed that between 1973 and 1986 the share of the US market in grand total has declined from 15.56 per cent in 1973 to less than 7 per cent in 1986. The Western European market share fluctuated between 19.53 per cent in 1984 at its lowest point and 31.30 per cent in 1976 at its highest point. The Asia–Pacific market rose steadily from 56 per cent to 65 per cent during this period. The Middle Eastern market rose from an insignificant share of less than 1 per cent in 1973 to over 3 per cent in 1986. These trends reflect the diversification of travel and trade to Thailand in the last few decades, showing an increasing influx from countries of the Asian continent and the Middle East, and the decreasing significance of the US and Western Europe.

Disaggregated data by countries within the Western European region and the Asia–Pacific region are presented in Tables 5.5 and 5.6 respectively. Table 5.5 shows that France, Germany, Italy and the United Kingdom constitute over half of the total Western European market. It is not possible to show how much of the percentage constitutes tourists who come for sexual services. However, as sex tourism does not occur exclusively through the agency of sex package tour operators but also occurs in the form of R&R for employees of TNCs in the Asian continent and the Middle East (oil fields, oil rigs, mining industry), the expansion and contraction of some segments of the Western European market may correspond to fluctuations in overseas employment, in addition to the usual change in preferences. As regards the data shown in Table 5.6 on the Asia–Pacific market, it may be noted that Japan and Malaysia constitute the major shares. Overall, Japan and Australia have a decreasing market share, while those of Singapore, Malaysia and India are growing.

Table 5.7 shows the sex ratio of visitors from 1977 to 1986. In general, there are more male than female tourists. On average, the sex ratio is 2:1 in favour of men. Since 1980, the ratio of male to female visitors has increased even more, with 73 per cent of the total number of international tourist arrivals in 1986 being male. If the high male sex ratio is associated with sex tourism, then the trend is increasing rather than decreasing.

Throughout the second half of the 1970s, tour operators based in Japan and Western European countries marketed cheap tours which included the sexual

Table 5.4
International Tourist Arrivals by Region, 1973–86

Year	Grand Total	%	USA	%	Western Europe	%	Middle East	%	Asia/Pacific	%
1973	1,037,737	100	161,444	15.56	264,774	25.51	8,297	0.80	579,598	55.85
1974	1,107,392	100	156,818	14.16	284,860	25.72	8,912	0.80	631,811	58.05
1975	1,180,075	100	116,190	9.85	324,336	27.48	11,790	1.00	699,269	59.26
1976	1,098,442	100	116,656	10.62	343,812	31.30	15,780	1.44	584,778	53.24
1977	1,220,672	100	124,082	10.17	350,616	28.72	25,750	2.11	677,441	55.50
1978	1,453,839	100	131,449	9.04	441,912	30.40	37,181	2.56	789,052	54.27
1979	1,591,455	100	114,595	7.20	495,321	31.12	43,604	2.74	882,215	55.43
1980	1,858,801	100	115,348	6.21	496,399	26.71	58,954	3.17	1,125,537	60.55
1981	2,015,615	100	119,895	5.95	499,757	24.79	67,792	3.36	1,254,071	62.22
1982	2,218,429	100	130,772	5.89	472,918	21.32	74,435	3.36	1,473,861	66.44
1983	2,191,003	100	140,401	6.41	443,035	20.22	78,226	3.57	1,459,304	66.60
1984	2,246,709	100	155,326	6.62	458,303	19.53	101,108	4.31	1,557,310	66.36
1985	2,438,270	100	171,247	7.02	488,347	20.03	104,813	4.30	1,595,353	65.43
1986	2,818,092	100	196,429	6.97	591,114	20.98	110,619	3.93	1,827,968	64.87

Definition: Western Europe includes Austria, Belgium, Denmark, Finland, France, West Germany, Italy, Netherlands, Norway, Portugal, Spain, Sweden, Switzerland, United Kingdom; Middle East includes Israel, Kuwait, Saudi Arabia, others; Asia/Pacific includes ASEAN countries, Australia, China, Hong Kong, Japan, South Korea, New Zealand, Taiwan ROC, India, Bangladesh, Nepal, Pakistan, Sri Lanka.

Source: Tourism Authority of Thailand.

Table 5.5
Tourist Arrivals from Western Europe, 1973–86

Year	Total Western Europe	%	France	%	West Germany	%	Italy	%	Netherlands	%	United Kingdom	%
1973	264,774	100	44,974	16.99	62,673	23.67	19,974	7.54	12,167	4.60	58,304	22.02
1974	284,860	100	42,572	14.94	69,394	24.36	23,814	8.36	12,769	4.48	65,444	22.97
1975	324,336	100	46,986	14.49	78,150	24.10	31,069	9.58	15,019	4.63	76,407	23.56
1976	343,812	100	48,540	14.12	85,956	25.00	28,498	8.29	20,399	5.93	72,777	21.17
1977	350,616	100	51,115	14.58	79,061	22.55	31,698	9.04	19,119	5.45	71,959	20.52
1978	441,912	100	64,002	14.48	91,452	20.69	48,737	11.03	24,427	5.53	98,485	22.29
1979	495,321	100	72,528	14.64	97,848	19.75	47,366	9.56	24,419	4.93	128,408	25.92
1980	496,399	100	72,095	14.52	95,535	19.25	42,053	8.47	25,152	5.07	138,808	27.96
1981	499,757	100	70,577	14.12	89,130	17.83	45,585	9.12	23,271	4.66	160,051	32.03
1982	472,918	100	64,618	13.66	84,94	17.97	40,474	8.56	23,226	4.91	152,916	32.33
1983	443,035	100	51,017	11.52	87,791	19.82	36,812	8.31	26,211	5.92	143,299	32.34
1984	458,303	100	60,500	13.20	95,705	20.88	38,282	8.35	28,348	6.19	133,209	29.07
1985	488,347	100	71,984	14.74	99,768	20.43	43,331	8.87	29,132	5.97	124,964	25.59
1986	591,114	100	100,439	16.99	119,441	20.21	52,039	8.80	34,061	5.76	147,221	24.91

Source: Tourism Authority of Thailand.

Table 5.6
Tourist Arrivals from Asia and the Pacific, 1973–86

Year	Total Asia/Pacific	%	Australia	%	India	%	Japan	%	Singapore	%	Malaysia	%
1973	579,598	100	48,222	8.32	18,898	3.26	151,947	26.22	31,754	5.48	190,827	32.92
1974	631,811	100	75,800	12.00	21,765	3.44	132,660	21.00	39,638	6.27	197,508	31.26
1975	699,269	100	78,907	11.28	22,021	3.15	146,986	21.02	46,531	6.65	227,826	32.58
1976	584,778	100	80,470	13.76	20,544	3.51	150,464	25.73	41,833	7.15	161,183	27.56
1977	677,441	100	69,465	10.25	21,300	3.14	173,988	25.68	44,273	6.54	271,412	40.06
1978	789,052	100	67,467	8.55	32,660	4.14	193,661	24.54	51,423	6.52	243,432	30.85
1979	882,215	100	61,720	7.00	49,227	5.58	200,333	22.71	60,652	6.87	254,515	28.85
1980	1,125,537	100	64,174	5.70	66,744	5.93	225,433	20.03	67,595	6.01	402,513	35.76
1981	1,254,071	100	68,015	5.42	83,109	6.63	214,628	17.11	86,381	6.89	446,657	35.62
1982	1,473,861	100	72,089	4.89	85,486	5.80	228,092	15.48	107,016	7.26	558,284	37.88
1983	1,459,304	100	73,295	5.02	108,408	7.43	223,614	15.32	120,879	8.28	576,116	39.48
1984	1,557,310	100	78,334	5.03	120,074	7.71	221,945	14.25	142,308	9.14	592,472	38.04
1985	1,593,353	100	92,813	5.83	128,140	8.04	221,485	13.90	159,608	10.02	554,979	34.83
1986	1,827,968	100	94,662	5.18	119,539	6.54	259,381	14.19	194,068	10.62	652,913	35.72

Source: Tourism Authority of Thailand.

services of Thai women. Generally, such sex package tours are purchased on an individual basis, but there is evidence that these tours were at one time sponsored by large companies and subsidiaries who provided them to their workers as a form of fringe benefit (Association of Anti-Prostitution Activities, March 1984). Sex package tours purchased on an individual basis were marketed in the Netherlands, Norway, West Germany, and the United Kingdom in the 1970s, and are still marketed in the 1980s, although less explicitly.

Table 5.7
Male and Female International Tourist Arrivals (percentages), 1977–86

Year	Male	Female
1977	66.02	33.98
1978	66.76	33.24
1979	69.21	30.39
1980	71.13	28.87
1981	70.34	29.66
1982	70.51	29.49
1983	70.21	29.79
1984	71.32	28.68
1985	71.66	28.34
1986	73.19	26.81

Source: Ayudhya et al (1982); Tourism Authority of Thailand.

At the end of the 1970s, visitors from Singapore, Malaysia and the Middle East became a substantial part of the total number of visitors. Throughout the 1970s, economic growth in these countries produced a new class of wealthy business executives who developed new tastes in leisure consumption and who became a significant market for the leisure industry (*Asian Business*, March 1984). With such an industry already developed, Thailand became a centre of attraction. According to a survey on leading tour operators in Bangkok, 90 per cent of visitors from the Middle East were men coming for the night life (*Business in Thailand*, January 1979). In so far as Singaporians and Malaysians are concerned, the problem of sex tourism and the spread of venereal diseases was at one point a source of irritation between the governments concerned, particularly between Malaysia and Thailand (*Far Eastern Economic Review*, 10 November 1983).

As a tourist attraction, prostitution is explicitly portrayed in advertising as a major instrument of marketing. As Uzzell (1984) argues, whether the message is implicit or explicit tourism advertisements provide a range of tools with which fantasy, meaning and identity can be created and constructed. Advertising on tourism and prostitution may be categorized into two types: (1) information provided by international tour operators to potential clients at the place of purchase (travel bureaux); and (2) information provided by the Thai business community to potential clients on the spot.

In the advertising campaigns of tour operators, fantasy and meaning centre around East–West differences, emphasizing the following: (1) the sexual availability of Thai women determined by the law of the market and local sexual norms: (2) the significance of male sexual satisfaction through the domination of females; and (3) the justification of prostitution by poverty, charity and curiosity. In the local campaign, emphasis is placed on female sexuality as an asset in the tourist venture and on its significance for national development and per capita income.

The following is an example of an advertisement by Rosie Reisen of West Germany:

> Thailand is a world full of extremes and the possibilities are unlimited . . . especially when it comes to girls. Still it appears to be a problem for visitors in Thailand to find the right places where they can indulge in unknown pleasures. It is frustrating to have to ask in broken English where you can pick up pretty girls. Rosie has done something about this. For the first time in history, you can book a trip to Thailand with erotic pleasures included in the price.[2]

Other advertisements for sex tours include the following.[3] (1) 'Slim, sun-burnt and sweet, they love the white man in an erotic and devoted way. They are master of the art of making love by nature, an art that we Europeans do not know' (Life Travel, Switzerland); (2) 'many girls from the sex world come from the poor northeastern region of the country and from the slums of Bangkok. It has become a habit that one of the nice looking daughters goes into the business in order to earn money for the poor family . . . you can get the feeling that taking a girl here is as easy as buying a package of cigarettes . . . little slaves who give real Thai warmth' (Kanita Kamha, Netherlands); (3) 'From Munich to Melbourne, the name Pat Pong evokes the image of go-go bars and massage parlours. As a sociological phenomenon, Pat Pong ought to be seen if not sampled' (Berlitz Travel Guide); or (4) 'there is real equality in Thailand, and not here in our part of the world where a man is lawless when in conflict with a woman. In Thailand, it is the market mechanism that rules, if there is a need somebody will emerge to satisfy this need' (Scan-Thai Travellers' Club, Norway). Less explicit examples of such marketing strategies include: (5) 'Bangkok is a captivating city, active, even at night . . . and the publicity about the famous massage parlours can only be tried out'; and (6) 'Taste the Orient, exhaust the charms of Thailand' (Vacances 2000, France).

Within the local business community, Thai women are portrayed as an asset that could lose its value owing to the fickle sexual tastes of rich clients. For example: 'The present favourable situation (of the Thai tourist industry) could easily change, for there are many alternative destinations for the tourist traffic. Increasing numbers of Germans have been going to Kenya and the Cameroun. And the Philippines, with their pleasant climate, fine beaches, cheaper beer, and other delights in every shape, size and colour could easily take a large share of Thailand's tourist trade' (*Business in Thailand*, January 1979: 124–5). Business journals also encourage visitors to visit newly opened tourist resorts in provincial areas where local residents have not been too receptive to tourists. For example: 'Everyone who has ever travelled widely in Thailand knows that indiscriminate love-making goes on in every hotel in the land with more enthusiasm in the South (Hai Yai and Phu Ket) . . . Love-making has a place in the Thai way of life too. The only difference is where you do it. The Thai consider love-making as an indoor sport. Foreigners are not so stereotyped' (*Business in Thailand*, March 1979: 11).

Tourist brochures and guides, available locally, explicitly advertise the range of sexual services, quoting addresses and standard prices as well as explaining that body massage is a service for which the woman uses her body, all of it, as an instrument of massage, and that this should not be confused with conventional massage (*Look East*, Vol. 15 (8), 1984).

Government authorities also take part in promotional campaigns. The Thai International airline is notorious for using women in its advertising, stressing female physical attributes and sexual services to attract customers. For example: 'Smooth as silk is a beautifully prepared meal served by a delicious hostess'; 'Some say it's our beautiful wide-bodied DC-10s that cause so many heads to turn at airports throughout the world. We think our beautiful slim-bodied hostesses have a lot to do with it'. Officials also endorse prostitution as a means to promote per capita income. In the words of the director of the Tourism Authority of Thailand: 'Yes, we have to admit that we have prostitution, but it is the same in every country . . . It might be partly true [that tourism encourages prostitution], but prostitution exists mainly because of the state of our economy, because everyone needs to earn their income. If we can create jobs, we can promote per capita income and do away with prostitution' (*Far Eastern Economic Review*, 9 January 1976).

Official endorsement of prostitution can also take the form of active persuasion, as in the case of the implementation of the tourism development master plan in provincial areas. In 1980 in a public speech, a former vice-premier of Thailand — now a well-known banker — encouraged provincial governors to create more sexual establishments as part of the tourism development strategy in the provinces:

> Within the next two years we need money. Therefore, I ask all governors to consider the natural scenery in your provinces, together with some forms of entertainment that some of you might consider disgusting and shameful because we have to consider the jobs that will be created. (*Business in* forms of entertainment should not be prohibited if only because you are morally fastidious. Yet explicit obscenities that may lead to damaging moral consequence should be avoided within a reasonable limit. We must do this because we have to consider the jobs that will be created. (*Business in Thailand*, November 1981: 44; Skronbanek, 1983: 39)

While it is not possible to draw firm conclusions as to how many tourists purchase the sexual services of Thai women, there is a clear interest among all parties (airlines, tour operators, hotels, entertainment places and leading official figures) in promoting prostitution as a tourist attraction.

Of particular importance in this promotional campaign are the discursive elements used in advertising and statements by policy makers which reflect the definition of Thai women as being 'other' than their counterparts elsewhere. The definition of the 'otherness' of Thai women legitimizes the sexual availability of Thai women to non-Thai men while at the same time helping to prevent the moral conscience of potential customers from questioning the legitimacy of sex tourism. In an era when issues related to human rights, women's rights and dignity are highly politicized, sex tourism can only be legitimized by incorporating either the issue of poverty, or the notion of prostitution as a reflection of women's autonomy to make decisions about their own lives and sexual conduct. For clients to overcome their feelings of guilt, prostitution must be defined as part of the culture of poverty, and/or part of a culture which has different moral and sexual terms of reference. Client participation in prostitution is legitimized by the idea of income redistribution, or by the cultural relativity of the exotic which permits them to adopt a non-committal engagement and to use and dispose of the women from whom they seek warmth and sexual satisfaction.[4]

By locating prostitution in the culture of poverty and the exotic, the question of human dignity becomes obscured and neutralized while Thai women become qualified as a 'new pasture' in which local entrepreneurs can invest and make profits, and over which rich clients can exercise their social and economic power by pursuing their sexual fantasies without guilt. Hidden behind the culture of poverty and the glossy image of the exotic is a process of accumulation from prostitutes' labour facilitated by a dubious juridical structure and the direct and indirect participation of members of the ruling class in the recruitment and utilization of prostitutes' labour.

Power and Production in Prostitution

During their 26 years of existence, the tourist and entertainment industries have been operating within an organized legal, financial and administrative framework which provides them with favourable conditions for growth and expansion. By contrast, sexual services are produced on the edge of legal ambiguity. Prostitution is criminalized under the Penal Code. At the same time it is formalized under the law governing industries. Under the Penal Code it is defined as 'a crime of promiscuity'. It is defined as 'personal services' under business law, and as 'special services' by the Police Department. The law recognizes 'personal services' as a business and ensures privileges to investors, and at the same time criminalizes workers in the business. Given the contradiction between the legality of 'personal services' enterprises and the illegality of prostitution, the relations of power and production in prostitution are bound to be complex and diverse.

Social relations of production in prostitution

In his book on the unprotected worker, Harrod (1987) suggests a number of useful guidelines to approach power and production from the perspective of multiple social relations. Harrod distinguishes power at four levels:

> Power in production, manifested by dominant–subordinated relationship within the production process; social power, which has been accrued by groups and class over time; political power as expressed through organizations which have the potential to control distribution and states; world power, which is the ability to extend power on a world scale. (1987: 8)

Power is expressed in a non-unitary way and its operation must be understood within the specific features of the different forms of social relations of production. Such relations bear the following aspects: objective, subjective and institutional. Objective aspects include the material means of production, accrued social power, political power, and the way in which the produce is distributed. Subjective aspects are the basic ethic governing the production process and the world-view of groups in production (consciousness). Institutional aspects include direct domination or the refusal to recognize conflict, and bargaining or the recognition of conflict and the creation of organizations to mediate conflict (Harrod, 1987: 13–14).

The issue of power in prostitution may thus be seen as follows. Power in production involves the dominant position of the pimp and the subordinated position of the prostitute. In Thailand, the pimp as a third party who mediates between clients and prostitutes is highly protected for reasons of class alliance. As previously shown, the initial pimps who offered the sexual services of Thai women to US military servicemen were members of the Thai military. Over the years, the military has accrued social and political power which enables it to control the state apparatus, policy decisions and the means of production in tourism and entertainment.

Police and military officers as well as government officials are known to be involved in hotels, entertainment places and prostitution and in the traffic in Thai women abroad (*Bangkok Post*, 7 November 1983; 19 May 1983). As has been officially stated, the problem of prostitution is very sensitive because it is connected with influential groups:

> Often, the police can't do anything because they know that the men behind the operation of some brothels are those whose pictures are frequently seen in the newspapers, attending big parties with top ranking policemen and government officials. (*Business in Thailand*, November 1982: 48)

A Police Department general gave four main reasons for the connivance of the Prostitution Suppression Act (Plukspongsawalee, 1982: 160), which may be summarized as follows:

1   Many policemen of both high and low rank have some relationship with the

owners of establishments, or in many cases own the establishments themselves. Consequently, many low-ranking honest policemen have been prevented from doing their duty for fear of harassment by their superiors. Petitions to investigate the conduct of certain policemen involved in the business are not taken seriously by the authorities. Those who are accused are usually tipped off and can get away.

2   When arrests are carried out, the women are arrested rather than the business operators, who are often informed in advance and disappear during the raid. They resume their function almost immediately after the raid. Women, on the other hand, are detained for trial. They can be released on bail (often bail money is advanced by their employers). Afterwards they have to work to pay back these loans.

3   During investigations, police officers make no attempt to trace and search for the operators of the business. If operators are caught, they need only to bribe dishonest policemen to look for legal loopholes or errors of facts to release them (they are usually charged with gambling or some other minor offence rather than prostitution).

4   When procurers who force women into prostitution (through trickery, or other means) are caught, they usually negotiate with the women concerned or with the families to pay compensation so that they drop the charges. Even though prostitution and procuring are public crimes which cannot be settled by individual parties, the police mediates to set these people free.

Apart from the involvement of official figures in the business which protects pimps from arrest and penalty, the enforcement of the law is arbitrary. Staged arrests are organized to show to the public that the police is enforcing the law. Older prostitutes are chosen as staged victims of such arrest. They are not bailed out by proprietors, owing to their deteriorating appearance and declining earning capacity. They are then turned over to the state welfare rehabilitation centres (Plukspongsawalee, 1982: 161).

Against this background, it may be stated that power in production in the entertainment industry which provides prostitutes' services is in the hands of an influential group which controls the means of production as well as the enforcement of the law. Law is enforced in such a way that the supply and control of prostitutes are ensured. Within this general pattern of power and domination, there are more specific patterns of social relations with specific effects on the conditions of prostitutes and their consciousness, for example:

1   Relations of confinement affecting mainly children and teenagers who are clothed and fed but receive no (or extremely low) wages;

2   Enterprise labour relations involving established entertainment places which employ 'special service girls' on a monthly or daily wage system, or less established places which employ women as waitresses but pay their wages in the form of a commission from the sale of drinks, rather than wages on a monthly or daily basis;

3   Self-employed labour relations involving escorts and call-girls who need a third party to provide information about their availability and to whom they pay a commission;

4   Primitive labour market relations involving ad-hoc street soliciting. This does not generally involve tourists as clients, since these tend to require a protected environment to negotiate prices and some accountability. The discussion will not include this category.

As regards the relation of confinement, a study conducted by a team from Thammasat University and summarized in the *Bangkok Post* (7 December 1983) found that among rescued child prostitutes (under 14 years of age) the majority were uneducated and came from low-income families from the North, followed by the Central and Northeastern regions. The working hours of the children depend on the places where they work, and can range from a full day to periods ranging between 6 and 13 hours. On average, they serve three customers per day, or maximally 12 to 15. Fresh and attractive children are paid between 50 and 150 baht per customer of which the owner takes a share. Less fortunate children sold into indentureship get a 5 baht allowance per day or as little as 20 baht per week until the debt has been fully covered. They may have days off during menstruation, although some are forced to work even during menstruation.

Rescued child prostitutes face criminal charges and are categorized as 'socially handicapped women'. Although there are on-going discussions about dropping criminal charges against rescued child prostitutes, it is not known how conclusive such discussions will be. Once rescued, child prostitutes are detained in rehabilitation centres where they are offered social and medical services as well as skill training for one year. Severe discipline and humiliating punitive measures are employed to make the prostitute recognize and repent her crime of promiscuity. The objective of such measures is to control the mind and the body and to forge a new identity out of child prostitutes, i.e. that of a chaste and submissive female (Hantrakul, 1983: 17–22). Upon completion of the year in detention, child prostitutes are given an allowance sufficient to make the trip back home. Once released from rehabilitation centres, they face the risk of being pushed back into prostitution, as there is no follow-up by the centres after the children have been released.

Under the relations of confinement in prostitution and under the legal framework which affects them once they are rescued, child prostitutes may be considered as the most powerless of the sex trade workers. The basic ethic governing their work is blatant coercion, violence and inhumanity. Their categorization as 'socially handicapped women' is equally inhumane and perpetuates the alienation they endure in prostitution. Both the legal and institutional practices of rehabilitation deprive them of their right to find their own identity. Rescued from the physical and sexual violence of prostitution, they continue to be subjected to physical, social and psychological violence. Rather than speculating on the kinds of consciousness these children have developed, it is better to stress that coerced repentance hardly changes the conditions of social alienation and isolation. Coerced repentance makes child prostitutes vulnerable to the sex syndicates who follow them and bring them back to prostitution.

As regards enterprise labour relations, the contractual relationship is somewhat less violent. As Harrod points out, under enterprise labour relations there is a direct relationship between the employer and employee within an enterprise, a certain degree of stability and some structure of employment (Harrod, 1987: 16). Such relations are found in the case of women working in massage parlours, bars and night-clubs. The contractual relationship has both objective and subjective dimensions. Objective dimensions include skill training, wage systems and working hours. Subjective dimensions include the ideology of patronage and protection.

In established massage parlours offering body massage and special techniques, employers may select promising workers — particularly young and attractive women — and invest in their skill training to increase their productivity. The price for a massage ranges from 140 to 350 baht per half hour depending on the nature of the services provided (Phongpaichit, 1982: 11). Women's earnings depend on the skills they acquire either through firm subsidies or on their own account, as the usual formula of payment is the distribution of the fees paid by clients in percentages (38 per cent to the masseuse and the rest to the owner of the establishment). In large-scale massage parlours, the woman gets a monthly wage which averages between 3,000 and 4,000 baht, and some medical attention. Earnings from prostitution within the establishment are permitted and some employers demand no cut (Phongpaichit, 1982: 18–21). The combination of the wage of a masseuse and earnings from prostitution can bring the total monthly income of some workers to a maximum of 25,000 baht per month (Phongpaichit, 1982: 19), compared to the average monthly income of a semi-skilled female worker of 840 baht (Tondugai, 1982: 8).

As regards bars and clubs, go-go dancers are usually trained on the job for a period of up to six months. As trainees, they get no wages, earning only a commission on the drinks they are able to persuade customers to buy. In some first-class institutions, a trained go-go dancer receives a monthly or daily wage. Daily wages average 60 baht. Some bars have rooms which are rented out on an hourly basis to clients who wish to buy the services of women within the establishment. If the client wants to take the woman outside the establishment, he is obliged to pay a bar fine. In less established bars, the woman gets a wage on an hourly basis or simply a commission. The gross income of go-go dancers includes the supplement earned from selling sexual services. In some places a fine is imposed on the woman for showing up late for work, e.g. one baht per minute (Truong, 1985a; 1986). There are no paid holidays nor is medical attention provided.

As regards the subjective dimension, in general patronage and protection are manifested by the responsibility taken by the employer to bail out workers when these are arrested. The worker must continue working to pay back the

where he is married to a Thai woman: "A beautiful people — as long as you have money".' Cohen also notes that such disenchanted foreigners often cease to have 'protracted liaisons altogether and entertain a sexual life-style characterized by a constant change of partners, whom they often choose from the fringe of the prostitution scene — girls who arrived only recently, and who are still more innocent, naive and pliant than those with longer experience'.

Conclusion

D'un petit garçon qui pleure
Les trop courtes journées
Et le bonheur impossible
Des vacances éternelles
Demain il n'y aura plus rien.
Il ne restera qu'une mare sans vie.
Une tâche d'océan
Vaccinée de puits de pétrole.
Demain il n'aura plus moyen
D'être un enfant

Jacques Danois, 1977: 11

The Problematic of Prostitution

Breaking away from the common conception of prostitution as promiscuity and vice, this study focuses on the social processes through which female sexuality is incorporated as labour into the sphere of production. The disassociation from the common conception of prostitution as promiscuity and vice is compelled by the finding of gaps in existing analytical frameworks in the social sciences and their effects on policies and strategies for change. The study is not engaged in the prescription of an alternative strategy, but points to areas of conceptual and strategic biases and their implications on prostitutes' lives and work. The study does not endorse an all-encompassing formula for change, but sees the value in sensitizing groups and individuals who are engaged in solving the problem of prostitution and prostitutes at various levels.

The study shows that theoretical explanations which reduce prostitution and sexual relations to biological instincts, or to cultural determinism are ahistorical and selective in their emphasis on the ideological and material basis of prostitution. Explanations based on the political economy of women's labour have adhered to an historical materialist approach to social relations and therefore can ground prostitution in the relations of production and reproduction. However, there remains a number of gaps which are consequential to the understanding of the social relations in prostitution.

Theoretical gaps originate at two levels. Conceptually, there is an ahistorical approach to the conception of the human body, and a conflation of the social and sexual aspects of prostitution. Explanations provided thus far tend to overemphasize the inter-relationship between prostitution and other forms of sexual relations along normative social lines. Similarities between prostitutes and women as a gender are highlighted, while many historical, cultural, economic and political differences are bypassed. The framework for the analysis of the political economy of women's labour has so far not bridged the gap between sexuality and economy. There is a strictly biological level of labour which can and has been incorporated in relations of production, but which has not been adequately dealt with. Also not examined are the diverse social relations in prostitution, their effects on prostitutes and on society at large.

Methodologically, such gaps stem from the tendency to add prostitution to the range of social issues which are pertinent to social movements emerging in defence of a particular interested position (labour emancipation, national emancipation, sexual emancipation or autonomy). Adding prostitution without adding the participation of prostitutes has not encouraged an understanding of prostitution in terms of the differentiated activities it entails and the social relationships embodied within it. This practice has encouraged the projection and assignment of specific qualities (e.g. social evil and disease, bourgeois decadence, male vice) to prostitution. The projection of particular values into prostitution mystifies the nature of the power relations in prostitution. It also facilitates the formulation of simplistic strategies to address complex social problems. Such strategies have been deduced from simplistic definitions which homogenize prostitutes rather than recognize the diversity of activities in prostitution, and of the social relations governing prostitutes' lives and work. Strategies to 'eradicate' and to 'combat' prostitution as a social evil so far have created juridical and social structures which do not achieve the stated purposes and are dis-enabling for prostitutes. They also ignore the role of the state, capital and consumers in the reconstitution of social relations, and in the creation of new forms of prostitution disguised within the leisure and entertainment industry.

Against this background, the present study proposes to disaggregate two main areas which are related to prostitution, namely sexuality and reproduction. Such a disaggregation permits a detailed analysis of the social relations which organize these two areas, showing the content of sexuality and reproduction and the origins of their expression through prostitution. Conclusions about the social position of prostitutes are drawn once the nature of their work, the relations of dominance and control are identified and understood.

Sexual Labour in Prostitution

Historical data show that the ideological base of prostitution tends to vary with social change, exhibiting diverse interpretations of what is natural, holy or criminal in sexual conduct and diverse social relations which organize prostitutes' labour. It is noted that there is an inversion process which occurs at the discursive and cognitive level as peripheral sexual subjects (prostitutes) become incorporated into dominant relations of production (e.g. from moral crime to lawful immorality; from moral crime to social utility and desirability). Given this inversion, it does not seem fruitful to depart from a specific quality attached to prostitution at any given time. It is more useful to examine prostitution from its base (i.e. sexual services under exchange relations), to look at how the nature of such services changes, and to understand the cognitive, institutional and economic conditions of their existence and transformation.

To grasp the content of sexuality and the process whereby it becomes incorporated into economic relations, the study focuses on three main questions: (1) what constitutes sex as a human need; (2) what is the material basis of the relations which organize the satisfaction of this need; and (3) how are these relations related to the relations of production? These questions require the location of the human body in social analysis and the recognition of biological issues as part of social processes.

Based on Foucault's concepts of discourse and power, the study cautions that the human body, its functions and needs cannot be treated as fixed, but must be understood in terms of their historical conception. Surrounding the human body are social interpretations and discursive practices which constitute sexual subjectivity, define sexual needs and construct sexual desire. Sexual subjectivity (the constitution of the sexual subject) operates at two levels of categorization, namely: (1) inter-subjectivity that occurs between groups (male and female, white and black, normal and abnormal, noble and common, bourgeois and working-class); and (2) intra-subjectivity which acts upon the body itself (mind and flesh, carnal and spiritual, chaste and unchaste, sexual and asexual). Through categorization and systematization at the level of cognition, mechanisms of inclusion and exclusion are established at the institutional level which direct human sexual practices. Sexual subjects are products of individual and collective cognition, as well as the operation of this cognition through institutional practices.

It is therefore not possible to presuppose that sexuality consists of an essence which is timeless. Sexual needs, desire and significance are constructed differently and do not manifest themselves in singular forms. In fact, there are conflicting forms of sexual subjectivity. Within the sphere of what is included as normal and universal, particular forms of sexual needs, desire and significance find their legitimacy. Excluded from this sphere is the otherness of the perverse and deviance, which lacks legitimacy, except the legitimacy to be persecuted. The predominance of particular kinds of cognition about sex, their discursive and institutional practices of inclusion and exclusion are bound to particular historical configurations, their social structures and material base.

In this study, Foucault's contribution to the understanding of sexual subjectivity is extended to link the constitution of the sexual subject through discourse, showing their material relevance in the organization of reproduction. identities — products of mechanisms of inclusion and exclusion — as its ideological basis. To show this link, the study breaks down the main elements of reproduction, separates its biological and social aspects, and looks at the social relations which organize them and how these relations are transformed. The main elements of reproduction are distinguished between biological sex (procreation and bodily pleasure) and social maintenance services. The social relations which organize reproduction and sexuality are examined at the level of household, community and state.

women's history and labour history (Walkowitz, 1980; Bujra, 1982; White, 1983a; 1983b; Stoler, 1985) that the wage-labour process has been accompanied by a process which incorporates women into the provision of reproductive services under exchange relations. While the disruption of natural forms of reproduction coincided with the emergence of the wage system and while commercial sex predates the emergence of wage labour, this disruption has been intensified and diversified with the penetration of capitalist relations in the area of reproduction. Rather than producing only use value, reproductive services in prostitution create surpluses that can be extracted by economic agents as well as by the state.

The study suggests that sexuality as a history of ideas about sex cannot be disconnected from concrete practices of the utilization of sexual labour. It is essential to understand how specific discursive elements have emerged, how they are applied, and their relationship with a given form of organization of sexual relations which fulfils certain reproductive functions. It must be recognized that there is a level of labour derived from the utilization of the body — particularly its sexual functions as an instrument. Whereas wage labour in production has been considered as productive, the productivity of sexual services for the purpose of reproduction under wage relations has been concealed by cognitive and institutional structures governing sexuality. This concealment permits an intensification of accumulation in prostitution, which impinges on the right of the state to persecute prostitutes in order to foster and enhance the relation of domination and dependency between them and their employers. Such a relation minimizes the effects of the wage system as a redistributive measure and permits the use of force to discipline sexual workers in order to increase productivity. Furthermore, legal persecution makes the labour process in prostitution fragmented, diversifies social relations of production on the basis of the selective recognition of what is moral and what is immoral and creates a plurality of consciousness among prostitutes. Legal persecution limits the space for resistance, or discounts resistance where space has been created.

Sexual Labour in International Tourism

Having discussed the relationship between sexual subjectivity and economic relations, the study moves on to explore the international dimension of this relationship. Here, the focus is placed on the entry of leisure into the international division of labour, showing how the interplay between discourse, culture and economy has conditioned the integration of developing countries and their female populations into the total structure of production of the leisure industry.

It is observed that the upsurge in the provision of leisure services in industrialized countries in the 1950s and 1960s was related primarily to two factors: (1) post-war economic growth in the West which created surplus income and surplus time through state intervention (holiday time by legislation); and   (2) the response of capital which aimed to absorb surplus income through the production of services utilized during surplus time. The emergence of long-distance leisure travel has been induced by innovations in the fields of air transport and information technology. Such innovations have created an enormous surplus of facilities which cannot be absorbed by the expansion of commerce and government activities alone.

Interest in the profitability of capital investment in the civil aviation industry spurred the dramatic growth of international tourism and its related sub-branches. This profitability was only realizable by two means: (1) the promotion of international tourism to absorb the disposable income of industrialized countries; and   (2) the creation of infrastructure and services at peripheral destinations. Against this background, the social and economic significance of international travel as a leisure activity became highlighted. The concept of tourism was incorporated in discursive practices in scientific and bureaucratic communities, and promoted via international organizations and governments under the guise of its educational and internationalist value. As international leisure travel in itself is an activity constrained by issues related to national sovereignty and priorities, new ideological frontiers had to be created to facilitate its smooth operation. In this connection, the economic potential of tourism became heavily emphasized as a development strategy for peripheral nations. The combination of technological innovations, capital integration and government policies have forged an economic and social doctrine of development. This doctrine has served to mobilize massive development funding to create the needed infrastructure.

A review of studies on the trends in international tourism production shows the significance of the interlocking interests between air carriers, tour operators and hotel companies which led to the formation of a new type of conglomerate specialized in the production of packages of services in tourism and travel. Mass production could only be met with substantial investment in local infrastructure. Such investment has been induced by policies geared towards the forging of tourism into an export-led industry based mainly on the provision of personal services.

Integration provides the conditions for these conglomerates to control the production process through the control of information and knowledge about the market. Information and knowledge are an essential component of international tourism as an 'experience good', i.e. a service to be consumed at the place of destination rather than the place of purchase. Information provided to potential buyers and to local producers of services is essential in synchronizing supply and demand. This entails a division of labour according to which peripheral countries play a passive role in providing the social infrastructure and facilities, with limited control over the process of production and distribution. Intensive efforts are made by local governments to encourage visitors to spend at the destination, in order to maximize earnings.

Given the salient feature of tourism as an 'experience good' which embodies the replication of household-related personal activities in a commercial context (hospitality service, accommodation, rest and psychological fulfilment), considerable emphasis has been placed on personal satisfaction and entertainment. As tourism shares a symbiotic relationship with advertising (which incorporates elements unrelated to tourism and transforms them into tourist products) the impingement of commercial relations on the area of the personal has created a homogenized culture in which the domain of sexuality is particularly emphasized in a fragmented manner. This has affected the ways in which local services are organized and provided.

In the case of Thailand, it has been found that beyond the general features of tourism depicted above, there are additional factors which contribute to the systematic incorporation of sexual services in tourism services. These include the character of gender relations rooted in religion and class structure and the specific geo-political situation of Southeast Asia in the 1960s. The legal persecution of prostitutes occurred almost simultaneously with the legal formalization of the entertainment industry, owing to an investment policy skewed towards capturing the 'Rest and Recreation' market during the Indochina conflict. The duality between the recognition and denial of prostitution, coupled with a massive arrival of US military servicemen, led to a proliferation of forms of prostitution disguised within the entertainment industry. Ad-hoc practices of hosting prostitution gradually became systemic as a result of the high rate of capital accumulation.

The industrial base and the pattern of employment created during this period suffered when the US forces withdrew from Indochina. Furthermore, the effects of Rest and Recreation tourism on the balance of payments were so substantial that when this market declined, alternatives had to be found to maintain the operation of the tourist infrastructure for investment returns and benefits.

The combination of shared vested interests led firms to incorporate diverse sexual services into a highly organized production process with diverse points of distribution on an international level. Of particular significance is the emergence of collective sex tourism through the agency of package tours purchased by individuals, groups, or by transnational firms as fringe benefits for their workers. This indicates that there is an on-going process of direct capital accumulation in the area of reproduction (maintenance and renewal of human working capacity) on a wide scale. In this connection, it is relevant to point out that the most congealed form of reproductive services under commercial relations, i.e. sex package tours, mirrors one contradiction in the internationalization of capitalist development. It is through the process of capitalist development that kinship relations have been broken down and subsequently reproductive services have become fragmented and incorporated into market relations. It is also through capitalist development that a re-integration of reproductive services can take place entirely under market relations.

As an outcome of this transformation, a new form of discourse and sexual subjectivity has emerged through advertising and pornographic media. In this new discourse, inter-subjectivity is established between East and West, emphasizing the 'otherness' of the East, the sexual availability of Eastern women and the culture of their poverty. The newly created inter-subjectivity appears to be related to two main purposes: (1) creating a distinct national identity to attract consumers; and   (2) legitimizing oppressive practices by relegating them to the culture of a particular ethnic group and thereby helping to ease the conscience of the consumers. Put into circulation, these discursive elements of sexuality not only support practices but also create a new 'apparatus of sexuality' which obfuscates mutual East/West cognition. An obscure legitimacy (national development) has been founded for the incursion of capital (international and local) and consumers into the domain of sexuality, breaking down more and more intra-subjective barriers.

Sex *Sans Frontières* and the Ethical Question

Rejection of the common conception of prostitution as vice and promiscuity and recognition of power relations in the domain of sexual subjectivity does not mean that there are no further issues of consequence to consider. The proposition that there exists a labour process in the area of reproduction and prostitution raises a number of new questions, some relating to the ethics of labour and the ethics of sexuality. The study has not dealt with these two questions in depth, but notes their pertinence for future work in this field.

On the question of labour, the study suggests that while theoretically the development of a capitalist system is defined as being based on 'free labour' (manual and mental), empirically various forms of indentured sexual labour have been a constituent, a fact which has been recognized by many. However, such recognition has been partial. From the standpoint of the ethics of the labour movement, the issue of prostitution has been discarded as a phenomenon of bourgeois decadence, repudiating the fact that empirically many prostitutes contribute to the reproduction (maintenance) of workers. From the standpoint of the state and organized religion, concern over public morality has led to the denial of the utility of prostitution and to pragmatic solutions geared towards the rehabilitation of individual prostitutes. This discounts the broader environment in which prostitution takes place and the complexity of human relations and labour relations.

If 'bourgeois decadence' is the issue, then empirically prostitution would wither away in socialist countries and the new working class would not purchase sex package tours. If the rehabilitation of individuals is necessary, the target group should include not only prostitutes, but also those who have found it legitimate to use prostitutes' labour for their own profits and pleasure while condemning them to moral, social and legal isolation. It is obvious that the reality of prostitution today directly confronts the ethics of labour and the ethics of public morality, about which more serious reflection is required.

It is not 'ethical' enough to incorporate the issue of prostitution into the centre of policy debates, or to add it as another issue of grievance against a particular system. Prostitutes' labour has benefited many layers of many societies. Prostitutes' demands for recognition and emancipation must be seriously considered. Recognition of their work would enable the provision of a certain political space for organization to articulate their needs, their perceptions of themselves and their relationship with society as a whole.

On the question of sexual ethics, the recognition of commercial sex as work directly confronts the ethics of the new sexual liberation movement. The recent sexual rebellion in the West which seeks to abandon old and repressive values to 'hammer out' new sexual values (*Time*, 12 April 1971: 49) is at an impasse. Previously, the 'shape' of such values was constrained within the politics of 'choice' (individual choice, plurality of choices), and 'autonomy' (Weeks, 1985). Sexual politics have failed to bring out the contradiction between personal politics and collective interests. The response of capital to the insufficiently charted domain of sexual ethics, often with the tolerance of the state, has been an invasion of the area of eroticism, sexual pleasure and desire, allowing capital to produce a proliferation of commoditized pleasure and eroticism.

Through the incursion of capital into the domain of sexuality and eroticism, a new process of sexual subjugation (the construction of a new subjectivity) has been initiated and affects society in a wide sense. It has created a new discursive field of sexuality monopolized by the pornographic media and the advertising industry. Here, new elements of sexual liberalism are incorporated in the discourse, and are transformed into a transnational image of the new sexual subject based on the glorification of what was formerly persecuted and despised (e.g. the shift from sexual prudery to the glorification of nakedness). Such an image is tied to the provision of new sexual practices offered conspicuously in a commoditized form and on a wide scale. Rather than a more progressive sexual morality, a new field of domination in sexuality and eroticism has emerged, affecting not only Western society but also those societies whose frontiers have been eroded by communication and the transfer of attributes.

Beyond the philosophical questions of sexual emancipation and progressiveness, the significance of the industrial production of ideas about, and practices of, sex and eroticism lies the labour process associated with it. The industrial production of sexual services and eroticism implies that a continuous supply of sexual labour must be ensured. The effect of this process has been an increase in the use of violence to locate and control sexual labour. Apart from the evidence found in Thailand and other countries in Asia, recent reports from Latin America and elsewhere on the traffic in women (*NRC Handelsblad*, 25 April 1984: 3; *Alerta*, April 1988) show that Asia is no exception. In this respect, it is not 'ethical' enough to provide plurality of choice. It is not 'ethical' enough to recognize prostitution as a praxis which confronts both patriarchal ideology and economic dependence. The traffic in women and children as a means to supply labour in prostitution cannot be treated as a separate issue from the plurality of sexual choices of which prostitution is one. The border of sexual ethics extends beyond the question of individual choices regarding practice, or consumption. It concerns the process of sexual domination which precedes the availability of such sexual choices. In other words, for the market to avail itself of sexual choices, sex as a source of life (emotions, vitality) of some people must be first appropriated. It is therefore important to keep in mind that to stop judging prostitution is one thing, but to cease imposing ethical boundaries on the use of sexual labour is quite another.

Bibliography

Books and Articles

Adam, B. D. (1985) 'Structural Foundations of the Gay World', *Contemporary Studies in Society and History*, Vol. 27, (4): 658–71.

Adorno, T. W. and M. Horkheimer (1979) *Dialectic of Enlightenment*, translated by J. Cumming, London, Verso Editions.

Anderson, M. H. (no date) *Transnational Advertising and the New World Information Order*, Transnational Corporations Research Project, Faculty of Economics, University of Sydney.

Arispez, L. (1977) 'Women in the Informal Sector', *Signs*, Vol. 3, (1): 25–38.

Arnold, F. and S. Piampiti (1984) 'Female Migration in Thailand', *Women in the Cities of Asia*, in J. T. Fawcett, et al. (eds), Boulder, Westview Press, Replica Edition.

Association of Anti-prostitution Activities (1984) *Anti-prostitution Activities in Japan*, Tokyo.

Ayudhya, S. D., S. Buraphadeja and S. Chuvanut (1982) *The Impacts of Transnational Companies in the Hotel and Tour Business*, Bangkok, Chulalongkorn University, Social Research Institute.

Balbus, I. (1986) 'Disciplining Women: Michel Foucault and the Power of Feminist Discourse', *Praxis*, Vol. 5, (4): 466–84.

Ballhatchet, C. (1980) *Race, Sex and Class under the Raj: Imperial Attitudes, Policies and Their Critiques, 1793–1905*, London, Weidenfeld and Nicolson.

Baretje, R. (1969) 'Le Mouvement de Concentration dans le Tourisme Moderne', *Revue de Tourisme*, Vol. 24, (4): 152–60.

Barry, K. (1981a) 'The Underground Economic System of Pimping', *Journal of International Affairs*, Vol. 35, (1): 10–17.

—— (1981b) *Female Sexual Slavery*, New York, Avon Books.

—— (ed.) (1984) *International Feminism: Networking Against Female Sexual Slavery*, New York, International Women's Tribune Center.

Beauge, G. (1985) 'Le Rôle de l'État dans les Migrations de Travailleurs et la Diversification Economique des Pays de la Péninsule Arabe'. *Tiers Monde*, Vol. 16, (103): 597–620.

Beauvoir, S. de (1974) *The Second Sex*, Harmondsworth, Penguin Books.

Beechey, V. (1979a) 'On Patriarchy', *Feminist Review*, (3): 66–82.

—— (1979b) 'Women and Production: a Critical Analysis of Some Sociological Theories of Women's Work', A. Kuhn and A. Wolpe (eds), in *Feminism and Materialism: Women and Modes of Production*, London, Routledge and Kegan Paul.

Bell, L. (ed.) (1987) *Good Girls, Bad Girls: Sex Trade Workers and Feminists Face to Face*, Toronto, The Women's Press.

Benedict, R. (1934) *Patterns of Culture*, Boston, Houghton Mifflin.

Beneria, L. (1979) 'Reproduction, Production and Sexual Division of Labour', *Cambridge Journal of Economics*, (3): 203–25.

Bergman, A. E. (1974) *Women in Vietnam*, San Francisco, The People's Press.

Boonsue, K. (1986) 'Buddhism and Gender Bias: An Analysis of the Jataka Tales', (unpublished research paper) Women and Development Programme, Institute of Social Studies, The Hague.

Boserup, E. (1969) *Women's Role in Economic Development*, London, Allen and Unwin.

Bosserman, P. (1981) 'The Impact of Leisure on Social Development in Modern Societies', paper prepared for the Research Committee on the Sociology of Leisure, 9th World Congress of Sociology, Uppsala, August.

Boxer, M. J. and J. H. Quataert (eds) (1978) *Socialist Women: European Socialist Feminists in the Nineteenth and Early Twentieth Centuries*, New York, Elsevier.

Brake, M. (ed.) (1982) *Human Sexual Relations: Towards a Redefinition of Sexual Politics*, Harmondsworth, Penguin Books.

Britton, S. (1980) 'Tourism and Economic Vulnerability in Small Pacific Island-States: the Case of Fiji', in R. T. Shand (ed.), *The Island States of the Pacific and Indian Oceans*, The Australian National University, Development Studies Centre, Monograph 23, Canberra.

—— (1982) 'The Political Economy of Tourism in the Third World', *Annals of Tourism Research*, Vol. 9, (3): 331–58.

Bromley, R. and C. Gerry (eds) (1979) *Casual Work in Third World Cities*, New York, John Wiley.

Brownmiller, S. (1975) *Against Our Will: Men, Women and Rape*, New York, Bantam Books.

Bujra, J. (1982) 'Prostitution, Class and the State', in C. Summers (ed.), *Crime, Justice and Development*, London, Heinemann.

Burkart, A. J. and S. Medlik (1976) *Tourism: Past, Present and Future*, London, Heinemann.

Capra, F. (1982) *The Turning Point: Science, Society and the Rising Culture*, London, Fontana Paperbacks.

Carmody, D. L. (1979) 'Women and Religion: Where Mystery Comes to the Center Stage', in E. C. Snyder (ed.), *The Study of Women: Enlarging Perspectives of Social Realities*, New York, Harper and Row.

Caspero, J. A. (1987) 'Labor in the Global Political Economy', in J. A. Caspero (ed.), *A Changing International Division of Labor*, Boulder, Colorado, Lynne Rienner Publishers, Inc.

Caufield, M. D. (1985) 'Sexuality in Human Evolution: What is "Natural" in Sex', *Feminist Studies*, Vol. 11, (2): 343–64.

Cazes, G. (1976) *Le Tiers Monde vu par les Publicités Touristiques: Une Image Géographique Mystifiante*, Aix-en-Provence, Centre des Hautes Études Touristiques, Université de Droit, d'Économie et des Sciences.

Chauvin, C. (1982) *L'Église et les Prostituées*, Paris, Éditions du Cerf.

Chodorow, N. (1978) *The Reproduction of Mothering, Psychoanalysis and the Sociology of Gender*, Berkeley, University of California Press.

Choonhavan, K. (1984) 'Thailand: Economic Development and Rural Poverty – A Country Report', *Unreal Growth: Critical Studies in Asian Development*, M. L. Ngo (ed.), Delhi, Hindustan Publishing Corporation.

Clement, H. (1961) *The Future of Tourism in the Pacific and Far East*, a report prepared by Checchi and Company under a contract with the United States Department of Commerce and co-sponsored by the Pacific Area Travel Association, Department of Commerce, Washington DC.

Cleverdon, R. (1979) *The Economic and Social Impacts of International Tourism on Developing Countries*, London, Economic Intelligence Unit Ltd.

Cohen, E. (1982) 'Thai Girls and Farang Men', *Annals of Tourism Research*, Vol. 9, (3): 403–28.

Comisky, H. A. (1977) 'The International Airlines and their Tour Operators: Competition on the Fringe of Regulation', *Journal of Air Law and Commerce*, Vol. 43, (1): 71–118.

Commission of Enquiry (into Traffic in Women and Children in The Far East) (1933) *Report to the Council*, Geneva, League of Nations.

Cordero, T. (1986) 'A Black Note on a White Sheet', unpublished notes from Second World Whores Congress held in Brussels, October 1–3 1986, Institute of Social Studies, The Hague.

Croll, E. (1984) 'The Exchange of Women and Property: Marriage in Post-Revolutionary China', in R. Hirschon (ed.), *Women and Property, Women as Property*, Kent, Croom Helm.

Curry, S. (1978) 'The Integration of Developed Countries and Underdeveloped Countries through Tourism', *Africa Development*, Vol. 3, (3): 29–50.

Damrong, H. R. H. Prince (1959) 'Siamese History Prior to the Founding of Ayudhya', *The Siam Society Journal*, Vol. 3: 32–100.

Danois, J. (1977) *Vent du Nord*, Paris, Prométhée.

Davis, K. (1937) 'The Sociology of Prostitution', *American Sociological Review*, Vol. 5, (2): 744–55.

—— (1948) *Human Society*, New York, Macmillan.

—— (1976) 'Prostitution', in R. K. Merton and R. Nisbet (eds), *Contemporary Social Problems*, fourth edition, New York, Harcourt Brace Jovanovich.

David Davis, H. (1968) 'Potentials for Tourism in Developing Countries', *Finance and Development*, Vol. 5, (4): 34–9.

—— and J. S. Simmons (1982) 'World Bank Experience with Tourism', paper presented at the International Conference on Trends in Tourism Planning and Development, Surrey, 1–3 September.

Dawkins, R. (1976) *The Selfish Gene*, New York, Oxford University Press.

D'Cunha, J. (1987) 'Prostitution in a Patriarchal Society: a Critical Review of the SIT Act', *Economic and Political Weekly*, November 7: 1919–25.

Delanay, J. M. et al. (1977) *The Curse: A Cultural History of Menstruation*, New York, Mentor Books.

Delphy, C. (1977) *The Main Enemy*, London, WRRC.

Dumazedier, J. (1968) 'Le Sociologie du Loisir', *La Sociologie Contemporaine*, Vol. 16, (1): 5–31.

Dunning, J. and M. McQueen (1981) *Transnational Corporations in International Tourism*, New York United Nations Centre for Transnational Corporations, United Nations.

—— (1982) 'Multinational Corporations in the International Hotel Industry', *Annals of Tourism Research*, Vol. 9, (1): 69–90.

Durkheim, E. (1951) *Suicide*, translated from the French by J. A. Spaulding and G. Simpson, New York, Free Press.

—— (1960) *The Division of Labor in Society*, translated from the French by G. Simpson, Glencoe, Illinois, Free Press.

—— (1979) 'The Normal and the Pathological', in D. L. Kelly (ed.), *Deviant Behavior*, New York, St. Martin's Press.

Easlea, B. (1981) *Science and Sexual Oppression: Patriarchy's Confrontation with Woman and Nature*, London, Weidenfeld and Nicolson.

Edholm, F., O. Harris and K. Young (1977) 'Conceptualizing Women', *Critique of Anthropology*, Vol. 3, (9–10): 101–30.

Eisenstein, Z. (1979) 'Developing a Theory of Capitalist Patriarchy and Socialist Feminism', in Z. Eisenstein (ed.), *Capitalist Patriarchy and the Case for Socialist Feminism*, New York, Monthly Review Press.

Elliot, D. L. (1978) *Thailand: Origins of Military Rule*, London, Zed Press.

Ellis, H. (1927) *Studies in the Psychology of Sex*, Philadelphia, F. A. Davis Company.

Elson, D. and R. Pearson (1981) 'The Subordination of Women and the Internationalization of Factory Production', in K. Young et al. (eds), *Of Marriage and the Market*, London, CSE Books.

Elzinga, K. G. (1978) 'The Travel Agent, the IATA Cartel and Consumer Welfare', *Journal of Air Law and Commerce*, Vol. 44, (1): 47–73.

Encyclopaedia Britannica: Macropaedia, (1973–74), Chicago/London, William Benton Publishers.

Eng, L. A. (1986) *Peasants, Proletarians and Prostitutes: A Preliminary Investigation into the Work of Chinese Women in Colonial Malaya*, Singapore, Institute of Southeast Asian Studies.

Engels, F. (1971) *The Conditions of the Working Class in England*, W. H. Chaloner (trans. and ed.), Oxford, Basil Blackwell.

—— (1981) *The Origins of the Family, Private Property and the State*, a reprint with an introduction from E. B. Leacock, Surrey, Unwin Brothers.

Enloe, C. (1983) *Does Khaki Become You? The Militarization of Women's Lives*, London, Pluto Press.

Erbes, R. (1973) *International Tourism and the Economy of Developing Countries*, Paris, OECD.

Ericsson, L. O. (1980) 'Charges Against Prostitution: an Attempt at a Philosophical Assessment', *Ethics*, Vol. 90, (April): 335–66.

Ewan, S. (1976) *Captain of Consciousness: Advertising and the Social Roots of the Consumer Culture*, New York, MacGraw-Hill.

Eyer, W. W. (1979) 'The Sale, Leasing and Financing of Aircraft', *Journal of Air Law and Commerce*, Vol. 45, (1): 217–74.

Farnsworth, B. (1978) 'Bolshevism, the Women Question and Aleksandra Kollontai', in M. J. Boxer and J. H. Quataert (eds) *Socialist Women: European Socialist Feminists in the Nineteenth and Early Twentieth Centuries*, New York, Elsevier.

Fawcett, J. T., S. E. Khod and P. C. Smith (eds) (1984) *Women in the Cities of Asia*, Boulder, Colorado, Westview Press, Replica Edition.

Ferguson, A. (1978) 'Women as a New Revolutionary Class', *Between Labor and Capital*, P. Walker (ed.), Montreal, Black Rose Books.

—— and N. Folbre (1981) 'The Unhappy Marriage Between Patriarchy and Capitalism', in L. Sargent (ed.), *Women, War and Revolution*, London, Pluto Press.

—— et al. (1984) 'Forum: The Feminist Sexuality Debate', *Signs*, Vol. 1, (10): 106–35.

Fernand-Laurent, J. (1983) *Report of the Special Rapporteur on the Suppression of the Traffic in Persons and the Exploitation of the Prostitution of Others*, delivered to the First Regular Session of the Economic and Social Council of 1983, N. 12 of the Provisional Agenda (Activities for the Advancement of Women: Equality, Development and Peace), United Nations, E/1983/7; 17 March.

Field, K. L. (1982) 'Allexandra Kollontai: Precursor of Eurofeminism', *Dialectical Anthropology*, Vol. 6, (3): 229–43.

Firestone, S. (1971) *The Dialectic of Sex: The Case for Feminist Revolution*, London, Jonathan Cape.

Foucault, M. (1980a) *The History of Sexuality: Vol. I, An Introduction*, New York, Vintage Books.

―――― (1980b) *Power/Knowledge: Selected Interviews and Other Writings 1972–1977*, C. Gordon (ed.), New York, Pantheon Books.

―――― (1983) 'Power, Sovereignty and Discipline', in D. Held et al. (eds), *States and Societies*, Oxford, Basil Blackwell.

―――― (1986) 'Disciplinary Power and Subjugation', in S. Lukes (ed.), *Power*, Oxford, Basil Blackwell.

Fox, M. G. (1960) 'Problems of Prostitution in Thailand', Memorandum dated 26 February 1957 from M. G. Fox, as United Nations Welfare Adviser, to Director-General, Department of Public Welfare, Thailand. Published in *Social Service in Thailand*, Bangkok, Department of Public Welfare, Ministry of Interior.

Gaboriau, M. (1970) 'Structural Anthropology and History', in M. Lane (ed.), *Structuralism: A Reader*, London, Jonathan Cape.

Gaddis, J. L. (1982) *Strategies of Containment: A Critical Appraisal of Post-war American National Security Policy*, New York, Oxford University Press.

Gage, M. J. (1893) *Woman, Church and State*, Reprint of 1980 with an introduction by M. Daly, Watertown, Massachusetts, Persephone Press.

Gagnon, J. H. (1968) 'Prostitution', *International Encyclopedia of Social Sciences*, Vol. 12, New York, Macmillan and Free Press.

Gane, M. (1983) 'Durkheim: Women as Outsider', *Economy and Society*, Vol. 12, (2): 227–70.

Gardiner, J. (1975) 'Women's Domestic Labour', *New Left Review*, (89): 47–58.

Garzon-Zapata, D. J. (1985) 'Estudio y Analysis Jurídico de la Prostitución', Unpublished Thesis, Universidad Central del Ecuador, Facultad de Juris-prudencia.

Generoso, L. C. (1980) *Consulta on the Problem of Prostitution: a Reaction from the Government*, NCR, MSSD (mimeo), Manila, Intramuros.

Giddens, A. (1985) *The Nation State and Violence*, London, Polity Press.

Gimenez, M. (1978) 'Structural Marxism on the Women Question', *Science and Society*, Vol. 42, (Fall): 301–23.

Goldman, R. (1983-84) 'We Make Weekends: Leisure in the Commodity Form', *Social Text*, Vol. 3, (2): 84–103.

Graburn, N. H. (1983) 'Tourism and Prostitution', *Annals of Tourism Research*, Vol. 10, (3): 437–42.

Gray, P. H. (1970) *International Travel – International Trade*, Lexington, Massachusetts, Heath Lexington Books.

Griswold, A. B. and Prasert na Nagara (1975) 'On Kingship and Society at Sukhodaya', in G. Skinner and A. T. Kirsch (eds), *Change and Persistence in Thai Society*, Ithaca, Cornell University Press.

Gross, R. M. (1980) 'Menstruation and Childbirth as Ritual and Religious Experience among Native Australians', in N. A. Falk and R. M. Gross (eds), *Unspoken Words, Women's Religious Lives in Non-Western Culture*, San Francisco, Harper and Row.

Grossman, R. (1981) 'Little Islands of America', *South East Asia Chronicle*, (78): 13–14.

Guldimann, W. (1981) 'Air Travel and Tourism Look Ahead to the Year 2000', *Impact of Science on Society*, Vol. 31, (3): 277–87.

Haanappel, P. P. (1978) *Rate Making in International Air Transport*, Deventer, Kluwer BV.

Hail, J. (1980) 'Our Sex Capital Image', *Focus*, November: 71–6.

Hamelink, C. J. (1984) *Transnational Data Flows in the Information Age*, Lund, Studentlitteratur, Chartwell-Bratt.

Hantrakul, S. (1983) 'Prostitution in Thailand', paper presented at the Women in Asia Seminar Series, Monash University, Melbourne, 22–24 July.

Harris, H. (1984) *Sex, Ideology and Religion: the Representation of Women in the Bible*, New York, Barnes and Noble.

Harris, M. (1980) *Cultural Materialism*, New York, Vintage Books.

—— and E. B. Ross (1987) *Death, Sex and Fertility: Population Regulation in Pre-industrial and Developing Societies*, New York, Columbia University Press.

Harrod, J. (1987) *Power, Production and the Unprotected Worker*, Vol. 2 in the four-volume Series, Power and Production, New York, Columbia University Press.

Hartmann, H. (1981) 'The Unhappy Marriage Between Marxism and Feminism', in L. Sargent (ed.) *Women and Revolution: The Unhappy Marriage Between Marxism and Feminism*, London, Pluto Press.

Hartsock, N. (1983) *Money, Sex and Power: Towards a Feminist Theory of Historical Materialism*, New York, Longman.

Haruhi, T. (1986) 'The Japanese Sex Industry', *Ampo*, Vol. 18, (2–3): 70–6.

Haug, F. (1984) 'Morals Also Have Two Genders', *New Left Review* (143): 51–96.

Hearn, J. (1987) *The Gender of Oppression: Men, Masculinity and the Critique of Marxism*, London, Wheatsheaf Books.

Hesselink, L. (1987) 'Prostitution: a Necessary Evil, Particularly in the Colonies – Views on Prostitution in the Netherlands Indies', in E. Locher-Scholten and A. Hiehof (eds), *Indonesian Women in Focus*, Dordrecht, Foris Publications.

Heyl, B. S. (1979) *The Madame as Entrepreneur: Career Management in House Prostitution*, New Brunswick, New Jersey, Transaction Books.

Heymann, H. Jr. (1964) *Civil Aviation and US Foreign Aid: Purposes, Pitfalls and Problems for US Policy*, Rand Corporation, Santa Monica, California.

Heyzer, N. (1986) *Working Women in South East Asia*, Milton Keynes, Open University Press.

Himmelweit, S. (1984) 'The Real Dualism of Sex and Class', *Review of Radical Political Economics*, Vol. 16, (1): 167–83.

Hirschon, R. (ed.) (1984) *Women and Property, Women as Property*, Kent, Croom Helm.

Hirst, P. (1972) 'Marx and Engels on Law, Crime and Morality', *Economy and Society*, Vol. 1, (1): 28–56.

Holden, P. (ed.) (1985) *Women's Religious Experience: Cross-Cultural Perspectives*, London, Croom Helm.

Horner, I. B. (1930) *Women Under Primitive Buddhism*, London, Routledge.

Hudson, E. (1972) *Vertical Integration in the Travel and Leisure Industry*, Paris Institut du Transport Aérien.

Hunziker, W. (1968) 'Statut Actuel et Tendances Évolutives de la Doctrine de l'Économie des Entreprises Touristiques', *Problèmes Actuels de l'Économie des Entreprises Touristiques*, report presented to the 19th Congress of the

Association Internationale d'Experts Scientifiques du Tourisme, Berne, Éditions Gurten.

Huynh, S. T. (1979) *The Heritage of Vietnamese Poetry*, New Haven, Yale University Press.

Ingleson, J. (1986) 'Prostitution in Colonial Java', in Essays in Honour of Professor J. D. Legge, D. P. Chandler and M. C. Ricklefs (eds), *Nineteenth and Twentieth Century Indonesia.*

International Committee for Prostitutes' Rights (1985) *World Charter of Prostitutes' Rights, (1985)*, in draft, Amsterdam, ICPR and de Graaf Stichting.

Jaget, C. (1980) *Prostitutes – Our Life*, Bristol, Falling Wall Press.

Jaggar, A. (1983) *Feminist Politics and Human Nature*, Sussex, Harvester Press.

James, S. (1983) 'Hookers in the House of Lords', in J. Holland (ed.), *Feminist Action*, London, Battle Axe Books.

Janssen-Jurreit, M. (1982) *Sexism: The Male Monopoly on History and Thought*, London, Pluto Press.

Jeffreys, S. (1985) 'Prostitution', in D. Rhodes and S. McNeil (eds), *Women Against Violence Against Women*, London, Only Women Press.

Jenkins, C. L. (1982) 'The Effects of Scale in Tourism Projects in Developing Countries', *Annals of Tourism Research*, Vol. 9, (2): 229–50.

Jocano, F. L. (1975) *Slums as a Way of Life*, Quezon City, University of the Philippines Press.

Jonsson, C. (1981) 'Sphere of Flying: The Politics of International Aviation', *International Organization*, Vol. 35, (2): 273–302.

Kabilsingh, C. (1984) 'Buddhism and the Status of Women', in B. J. Terwiel and S. Sahai (eds), *Buddhism and Society in Thailand*, Gaya, Centre for South Asian Studies.

de Kadt, E. J. (ed.) (1979) *Tourism: Passport to Development?* New York, Oxford University Press.

Keesmaat, M. (1985) *Forum 1985 – Nairobi Report on the Prostitution Workshop*, (mimeo) Amsterdam, De Regenboog.

Kelly, D. H. (ed.) (1979) *Deviant Behavior*, New York, St. Martin's Press.

Kemp, T. (1936) *Prostitution: An Investigation of its Causes Especially with Regard to its Hereditary Factors*, Copenhagen, Levin and Munksgaard.

Keyes, C. (1977a) *The Golden Peninsula: Culture and Adaptation in Mainland South East Asia*, New York, Macmillan.

—— (1977b) 'Millennialism, Therevada Buddhism and Thai Society' *Journal of Asian Studies*, Vol. 36, (2): 283–302.

Kieckhefer, R. (1976) *European Witch Trials: Their Foundations in Popular and Learned Culture – 1300–1800*, Berkeley, University of California Press.

Kirsch, A. T. (1977) 'Complexity in the Thai Religious System: An Interpretation', *Journal of Asian Studies*, Vol. 36, (2): 241–66.

—— (1984) 'Cosmology and Ecology as Factors in Interpreting Early Thai Social Organization', *Journal of Southeast Asian Studies*, Vol. 15, (2): 245–52.

Kollontai, A. (1972) *Sexual Relations and the Class Struggle: Love and the New Morality*, translated and introduced by A. Holt, Bristol, Falling Wall Press.

—— (1977) *Selected Writings*, translated by A. Holt, London, Allison and Busby.

Korean Church Women United (1984) *Kisaeng Tourism, A Nation-wide Survey Report on Conditions in Four Areas, Seoul, Pusan, Cheju, Kyongju*, Research Material, Issue No. 3, Seoul, Catholic Publishing House.

Kosters, M. J. (1984) 'The Deficiencies of Tourism Science without Political Science: Comment on Ritcher', *Annals of Tourism Research*, Vol. 11, (4): 609–12.

Krippendorf, J. (1971) 'Marketing et Tourisme', *Études Bernoises de Tourisme*, Cahier (7), Berne.

Kuhn, A. and A. Wolpe (eds) (1978) *Feminism and Materialism: Women and Modes of Production*, London, Routledge and Kegan Paul.

Lane, M. (ed.) (1970) *Structuralism: A Reader*, London, Jonathan Cape.

Lanfant, M. F. (1980) 'Tourism in the Process of Internationalization', *International Social Sciences Journal*, Vol. 32, (1): 14–43.

Leach, E. (1967) 'Men and Morality: The Fourth of the Reith Lectures', *The Listener*, Vol. 78 (2019).

Leacock, E. (1980) *The Myths of Male Dominance: Collected Articles on Women Cross-Culturally*, New York, Monthly Review Press.

——— (1983) 'Interpreting the Origins of Gender Inequality', *Dialectical Anthropology*, Vol. 7, (4): 263–84.

Lefèbvre, H. (1976) *The Survival of Capitalism*, London, Allison and Busby.

Lemert, E. M. (1951) *Social Pathology: a Systematic Approach to the Theory of Sociopathic Behavior*, New York, MacGraw-Hill.

Lenz, I. (1978) *Prostitutional Tourism in South East Asia*, (mimeo), Berlin, Freie Universität Berlin.

Lerner, G. (1986) *The Creation of Patriarchy*, New York, Oxford University Press.

Lévi-Strauss, C. (1969) *Elementary Structures of Kinship*, Boston, Beacon Press.

——— (1970) 'The Sex of the Heavenly Bodies', in M. Lane (ed.), *Structuralism: A Reader*, London, Jonathan Cape.

——— (1985) 'Structuralism and Ecology', *The View From Afar*, translated by J. Neugroschel and P. Hoss, Oxford, Basil Blackwell.

Lewontin, R. C., S. Rose and L. Kamin (1984) *Biology, Ideology and Human Nature: Not in Our Genes*, New York, Pantheon Books.

Lindsey, K. (1979) 'Madonna or Whore', *ISIS International Bulletin (13)*: 4–5.

Lowe, M. (1978) 'Sociobiology and sex differences', *Signs*, Vol. 4, (1): 118–24.

Lowenfeld, A. (1975) 'A New Takeoff for International Air Transport', *Foreign Affairs*, Vol. 51, (1): 36–50.

——— and A. I. Mendelson (1979) 'Economics, Politics and Law: Recent Developments in the World of International Air Charters', *Journal of Air Law and Commerce*, Vol. 45, (3): 479–508.

Lubeigt, G. (1979) 'L'Économie, Tourisme et Environement en Thailande', *Cahiers d'Outre-Mer*, N. 128 (Octobre–Décembre): 371–99.

MacCormack, C. P. (1980) 'Nature, Culture and Gender: A Critique', in C. P. MacCormack (ed.), *Nature, Culture and Gender*, London, Cambridge University Press.

MacIntosh, M. (1981) 'Gender and Economics: The Sexual Division of Labour and the Subordination of Women', in K. Young et al. (eds), *Of Marriage and the Market*, London, CSE Books.

MacKinnon, C. (1982) 'Feminism, Marxism, Method and the State: An Agenda for Theory', in N. O. Keohane et al. (eds), *Feminist Theory: A Critique of Ideology*, Sussex, Harvester Press.

Malinowski, B. (1932) *The Sexual Life of Savages in North-western Melanesia*, Third Edition with a Special Foreword, London, Routledge and Kegan Paul.

——— (1960) *Sex and Repression in Savage Society*, London, Routledge and Kegan Paul.

Malos, E. (ed.) (1980) *The Politics of Housework*, London, Allison and Busby.

Mandel, E. (1977) *Marxist Economic Theory*, London, Merlin Press.

Marcuse, H. (1962) *Eros et Civilisation*, translated by J. G. Neny, Paris, Éditions Anthropos.
—— (1968) *Negations*, translated by J. Shapiro, Boston.
Marglin, F. A. (1985) *Wives of the God-King: the Rituals of the Devadasis of Puri*, Delhi, Oxford University Press.
Marr, D. (1976) 'The 1920s Women's Rights Debates in Viet-Nam', *Journal of Asian Studies*, Vol. 355, (3): 371–89.
Martin, M. K. and M. Voorhies (1975) *Female of the Species*, New York, Columbia University Press.
Marx, K. (1973) *Grundrisse: Foundations of the Critique of Political Economy*, New York, Vintage Books.
—— (1974) *Capital: A Critique of Political Economy*, Vol. I, II and III, Moscow, Progress Publishers.
—— and F. Engels (1970) *The German Ideology*, New York, International Publishers.
Matejko, A. (1971) 'Culture, Work, and Leisure', *Society and Leisure*, (2): 21–42.
Matthews, H. G. (1978) *International Tourism: a Political and Social Analysis*, Cambridge, Schrenkman Publishing Company.
McDonough, R. and R. Harrison (1978) 'Patriarchy and Relations of Production', in A. Kuhn and A. Wolpe (eds), *Feminism and Materialism: Women and Modes of Production*, London, Routledge and Kegan Paul.
McGough, J. (1981) 'Deviant Marriage in Chinese Society', in A. Kleinman and D. Tsung-Yi-Lin (eds), *Normal and Abnormal Behaviour in Chinese Culture*, Dordrecht, Reidel Publishing Company.
McLeod, E. (1982) *Women Working: Prostitution Now*, Kent, Croom Helm.
McQueen, M. (1983) 'Appropriate Policies Towards Multinational Hotel Corporations in Developing Countries', *World Development*, Vol. 11, (2): 141–52.
Mead, M. (1949) *Male and Female*, New York, Mentor Books.
Medvedev, R. (1974) 'On Gulag Archipelago', *New Left Review*, (85): 25–36.
Mernissi, F. (1982) *Beyond the Veil: Male and Female Dynamics in a Modern Muslim Society*, London, Wiley and Son.
Mies, M. (1982) *The Lace Makers of Narsapur*, London, Zed Press Ltd.
—— (1986) *Patriarchy and Accumulation on a World Scale: Women in the International Division of Labour*, London, Zed Books Ltd.
—— and K. Jayawardena (1981) *Feminism in Europe*, The Hague, Institute of Social Studies.
Millett, K. (1971) *Sexual Politics*, London, Hart-Davis.
—— (1975) *The Prostitution Papers*, London, Paladin.
Mitchell, J. (1971) *Woman's Estate*, Harmondsworth, Penguin Books.
—— (1975) *Psychoanalysis and Feminism*, Harmondsworth, Penguin Books.
Molyneux, M. (1979) 'Beyond the Domestic Labour Debate', *New Left Review*, (116): 3–27.
Morgan, R. (1984) *The Anatomy of Freedom: Feminism, Physics and Global Politics*, Garden City, New York, Doubleday.
Moselina, L. M. (1981) 'Olongapo's R & R Industry: a Sociological Analysis of Institutionalized Prostitution', *Ang Makatao*, Vol. 1, (1): 4–34.
Mowlana, H. (1986) *Global Information and World Communication: New Frontiers in International Relations*, New York/London, Longman.
Nakamura, H. (1976) 'The Basic Teachings of Buddhism', in H. Dumoulin and J.

C. Haraldo (eds), *Buddhism in the Modern World*, London, Collier/Macmillan.

Nakornjarupong, W. (1981) 'Patronage and the Night Queens', *Business in Thailand*, November: 40–52.

Nananukool, S. (1980) 'Case Studies of Tourism Financing by Commercial Banks', *Proceedings of the ESCAP/WTO Seminar-Cum-Workshop on Investment and Financing of Tourism Development Projects and Related Infrastructures*, held in Phu-Ket, Thailand, United Nations/ESCAP, Bangkok, 19–25 February.

Na-Rangsi, S. (1984) 'The Significance of Buddhism for Thai Studies', in B. J. Terwiel and S. Sahai (eds), *Buddhism and Society in Thailand*, Gaya, Centre for South Asian Studies.

Nartsupha, C. and S. Prasartset (1976) *The Political Economy of Siam 1851–1910*, Bangkok Social Science Association of Thailand.

Nelson, N. (1978) 'Women Must Help Each Other: the Operation of Personal Networks among Buzaa Beer Brewers in Mathare Valley, Kenya', in P. Kaplan and J. Bujra (eds), *Women United, Women Divided*, London, Tavistock Publications.

——— (1979) 'How Women and Men Get By: The Sexual Division Of Labour in the Informal Sector in a Nairobi Squatter Settlement', in R. Bromley and C. Gerry (eds), *Casual Work and Poverty in Third World Cities*, Chichester/New York/Brisbane, Wiley and Sons.

Neumann, L. (1979) 'Hospitality Girls in the Philippines', *South East Asia Chronicle* (66): 18–22.

Noronha, R. (1979) *Social and Cultural Dimensions of Tourism*, World Bank Staff Working Paper, N. 326, Washington, DC, International Bank for Reconstruction and Development.

Ohse, U. (1985) *Forced Prostitution and the Traffic in Women in West Germany*, Edinburgh, Human Rights Group.

Ortner, S. (1974) 'Is Female to Male as Nature to Culture', in M. Z. Rosaldo and L. Lamphere (eds), *Women, Culture and Society*, Stanford, Stanford University Press.

Parker, S. (1975) 'The Sociology of Leisure: Progress and Problems', *British Journal of Sociology*, Vol. 26, (1): 91–101.

Parrinder, G. (1980) *Sex in the World's Religions*, London, Sheldon Press.

Parsons, T. and R. F. Bales (1956) *Family: Socialization and Interaction Process*, London, Routledge and Kegan Paul.

Paul, D. (1979) *Women and Buddhism: Image of the Feminine in Mahayana Tradition*, Berkeley, California, Asian Humanity Press.

Peet, J. R. (1982) 'International Capital, International Culture', in M. Taylor and N. Thrift (eds), *The Geography of Multinationals*, Kent, Croom Helm.

Permtanjit, G. (1982) *Political Economy of Dependent Capitalist Development: Study on the Limits of the Capacity of the State to Rationalize in Thailand*, Bangkok, Chulalongkorn University, Social Research Institute.

Perry, M. E. (1985) 'Deviant Insiders: Legalized Prostitutes and a Consciousness of Women in Early Modern Seville', *Contemporary Studies in Society and History*, Vol. 27, (1): 138–58.

Peters, M. (1969) *International Tourism: the Economics and Development of the International Tourist Trade*, London, Hutchinson.

Philip-English, E. (1986) *The Great Escape: an Examination of North–South Tourism*, Ottawa, North–South Institute.

Phongpaichit, P. (1980a) 'The Open Economy and its Friends: the "Development" of Thailand', *Pacific Affairs*, Vol. 53, (3): 440–60.

—— (1980b) *Economic and Social Transformation in Thailand: 1957–1976*, Bangkok, Chulalongkorn University, Social Research Institute.

—— (1982) *From Peasant Girls to Bangkok Masseuses*, Geneva, ILO.

Piampiti, S. (1977) *Female Migrants in the Bangkok Metropolis*, Bangkok, School of Applied Statistics, National Institute of Development Administration.

Piñeda, R. V. (1981) 'Domestic Outwork for Export Oriented Industries', *Philippine Social Sciences and Humanities Review*, Vol. XLV, (1–4).

Piñeda-Ofreneo, R. V. (1985) 'Issues in the Philippines Electronics Industry: A Global Perspective', *Economic and Industrial Democracy*, Vol. 6, (2): 185–207.

Piampiti, S. (1977) *Female Migrants in the Bangkok Metropolis*, Bangkok, School of Applied Statistics, National Institute of Development Administration.

Piñeda, R. V. (1981) 'Domestic Outwork for Export Oriented Industries', *Philippine Social Sciences and Humanities Review*, Vol. XLV, (1–4).

Piñeda-Ofreneo, R. V. (1985) 'Issues in the Philippines Electronics Industry: A Global Perspective', *Economic and Industrial Democracy*, Vol. 6, (2): 185–207.

Pittin, R. I. (1979) 'Marriage and Alternative Strategies: Career Patterns of Hausa Women in Katsina City', unpublished PhD dissertation in Anthropology, School of Oriental and African Studies, University of London.

Plukspongsawalee, M. (also spelled Pruekponsawalee) (1982) 'Women and the Law', in S. Prasith-Rathsint and S. Piampiti (eds), *Proceedings of the Seminar on Women in Development: Implications for Population Dynamics in Thailand*, Bangkok, The National Institute of Development Administration.

Polsky, N. (1967) *Hustlers, Beats, and Others*, Chicago, Adline.

Poster, M. (1984) *Foucault, Marxism and History*, Cambridge, Polity Press.

Potter, J. M. (1976) *The Thai Peasant Social Structure*, Chicago, University of Chicago Press.

Poumisak, J. (1987) 'The Real Face of Thai Saktina Today', published under his penname as S. Srisudravarna C. Reynolds (ed.), *Thai Radical Discourse: The Real Face of Thai Feudalism Today*, Ithaca, Cornell University Press.

Pramoj, S. (1959) 'King Mongkut as a Legislator', *The Siam Society Journal*, Vol. 4: 203–37.

Ramesh, A. and H. P. Philomena (1984) 'The *Devadasi* Problem', in K. Barry et al. (eds), *International Feminism: Network Against Sexual Slavery*, New York, International Women's Tribune Centre, Inc.

Reddock, R. (1984) 'Women, Labour and Struggle in Trinidad and Tobago – 1898–1960', unpublished PhD dissertation, University of Amsterdam, Amsterdam.

Reed, E. (1975) *Women's Evolution*, New York, Pathfinder Press.

—— (1978) *Sexism and Science*, New York, Pathfinder Press.

Reynolds, C. J. (1976) 'Buddhist Cosmography in Thai History, with Special Reference to Nineteenth-Century Cultural Change', *Journal of Asian Studies*, Vol. 35, (2): 203–20.

—— (1977) 'A Nineteenth Century Thai Buddhist Defense of Polygamy and Some Remarks on the Social History of Women in Thailand', paper prepared for the Seventh Conference, International Association of Historians of Asia, University of Chulalongkorn, Bangkok, 22–26 August.

Reynolds, F. E. (1977) 'Civic Religion and National Community in Thailand', *Journal of Asian Studies*, Vol. 36, (2) 267–82.

Rhodes, D. and S. McNeill (eds) (1985) *Women Against Violence Against Women*, London, Only Women Press.

Richter, L. (1983) 'Tourism Politics and Political Science: A Case of Not So Benign Neglect', *Annals of Tourism Research*, Vol. 10, (3): 313–36.

Rodman, H. (1971) *Lower-class Families: The Culture of Poverty in Negro Trinidad*, New York, Oxford University Press.

Rojanasoonthon, T. (1982) 'Thailand', in *Social and Economic Impact of Tourism on the Asian Pacific Region*, Tokyo, Asian Productivity Organization.

Rose, S. and H. Rose (1986) 'Less Than Human Nature: Biology and the New Right', *Race and Class*, Vol. 27, (3): 47–66.

Rosenblum, K. E. (1975) 'Female Deviance and the Female Sex Role: a Preliminary Investigation', *British Journal of Sociology*, Vol. 26, (2): 169–85.

Ross, E. and R. Rapp (1981) 'Sex and Society: a Research Note from Social History and Anthropology', *Comparative Studies in Societies and History*, Vol. 23, (1): 51–72.

Rowbotham, S. (1973) *Women's Consciousness, Man's World*, New York, Penguin.

Rubin, G. (1975) 'The Traffic in Women: Notes on the Political Economy of Sex', in R. Rapp Reiter (ed.), *Towards an Anthropology of Women*, New York, Monthly Review Press.

Ruse, M. (1979) *Sociobiology: Sense or Nonsense*, London, Reidel Publishing Company.

Russell, M. (1977) 'Black Eyes Blues Connections', in C. Kramarae and P. A. Treichler (eds), *Feminist Dictionary*, Boston, London and Henley, Pandora Press.

Ruthven, K. K. (1979) *Critical Assumptions*, Cambridge, Cambridge University Press.

Salmon, Mr. (1725) *Modern History: The Present State of All Nations*, Vol. 1, Third Edition, London, Fleet Street, James Crokate.

Sampson, A. (1985) *Empires of the Sky: The Politics, Contests and Cartels of World Airlines*, Kent, Coronet Books.

Sargent, L. (ed.) (1981) *Women, War and Revolution: a Discussion of the Unhappy Marriage of Marxism and Feminism*, London, Pluto Press.

Sayers, J. (1982) *Biological Politics: Feminist and Anti-feminist Perspectives*, London, Tavistock Publications.

Schiller, H. (1981) *Who Knows: Information in the Age of the Fortune 500*, Norwood, New Jersey, Ablex Publishing.

Schwartz, A. C. (1981) 'Airports in Developing Nations: World Bank Helps with Financing, Expert Guidance', *Impact of Science on Society*, Vol. 31, (3): 313–21.

Senftleben, W. (1986) 'Tourism, Hot Spring Resorts and Sexual Entertainment, Observations From Northern Taiwan: A Study in Social Geography', *Philippine Geographical Journal*, Vol. 30, (1 & 2): 21–41.

Sereewat, S. (1983) *Prostitution: Thai–European Connection*, Geneva, World Council of Churches.

Sessa, A. (1969) 'Les Entreprises Touristiques et la Concurrence Internationale', *Revue de Tourisme*, Vol. 24, (2): 46–52.

Skrobanek, S. (1983) 'The Transnational Sex-exploitation of Thai Women' (unpublished research paper) Women and Development Programme, Institute of Social Studies, The Hague.

—— (1985) 'In Pursuit of an Illusion: Thai Women in Europe', *South East Asia Chronicle*, (96): 7–13.

Smart, B. (1983) *Foucault, Marxism and Critique*, London, Routledge and Kegan Paul.

Smart, C. (1976) *Women, Crime and Criminology: a Feminist Critique*, London, Routledge and Kegan Paul.

Smith, V. (ed.) (1977) *Host and Guests: The Anthropology of Tourism*, Philadelphia, University of Pennsylvania Press.

Smith, J., I. Wallerstein and H. D. Evers (eds) (1984) *Households and the World Economy*, Beverly Hills, Sage Publications.

Snitow, A., C. Stansell and S. Thompson (eds) (1983) *The Powers of Desire*, New York, Monthly Review Press.

Srinivasan, A. (1985) 'Temple Prostitution and Community Reforms: The Devadasi Case', paper presented at the Asian Regional Conference on 'Women and the Household', Indian Institute of Statistical Studies and Jawaharlal Nehru University, Delhi, 27–31 January.

—— (1988) 'Reform or Conformity? Temple "Prostitution" and the Community in the Madras Presidency', B. Agarwal (ed.), *Structures of Patriarchy: State, Community and Household in Modernising Asia*, New Delhi, Kali For Women; London, Zed Books.

Stol, A. (1980) *Charter Naar Bangkok*, Rotterdam, Ordeman.

Stoler, A. (1985) *Capitalism and Confrontation in Sumatra's Plantation Belt 1880–1979*, New Haven, Yale University Press.

Stone, L. (1977) *The Family, Sex and Marriage in England, 1500–1800*, London, Weidenfeld and Nicolson.

Suksamran, S. (1982) *Buddhism and Politics in Thailand*, Singapore, Institute of South East Asian Studies.

—— (1984) 'Buddhism and Political Authority: A Symbiotic Relationship', in B. J. Terwiel (ed.), *Buddhism and Society in Thailand*, Gaya, Centre for South East Asian Studies.

Sutton, W. A. Jr. (1967) 'Travel and Understanding: Notes on the Social Structure of Touring', *International Journal of Comparative Sociology*, Vol. 8, (2): 218–23.

Tambiah, S. J. (1976) *World Conqueror and World Renouncer: a Study of Buddhism and Polity in Thailand Against a Historical Background*, Cambridge, Cambridge University Press.

Tanner, N. and A. Zihlman (1976) 'Women in Evolution', *Signs*, Vol. 1, (3): 585–608.

Thai Delegation (1985) 'Country Paper', presented at the Workshop of Experts on Prevention and Rehabilitation Schedule for Young Women in Prostitution and Related Occupations, UN/ESCAP, Bangkok, 17–21 June.

Thailand National Council of Women's Affairs (1982) *Summary of Long-term Women's Development Plan (1982–2001)*, Bangkok, The Thai Royal Government.

Theuns, H. L. (1976) 'Notes on the Economic Impact of International Tourism in Developing Countries', *Revue de Tourisme*, (3): 1–10.

—— (1985) 'Ontstaan en Ontwikkeling van het Massatoerisme naar de Derde Wereld', *ESB*, (70) 31 Juli: 752–9.

Thitsa, K. (1980) *Providence and Prostitution*, London, Change International Reports.

—— (1983) *Nuns, Mediums and Prostitutes in Chiang Mai: a Study on Some Marginal Categories of Women*, Occasional Paper, University of Canterbury, Elliot.

Thurot, J. M. and G. Thurot (1983) 'The Ideology of Class and Tourism: Confronting the Discourse of Advertising', *Annals of Tourism Research*, Vol. 10, (1): 173–91.

Tiger, L. and R. Fox (1974) *The Imperial Animal*, New York, Dell.

Tongudai, P. (1982) 'Women, Migration and Employment: a Study of Migrant

Workers in Bangkok', unpublished PhD thesis, New York University.

Tourism Authority of Thailand (1980 to 1986) *Annual Statistical Reports*, Bangkok.

Tragen, I. G. (1969) *Tourism: Resource for Development – A Study of the Benefits to Developing Countries From Investment in Hotels and Motels*, Senior Seminar in Foreign Policy, Department of State, Washington DC.

Trivers, R. L. (1972) 'Parental Investment and Sexual Selection', in B. Campbell (ed.) *Sexual Selection and the Descent of Man*, Chicago, Aldine.

Truong, T. D. (1983) 'The Dynamics of Sex Tourism', *Development and Change*, Vol. 14, (3): 533–53.

—— (1985a) 'Touring the Sex Industry', *Spare Rib*, October: 6–8 and 32–3.

—— (1985b) 'Letter from Amsterdam', unpublished fieldnotes on the First World Whores Congress held in Amsterdam in February, 1985.

—— (1986) *Vice, Virtue, Order, Health and Money: Towards a Comprehensive Perspective on Female Prostitution in Asia*, Bangkok, United Nations Economic Commission for Asia and The Pacific.

Turner, L. (1976) 'The International Division of Leisure: Tourism and the Third World', *World Development*, Vol. 4, (3): 253–60.

—— and L. Ash (1975) *The Golden Hordes: International Tourism and the Pleasure Periphery*, London, Constable.

Turton, A. (1980) 'Thai Institutions of Slavery', in J. L. Watson (ed.), *Asian and African Systems of Slavery*, Oxford, Basil Blackwell.

United Nations (1984) *Statistical Yearbook for Asia and the Pacific*, Bangkok, Economic and Social Commission for Asia and the Pacific.

UNCTAD Secretariat (1971) *Elements of Tourism Policy in Developing Countries*, TD/B/C.3/89, Geneva.

United Nations (1963) Conference on International Travel and Tourism *Recommendations: International Travel and Tourism*, Rome, 21–25 September.

—— (1984) *Statistical Yearbook for Asia and the Pacific*, Bangkok, Economic and Social Commission for Asia and the Pacific.

United Nations/ECAFE (1973) *Review of Current Developments in Tourism*, Sub-committee on Tourism and Facilitation of International Traffic, Bangkok, Doc. N. Trans/Sub.5/CR/1, 24 September.

United Nations/ECOSOC (1980) *Studies on the Effects of the Operations and Practices of Transnational Corporations in International Tourism*, Report of the Secretariat, New York, Doc. N. E/C.10/68, 8 April.

United Nations/ESCAP (1980) *Proceedings of the ESCAP/WTO Seminar-Cum-Workshop on Investment and Financing of Tourism Development Projects and Related Infrastructures*, Phu-Ket, Thailand, 19–25 February, Bangkok, Economic Commission for Asia and the Pacific.

Uzzell, D. (1984) 'An Alternative Structuralist Approach to the Psychology of Tourism Marketing', *Annals of Tourism Research*, Vol. 11, (1): 79–100.

van den Berghe, P. L. (1978) *Man in Society: A Biosocial View*, (Second Edition) New York/Oxford, Elsevier.

van de Velden, L. (1981) *Visitors and Tourists to Thailand and Their Eventual Sexual Demands for Prostitution*, (mimeo), University of Amsterdam.

von Werlhof, C. (1980) 'Notes on the Relation Between Sexuality and Economy', *Review*, Vol. 4, (1): 33–42.

Vries, J. C. de (1985) *Onderzoek Naar Sextoerisme* (mimeo), Leiden, Noordeinde 25, 2311 CA.

Walkowitz, J. (1980) *Prostitution and Victorian Society: Women, Class and the State*, Cambridge, Cambridge University Press.

Wallerstein, I., W. Martin and T. Dickinson (1982) 'Household Structures and Production Processes: Preliminary Theses and Findings', *Review*, Vol. 3, (3): 437–58.

Watson, J. L. (ed.) (1980) *Asian and African Systems of Slavery*, Oxford, Basil Blackwell.

Wedel-Pattanapongse, Y. (1982) *Modern Thai Radical Thought: the Siamization of Marxism and Its Theoretical Problems*, Bangkok, Thai Khadi Research Institute, Thammasat University.

Weeks, J. (1980) *Sex, Politics and Society*, London and New York, Longman.

—— (1985) *Sexuality and its Discontents*, London, Routledge and Kegan Paul.

—— (1987) *Sexuality*, Chichester, Ellis Norwood Limited; New York, Tavistock Publications.

White, L. (1977) *Women's Domestic Labor in Colonial Kenya: Prostitution in Nairobi – 1909–1950*, African Studies Center Working Papers, Brookline, Massachusetts, Boston University.

—— (1983a) 'A Colonial State and an African Petty Bourgeoisie: Prostitution, Property, and Class Struggle in Nairobi, 1936–1940', in F. Cooper (ed.) *Struggle for the City: Migrant Labour, Capital and the State in Urban Africa*, London, Sage Publications.

—— (1983b) 'Vice Centers and Vagrants: Prostitution and Unskilled Labor in Nairobi in the Mid-1930s', paper presented at the Conference on the History of Law, Labour and Crime, University of Warwick, September.

—— (1986) 'Prostitution, Identity, and Class Consciousness in Nairobi During World War II', *Signs*, Vol. 11, (2): 255–73.

Whitehead, A. (1979) 'Some Preliminary Notes on The Subordination of Women', *IDS Bulletin*, Vol. 10, (3): 10–14.

—— (1981) 'I'm Hungry Mum: the Politics of Domestic Budgeting', in K. Young et al. (eds), *Of Marriage and the Market*, London, CSE Books.

Wihtol, R. (1982) 'Hospitality Girls in the Manila Tourist Belt', *Philippine Journal of Industrial Relations*, Vol. 4, (1–2): 18–41.

Wilson, E. O. (1975) *Sociobiology: The New Synthesis*, Cambridge, Massachusetts, Harvard University Press.

Wolf, G. (1967) *Die Entwicklung des Weltluftverkehrs nach dem Zweiten Weltkrieg*, Tübingen, J. C. Mohr, Paul Siebeck.

Wood, R. E. (1980) 'International Tourism and Cultural Change in South East Asia', *Economic Development and Cultural Change*, Vol. 23, (3): 561–81.

—— (1981) 'The Economics of Tourism', *South East Asia Chronicle*, (78): 2–11.

—— (1984) 'Ethnic Tourism, the State and Cultural Change in South East Asia', *Annals of Tourism Research*, Vol. 11, (3): 353–74.

World Bank (1972) *Tourism Sector*, Working Paper, Washington, DC, International Bank for Reconstruction and Development.

World Tourism Organization (WTO) (1983) *Monograph on Tourism in East Asia and The Pacific*, Mon/AP/83, Madrid.

Wyatt, A. T. (1984) 'Law and Social Order in Early Thailand: An Introduction to the *Mangraisat*', *Journal of Southeast Asian Studies*, Vol. 15, (2): 245–52.

Youdorf, B. (1979) 'Prostitution as a Legal Activity', *Policy Analysis*, Vol. 5, (4): 418–33.

Young, K. et al. (eds) (1981) *Of Marriage and the Market*, London, CSE Books.

Zetkin, C. (1951) 'Lenin on the Woman Question', *The Woman Question: Selections from the Writings of K. Marx, F. Engels, V. I. Lenin, J. V. Stalin*, New York, International Publishers Co. Inc.

—— (1973) 'Lenin on the Woman Question', *Women and Communism: Selections from the Writings of Marx, Engels, Lenin and Stalin*, Westport, Connecticut, Greenwood Press.

Zinder, H. and Associates, Inc. (1969) *The Future of Tourism in the Eastern Caribbean*, a Report Prepared Under Contract With the Agency for International Development, Washington, DC.

Zuzanek, J. (1981) 'Leisure Services and Leisure Research in North America from a Historical Perspective', paper presented to the Third Canadian Congress on Leisure Research, Alberta, August 17–21.

Newspapers, Newsletters, Weeklies and Miscellaneous

Alerta (Amsterdam); *Asian Business* (Hong Kong); *Asian Women's Liberation* (Tokyo); *Bangkok Bank Monthly Review* (Bangkok); *Bangkok Post* (Bangkok); *Business in Thailand* (Bangkok); *Congress and the Nation* (Washington, DC); *English Collective of Prostitutes Newsletter* (London); *Far Eastern Economic Review* (Hong Kong); *Human Rights in Thailand* (Bangkok); *IMF International Financial Statistics* (Washington, DC); *International Tourism Quarterly* (London); *ISIS International Bulletin* (Geneva); *Le Monde Diplomatique* (Paris); *Look East* (Bangkok); *NCR Handelsblad* (Rotterdam); *Off Our Backs* (Washington DC); *South* (London); *Thailand Development Newsletter* (Bangkok); *The Investor* (Hong Kong); *The Nation* (Bangkok); *The Observer* (London); *Time* (New York).

Index